Volume 1 (2016)

Contents

JIQSA 1 (2016): 3–9

EDITORS' INTRODUCTION: THE QUR'ĀN BETWEEN BIBLE AND *TAFSĪR*

MICHAEL E. PREGILL AND VANESSA DE GIFIS

JIQSA is being launched at a crucial time for the growth and development of Qur'ānic Studies as a scholarly field. While there has been a surge of advances in just the last fifteen years, the field at times appears incoherent, seeming to lack a clear disciplinary identity. As greater numbers of scholars devote their efforts to the study of the Qur'ān, there is a natural diversification of research aims and methods, stimulating attempts to define Qur'ānic Studies "proper"—to distinguish those aims and methods that are central to the field from those that are peripheral, and determine how (and whether) the center and peripheries are meaningfully related. At the forefront of this drive currently are two major questions aimed at situating Qur'ānic Studies as an emergent field in its own right vis-à-vis those disciplines with which it has been linked historically:

(1) How is Qur'ānic Studies related to Biblical Studies?
(2) How is Qur'ānic Studies related to *Tafsīr* Studies?

Inherent to these field-orienting questions are more fundamental questions about how to situate the qur'ānic text itself in the contexts of Late Antiquity on the one hand and Islamic religion, culture, and society on the other. What does it mean to study the qur'ānic text on its own terms, and how can such study enhance, and be enhanced by, studies of other late antique scriptural, parascriptural, and exegetical texts, as well as the study of Islamic literature?

As a field, Qur'ānic Studies is presently grappling with two major problems provoked by revisionism—epitomized by the groundbreaking but problematic work of John Wansbrough and his students that revolutionized the study of the Qur'ān and early Islam some forty years ago. First, how can the text of the Qur'ān be meaningfully distinguished from classical Islamic exegeses thereof, separating the qur'ānic text as an artifact of its time from the dogmatic, social, and political concerns of later eras? Second, how can extra-Islamic sources (especially the scriptural and parascriptural traditions of Late Antiquity) be responsibly and critically recruited for the study of the Qur'ān's textual history and originating socio-historical milieu?

doi: http://dx.doi.org/10.5913/jiqsa.1.2017.a001

Much contemporary work in Qur'ānic Studies may be labeled 'post-revisionist'—grounded in a carefully negotiated synthesis of these two concerns. The best contemporary scholarship seeks on the one hand to re-engage Islamic exegetical traditions in ways that illuminate rather than overshadow the study of the qur'ānic text itself, and on the other hand to reconceptualize the relationship between the Qur'ān and biblical tradition, moving from a model focusing on "influences" to one focusing on "intertexts." A major aim of *JIQSA* is to contribute to a redefinition of the field by facilitating these ongoing efforts, showcasing research that consciously and actively intervenes in debates about theory, sources, and methodologies within Qur'ānic Studies as an increasingly discrete and well-established field in its own right, as well as in conjunction with other relevant fields.

The Qur'ān and Biblical Tradition

It is clear that we have moved away (or are moving away) from the dominance of the influence paradigm, the view of the Qur'ān as borrowing or derived from various biblical, Jewish, and occasionally Christian prototypes. Beginning in the 1970s, the emphasis on uncovering the sources of the Qur'ān began to give way to new conceptions of its relationship to older monotheistic traditions.

There are two main grounds on which to assert a meaningful connection between Biblical Studies and Qur'ānic Studies: the historical-contextual and the methodological. With the former, the Qur'ān may be seen as an "Abrahamic" scripture, emerging out of the matrix of late antique "Judeo-Christian" scripturalism. With the latter, one may attempt to shape and frame Qur'ānic Studies on the model of Biblical Studies, proceeding in a philological and historical-critical vein, and (at least theoretically) branching out into myriad subfields dedicated to textual, contextual, material, literary, and cultural facets of the genesis, development, production, and reception of the text.

Resistance to comparison of Bible and Qur'ān, or to assertions of similarity and filiation, is caused, at least in part, by anxieties about reductionism—a tendency that is foundational in the field. From the early nineteenth century, many scholars employed philological or historical analyses in the quest for the sources of the Qur'ān, and maintained a basic thesis that Muḥammad had produced the Qur'ān through extensive borrowings from Jews, and thus that Islam was profoundly indebted to Judaism from the very start. Other scholars sought to redirect inquiry from rabbinic Jewish to Eastern Christian sources—shifting the putative vectors of influence but hardly altering the basic presuppositions that informed older scholarship.

In light of this history, it is unsurprising that demographic changes in scholarship in both Anglophone and European university cultures in the later twentieth century, particularly the inclusion of Muslim students and scholars as full participants in a scholarly discourse from which they were formerly excluded, led to resistance to such conjectures about "influence." Until quite recently, a countervailing sympathy for the conventional account of Islam's origins, at least in its broad contours, discouraged direct discussion of the possible literary influences on the Qur'ān—to say nothing of the question of its authorship. The exception to this trend was the aforementioned work of scholars of the so-called revisionist school, whose impact on the larger field of Islamic Studies was relatively marginal until the recent resurgence of interest in their ideas.

Much attention is now being given to Syriac literature as providing the primary comparanda of interest for investigation of the literary, cultural, and religious background to the Qur'ān, especially of the echoes of biblical tradition found therein. A new consensus is emerging that this corpus of literature appears to provide the most apposite parallels for understanding both qur'ānic *contexts* and *subtexts*. (Perhaps this is comparable to the significance of the discovery of the literary remains of Ugarit in revolutionizing the study of the oldest strata of the Hebrew Bible and investigation into the origins of ancient Israel.) But this shift in direction in the field needs to be managed carefully, and arguments about the relevance of this material constructed thoughtfully and self-consciously. What do we mean when we compare, when we draw parallels, when we excavate sources, when we point to the language, themes, and style of (for example) Syriac *memrē* as meaningful for understanding the Qur'ān? If we do not refine our conceptual models and approaches, then we risk falling into the same reductionist trap into which scholars fell in the past, and the work of those who now strive to articulate a new historical-critical approach to the Qur'ān may justifiably be criticized as improving little upon the insights of a century ago. Further, we also run the risk of alienating an audience that may be apprehensive about attempts to draw Biblical Studies and Qur'ānic Studies closer together, an enterprise that has great constructive potential.

Recent advances in the field of Qur'ānic Studies have to a large degree involved looking backwards, revisiting older work on comparanda and the late antique historical context of the Qur'ān—but now, at least ideally, reconfiguring or re-envisioning comparanda in order to explore the cultural and literary frame of reference reflected in the Qur'ān, rather than merely cataloguing passively received "influences" *per se*, and thus shedding some of the problematic baggage of older scholarship. Despite these attempts to proceed in a more nuanced and less reductionist way, concern with the Qur'ān's background in older scripturalist traditions is sometimes still perceived and represented as being dated, retrograde, and politically and ideologically suspect. At worst, the critical study of qur'ānic origins may be portrayed as the essence of Orientalism, a Western colonization of the Qur'ān that subordinates it to a Judeo-Christian tradition presupposed to be more original and authentic.

However, any contextualist or historical-critical approach to the Qur'ān must of necessity seek to locate its origins—as a discourse and living revelation before the emergence of the *textus receptus*—in an older context in which there was in fact no Islam. Logically, the Qur'ān in its originating context can only make sense in terms of the Bible and contemporary Judaism and Christianity, with its primary comparanda being those literatures with which Biblical Studies and related fields are concerned. Thus, while some may deem Biblical Studies to be marginal to Islamic Studies, it cannot be deemed marginal to Qur'ānic Studies.

Further, although the attempt to assert the Qur'ān's autonomy from Biblical Studies is an understandable response to the once-ubiquitous Orientalist assertion of the Qur'ān's dependence on—and, implicitly, its inferiority to—Judaism and Christianity, there is a danger of going too strongly in the other direction. To overstate the Qur'ān's autonomy from the Bible and the Judaism and Christianity of its time and sever it from its most salient frameworks of meaning in its original context is to slip into another Orientalizing trap—that of rendering the Qur'ān irresolvably alien to these traditions, and thus estranging Islam from its roots in the same historical contexts, discourses, and experiences that informed historical Judaism and Christianity, anchored in the late antique *oikoumene* of the Near East and Mediterranean. The isolation of Qur'ānic Studies from Biblical Studies, the insistence that the Qur'ān is *sui generis*, can be a danger to constructive study of the Qur'ān and substantive dialogue about its meaning and historical significance.

Resistance to drawing Biblical Studies and Qur'ānic Studies closer together also seems to be based on a poor understanding of significant developments in Biblical Studies over the last few decades. "The Bible" as a construct has been rigorously interrogated for decades now, and the hegemony of the canonical text has been more or less decisively overthrown, in the sense that the field is no longer defined exclusively or primarily by an attempt to dissect a single canonical Hebrew Bible into its constituent parts, each of which represents an artifact of one or another era in the emergence of Israelite monotheism. Contemporary Biblical Studies is marked by significant disagreement and continuing debate between traditionalists and revisionists, those who in some way seek to revitalize the Documentary Hypothesis and rehabilitate some version of source criticism for the twenty-first century and those who would see such attempts as hopelessly naïve. A general consensus on the most suitable analytical approach to the text as an historical artifact remains elusive, and perhaps should remain so.

Moreover, to many Bible scholars, there is no single "Bible" that is the universal object of concern of both ancient exegetes and modern scholars. Rather, in the ancient world predating the rise of Islam, the canon is not a reified or unitary thing but rather represents a *discursive posture.* In this period, there are multiple canonical bibles of Jews, multiple canonical bibles of Christians, and a great many parascriptural traditions reflecting engagements with one or another canonical or quasi-canonical text. The Qur'ān as a late antique document reflects the impact of a wider discourse regarding the canonical, the elaboration of the paracanonical, how the two are related, and so forth.

This is all to say that Biblical Studies, like Qur'ānic Studies, continues to evolve, with increasing attention paid to the *Nachleben* or "afterlife" of biblical traditions—the complex processes of canonization, exegesis, and reception in later works. It is true that Qur'ānic Studies has never elaborated anything similar to the Documentary Hypothesis, or developed a serious equivalent of the well-established methodologies of source criticism, form criticism, and the like that are the foundation of the historical-critical study of the Bible. And yet, the contemporary study of the Qur'ān is rather similar to the contemporary study of the Bible, at least in broad terms: each represents a wealth of complementary and competing approaches, a network of overlapping and interconnected methods informed by different presuppositions that may nevertheless enrich each other in a variety of ways. Both Biblical Studies and Qur'ānic Studies have transcended their disciplinary origins, and while the resulting riot of perspectives may seem incoherent, we would argue that this diversity is salutary, reflecting the continuing vitality of both fields.

The Qur'ān and Islamic Tradition

It is worth noting that for much of its history, the study of the Qur'ān in the Anglo-European tradition has actually *not* been modeled on Biblical Studies but rather on Muslim approaches to the text. This is demonstrated by the profound reliance on *tafsīr* in early modern interpretations and translations of the text, as well as by the fundamental reliance on the *sīrah* literature as the primary account of its historical context. Most modern attempts to make sense of the Qur'ān as a discourse have simply taken for granted that the text's meaning could only be brought into focus through the lens of traditional *tafsīr*. Given their closer proximity in time to the composition of the Qur'ān, the works of early and classical Muslim exegetes were assumed to more reliably approximate—and, taken cumulatively, fully capture—the text's "original" meaning. But in more recent years, scholars of the Qur'ān have become increasingly aware of how the "original" meaning located in the text *per se* may be apprehended apart from early readers' perceptions and constructions of its meaning, and of the inherent subjectivities of *tafsīr* texts (indeed, of all scholarly texts). Serious questions are thus being raised about the relevance and credibility of the *tafsīr* literature for understanding the qur'ānic text on its own terms. Inasmuch as studying the Qur'ān on its own terms is the definitive aim of Qur'ānic Studies proper, there is a growing and persistent call to free the discipline from the presuppositions of *tafsīr* in order to achieve something resembling a more objective assessment of the qur'ānic text and its meaning.

Some participants and observers in the field might construe "objective" here to mean culturally unbiased or ideologically disinterested, but in reality, no position or approach can be entirely free of bias or devoid of interest, so such an agenda is at best aspirational. However, it is not futile to aim to produce scholarship that self-consciously acknowledges and controls for biases and corrects for ideological motivations, and thus seeks to be as objective as realistically possible. Further, it is not difficult to imagine how a deliberate focus on the qur'ānic text as an object presented to scholarly consciousness and read primarily in the light of qur'ānic discourse itself (or its historical context), rather than an uncritical reliance on the subjectivities of individual exegetes or received Muslim tradition, may be productive.

Meanwhile, there has been increasing interest among scholars to study *tafsīr* in its own right—as a literary genre, hermeneutic exercise, and mode of social discourse—in order to better understand how Muslim exegetes have gone about the business of qur'ānic interpretation. Since the early 2000s, we have seen the emergence of three major monograph series in the field of Qur'ānic Studies: Brill's *Texts and Studies on the Qur'an*, published since 2003; the *Qur'anic Studies Series* jointly published by Oxford University Press and the Institute of Ismaili Studies since 2004; and *Routledge Studies in the Qur'an*, published since 2008. Collectively, more than half the books published to date in these series are in actuality devoted to the study of *tafsīr*. It is thus clear that *tafsīr* is no longer being studied merely instrumentally, as a means of making sense of the Qur'ān, but rather ultimately, for the sake of making sense of *tafsīr* itself. *Tafsīr* Studies has thus emerged as a distinctive field of academic specialization, which yet remains intermixed theoretically and practically with Qur'ānic Studies proper. Nowadays a major question across the intermingled disciplines of Qur'ānic Studies and *Tafsīr* Studies is whether they should continue to overlap, and, if so, how.

The pitfalls of consulting *tafsīr* in an "objective" study of the Qur'ān should not be overstated, though some scholars have suggested that Qur'ānic Studies proper should be wholly extricated from the tradition. This attitude is particularly dangerous when it leads to the prejudicial conclusion that confessionally informed perspectives on the Qur'ān—whether in the past or the present—are uniquely fraught with problems, insufficiently rigorous, or lack value for objective approaches. Such prejudice plays into old "insider" versus "outsider" dichotomies, leading to skepticism, even cynicism, about motivations that is hardly salutary for the field. What is more, excluding scholarship on *tafsīr* from Qur'ānic Studies deprives us of a wealth of knowledge about the qur'ānic text. Many traditional exegetes exhibit a concern for the plain sense of the text—what we would call "objective" textual meaning—and deploy a variety of scholarly approaches to apprehend it, including philological analysis and rationalist arguments akin to those valued and practiced in modern non-confessional academic circles. At the very least, authors of traditional *tafsīr*, despite all their theological and methodological diversity, have one basic thing in common with modern scholars in Qur'ānic Studies: they seek to engage directly with the scripture as their primary object of study. From this perspective, it seems both unnecessary and unprofitable to sever the *tafsīr* tradition from the intellectual and literary heritage upon which modern cosmopolitan scholars of the Qur'ān may draw.

Thus, it is clear that *Tafsīr* Studies as an academic field today should not be severed from Qur'ānic Studies. If *tafsīr* texts are to remain useful in "objective" studies of the Qur'ān, we must better understand their subjectivities and the social, historical, literary, and intellectual contexts that shape them. Studies of *tafsīr* foster a deeper consciousness of the complex interrelationship between text and reader, the rich variety of methodologies in qur'ānic exegesis, and the virtually innumerable ideas about what the Qur'ān means that have come before. More clarity on all these matters equips Qur'ān scholars today with a sharper sense of their own work in historical and cultural context, and a greater dexterity in the use of *tafsīr* texts not as conclusive but as contributing sources for better understanding the Qur'ān itself.

On the other hand, studies of the Qur'ān on its own terms, including linguistic, literary, and historical studies—with all their various methodological advances—enhance our understanding of the text with which the authors of *tafsīr* were concerned, equipping scholars of the Qur'ān and *tafsīr* alike with a deeper empathy for how the *mufassirūn* dealt with shared concerns about the features and history of the text of the Qur'ān.

The fundamental distinction between Qur'ānic Studies and *Tafsīr* Studies today would seem to boil down to what the ultimate object of study is, the qur'ānic text or *tafsīr* texts, and hence to the status one might assign to *tafsīr* literature as a secondary or rather primary source. Since both the text of the Qur'ān and texts of *tafsīr* deserve to be studied for their own sake, the bifurcation of qur'ānic and *tafsīr* study is both natural and beneficial. At the same time, insofar as both fields explore (in more or less direct ways) qur'ānic textual meaning, they may potentially benefit all the more from ongoing conversation and cross-fertilization.

JIQSA 1 (2016): 11–22

THE PROBLEMATIC OF PROPHECY: 2015 IQSA PRESIDENTIAL ADDRESS

REUVEN FIRESTONE

When Muḥammad began to gain followers in Mecca, the leaders of the town sent trusted emissaries to the Jews of Yathrib/Medina to ask their opinion about whether or not Muḥammad was a true prophet. Al-Nadhr b. al-Ḥārith and ʿUqbah b. Abī Muʿayṭ traveled the 200 or so miles to Medina. When they got there, they were instructed by the Jewish leadership, "Ask Muhammad three questions. If he can answer them, he is a true prophet, but if not, then he is an imposter."[1]

The Medinan Jews soon became curious enough about the alleged prophet to send a learned and rather corpulent rabbi named Mālik to Mecca in order to find out what he could about him. When Mālik met Muḥammad, he was outwitted by a surprise question Muḥammad posed to him about his chubbiness, for which he was totally unprepared. Outmaneuvered, Mālik returned to Medina, humiliated by his failure to interrogate the alleged prophet successfully.[2]

Shortly thereafter, when Muḥammad made his hijrah to Medina, he stayed with the Banū ʿAmr b. ʿAwf in Qubāʾ. A learned Jew named ʿAbd Allāh b. Salām was up in a date palm, probably to pollinate it for harvest, when he heard that Muḥammad had reached the outskirts of Medina. He immediately exclaimed "*Allāhu akbar*" at the news of Muḥammad's arrival, to which his aunt Khālidah bt. al-Ḥārith, who was working below him on the ground, replied, "Is he the prophet whom we have been told will be sent at this very time?"[3] According to ʿAbd Allāh he certainly was, for he said, "When I heard about the Messenger of God, I knew by his description, his name, and his time [i.e., when he appeared] that he was the one we were

1. See Hartwig Hirschfeld, "Historical and Legendary Controversies between Mohammed and the Rabbis," *JQR* (First Series) 10 (1898): 100–116, 100.

2. Ibid., 102.

3. Ibn Hishām, *Al-Sīrah al-nabawiyyah li-Ibn Hishām* (2 vols.; Beirut: Dār al-Thiqāfah al-ʿArabiyyah, n.d.), 1:516–517; Alfred Guillaume (trans.), *The Life of Muhammad: A Translation of Isḥāq's* [sic] Sīrat Rasūl Allāh (Karachi: Oxford University Press, 1967), 240–241.

doi: http://dx.doi.org/10.5913/jiqsa.1.2017.a002

waiting for."[4] ʿAbd Allāh promptly sought out Muḥammad and became a devoted follower. So did Mukhayrīq, another learned Jewish scholar (*wa-kāna ḥabran ʿāliman*), who not only followed him but gladly gave his life during the battle of Uḥud.

Toward the end of Muḥammad's life, the Companion Muʿādh b. Jabal served as the governor of Janad in central Yemen. At that time, most of the inhabitants of Janad were Jewish. When a group of Jews there questioned Muʿādh about the keys of Paradise, "He not only gave them the right answer, but also told them that Muḥammad had anticipated their question…"[5] Muʿādh, who had been a Jew before joining up with the Prophet, succeeded in leading a mass conversion of the area's Jews at the mosque of Janad.[6]

Most of the Jews of Medina, however, did not follow ʿAbd Allāh, Mukhayrīq, or Muʿādh's example. Perhaps it is more accurate to put it this way: while several individual Jews—including at least a few who were well-educated in Jewish tradition and practice—followed Muḥammad, the Jewish community as a community did not. Ibn Isḥāq (d. 150/767) provides the names of certain *aḥbār al-yahūd* (learned Jews) who consistently tried to annoy Muḥammad with difficult questions.[7] They aggravated the Prophet in other ways as well. Once, when Muḥammad's camel wandered off, a Jewish *ḥabr* named Zayd b. al-Luṣayt asked how he could be a true prophet when he did not even know where his camel was.[8] The continued questioning suggests that most of the Jews of Medina were not convinced of Muḥammad's prophethood. But it is interesting to note that, despite their skepticism, they seem to have continued to ask the questions for some time before the differences between Muḥammad and the Jews of Medina broke down into violence.

Now it is well-known that all of these stories are open to question and criticism according to careful historians of Late Antiquity and early Islam. Cautious scholars take great care when considering whether these episodes could have occurred as depicted or whether something like them happened at

4. Ibid.

5. Michael Lecker, "The Jewish Reaction to the Islamic Conquests," in Volkhard Krech and Marion Steinicke (eds.), *Dynamics in the History of Religions between Asia and Europe* (Leiden: Brill, 2012), 177, n. 2.

6. Ibid., 177. Lecker, who identifies Muʿādh as a Jew, is the leading Western scholar of the intricate genealogies of the Meccan and Medinan communities. On the problem of the meaning of conversion, see Richard Bulliet, "Conversion Stories in Early Islam," in Michael Gervers and Ramzi Jibran Kighazi (eds.), *Conversion and Continuity: Indigenous Christian Communities in Islamic Lands, Eighth to Eighteenth Centuries* (Toronto: Pontifical Institute of Medieval Studies, 1990), 123–133.

7. Ibn Isḥāq, *Sīrah,* 1.513–514.

8. Ibn Isḥāq, *Sīrah,* 1.527, 2.522–523.

all. But whether or not they can be relied upon as historically accurate, I think they reveal a great deal about what concerned the early actors and observers of the period, and they raise a number of important questions for students of early Islam, of the Qur'ān, and of religion and scripture in general.

Why were the Jews of Medina depicted as instructing the Meccan pagans about how to test Muḥammad's prophetic status? Why did they send their own emissary? Why did they continue to ask him annoying questions?

Were the Jews of Arabia expecting a prophet?

This is actually an old question in modern scholarship, and it reflects an issue that turns up quite a bit in the polemical literatures of both Muslims and Jews. Medieval Muslim polemicists from Ibn Ḥazm in Spain to Ibn Kathīr in Syria argued that Jews had moved to Arabia expecting a prophet based on biblical testimony.[9]

But the early Muslim sources are *also* quite certain that the Jews of Arabia were expecting a prophet. Ibn Isḥāq wrote about a pious, elderly Jew named Ibn al-Hayyabān who had moved to Medina from Syria and was known for his ability to bring rain through his devoted prayers. When Ibn al-Hayyabān was about to die he said, "O Jews, what do you think caused me to leave a land of wine and bread to a land of suffering and hunger?... I came to this country expecting the appearance of a prophet whose time had come!"[10] Ibn Isḥāq also referred to a Medinan Jew from the Banū'l-Ashhal who preached to the local polytheists about "*al-qiyāmah wa'l-baʿth wa'l-ḥisāb wa'l-mīzān wa'l-jannah wa'l-nār* (the Resurrection, the Reckoning, the Scales of Judgment, Paradise, and Hell)." When asked by the locals for a sign to confirm his views, he said, "A prophet will be sent from the direction of this land," and he pointed with his hand toward Mecca and the Yemen.[11]

Ibn Saʿd (d. 230/845) records similar reports. A Jewish merchant living in Mecca came one night to an assembly of Quraysh, the dominant tribe in Mecca, and informed them that a future prophet named Aḥmad had just been born there. He asked if any of them had begotten a child that night.[12] Ibn Saʿd cites a report about Tubbaʿ the king of Yemen, who encamped before Yathrib (that is, Medina) intending to destroy the Jews of the town. When he informed them of his desire to rid the town of Judaism, the most learned Jew of the town, whose name was Sāmūl, informed the king that that city was the place of hijrah of a future prophet named Aḥmad from the

9. The biblical texts referred to most frequently are Deut 33:1–2; Hab 3:1–3; Isa 63:1.

10. Ibn Isḥāq, *Sīrah*, 1.213–214.

11. Ibid., 1.112.

12. Muḥammad b. Saʿd b. Manīʿ al-Hāshimī, *Al-Ṭabaqāt al-kubrā* (9 vols.; Beirut: Dār al-Kutub al-ʿIlmiyyah, 1418 [1997]), 1.129.

children of Ishmael. Sāmūl proceeded to describe Muḥammad and told of his future battles during which he would first be defeated and then prevail.[13] In another tradition cited by Ibn Saʿd, the most learned of Medinan Jews was a man named al-Zabīr b. Bāṭā. He knew from a book owned by his father that Muḥammad (in the book the name is Aḥmad) was described as the awaited prophet who would be raised up in Mecca. But when he learned about the *actual* Muḥammad, the flesh-and-blood Muḥammad, al-Zabīr blotted out the prophecy about him that was in the book.[14] That the Jews did not accept the prophethood of Muḥammad was due, one would surmise from these stories, simply to their willful stubbornness and obstinate selfishness.

When we move to Jewish sources we also find some interesting material. Certain biblical texts were understood by some Jews to suggest the geographical direction from which a future redeemer or messianic figure would come. The most suggestive for our purposes are from the prophets Isaiah and Habakkuk, who hint at a future redemptive figure coming from Teman (Yemen), Paran, and Edom. These three locations are associated with Arabian geography in pre-Islamic Jewish texts from both Bible and Talmud. That association was very enticing to later Muslims. The great geographer Shihāb al-Dīn Yāqūt b. ʿAbd Allāh al-Ḥamawī (d. 626/1229), for example, wrote the following regarding Paran (*Fārān* in Arabic): "*Fārān*… An Arabized Hebrew word. It is one of the names of Mecca mentioned in the Tawrāt [Torah]. It is said that it is a name for the mountains of Mecca…"[15]

Some Jewish sources, perhaps produced during or shortly after the Muslim (or Arab) conquests, clearly wondered whether the military victories of the early caliphs were the beginnings of redemption according to Jewish tradition. Here is an example of an apocalyptic Hebrew poem that raises the question ("Israel" is a designation for the Jewish people in traditional Jewish texts):

> On that day when the Messiah, son of David, will come to a downtrodden people,
> These signs will be seen in the world and will be brought forth:
> Earth and heaven will wither…
> The king of the West and the king of the East
> Will be ground one against the other,
> And the armies of the king of the West will hold firm in the land.
> And a king will go forth from the land of Yoqtan[16]

13. Ibn Saʿd, *Ṭabaqāt*, 1.126.

14. Ibid.

15. Yāqūt, *Muʿjam al-buldān*, ed. Farīd ʿAbd al-ʿAzīz al-Janūdī (Beirut: Dār al-Kutub al-ʿIlmiyyah, 1410/1990), 4.255.

16. Considered in some Arab genealogies to be Qaḥṭān.

> And his armies will seize the Land,
> And dwellers of the world will be judged
> And the heavens will rain dust on the earth,
> And winds will spread in the Land.
> Gog and Magog will incite one another
> And kindle fear in the heart of the Gentiles.
> And Israel will be freed of all their sins
> And will no more be kept far from their house of prayer...
> The kings from the land of Edom will be no more,
> And the people of Antioch will rebel and make peace...
> Edomites and Ishmael[17] will fight in the valley of Acco
> 'Til the horses sink in blood and panic.
> Gaza and her daughters will be stoned
> And Ashkelon and Ashdod will be terror-stricken.
> Israel will go forth from the City and turn eastwards,
> And taste no bread for five and four days.
> And their Messiah will be revealed and they will be consoled...[18]

This and a few other Jewish texts are extremely enticing, but it must be kept in mind that in the Jewish sources, which certainly expected a redemptive figure, that person is always a *messianic* redeemer and not a new *prophet*. As the Talmud remarks, prophethhood ceased with the end of the last biblical prophets, Haggai, Zachariah, and Malachi.[19] And Ibn Isḥāq notes that five Jews confronted ʿAbd Allāh b. Salām, the man who left the Jewish community, when he joined Muḥammad. Kaʿb b. Asad, Abū Rāfiʿ, Ashyaʿ, and Shamwīl b. Zayd said to ʿAbd Allāh: ما تكون النبُوَّة في العرب، ولكن صاحبك ملك ("there will be no prophecy among the Arabs. Your master is [only] a king").[20]

17. The name Edom or Edomites is often used in Jewish literature as a coded reference to Christians, and Ishmael or Ishmaelites to Muslims. Edom derives from Jacob's brother Esau according to the Hebrew Bible (Gen 25:25, 30; 36:1). See Gerson D. Cohen, "Esau as Symbol in Early Medieval Thought," in Alexander Altmann (ed.), *Jewish and Medieval and Renaissance Studies* (Cambridge, MA: Harvard University Press, 1967), 19–48; *Pirqe Rabbi Eliezer*, Chapter 30, trans. Gerald Friedlander (North Straford, NH: Ayer, 2004), 250–251.

18. Various versions of this can be found in Bernard Lewis, "An Apocalyptic Vision of Islamic History," *BSOAS* 13 (1950): 308–338.

19. b. Sotah 48a; b. Sanh. 11a. A number of cutoff dates are provided by rabbinic literature, and Urbach and Weinfeld have provided data that can be understood to demonstrate how the endpoint of prophecy may have correlated with the long process of canonization of the Hebrew Bible. See Ephraim Urbach and Moshe Weinfeld, "When Did Prophecy End?" [Heb.], *Tarbiz* 18 (1947–1948): 1–27.

20. Ibn Isḥāq, *Sīrah*, 1.571.

We are not informed by the sources that any Christian communities lived with Muḥammad and his followers, as did the Jews of Medina. In fact, it would be interesting to consider how the Qur'ān's generally more positive perspective toward Christians might have been different had the hijrah of the Prophet been to the town of Najrān, in which a substantial Christian community lived, rather than Medina, a town with a large Jewish population. The real conflict between Muslims and Christians historically would emerge only later, after the death of Muḥammad and the end of revelation, when the sting of Christian rejection of Muḥammad's prophethood could not enter in the qur'ānic record of divine disclosure.

The early post-qur'ānic Islamic sources, however, are a different matter. They refer to the story of a Christian monk sometimes named Baḥīrah ("chosen one" in Christian Aramaic), who through various signs, including in some versions a "mark of prophecy" on the young Muḥammad's back, confirmed that the boy would become a great prophet expected also by Christians.[21] Some sources go even further in their clarity about the expectation of a prophet. According to Ibn Isḥāq, virtually all the learned and informed inhabitants of the peninsula knew that a new and uniquely Arabian prophet was at hand before the appearance of Muḥammad. As he put it:

وكانت الأحبار من اليهود والرهبان من النصارى والكهان من العرب قد تحدثوا بأمر رسول الله صلى الله عليه وسلم قبل مبعثه.

> The Jewish rabbis, Christian monks, and pagan Arab soothsayers [all] spoke of the circumstances of the Messenger of God before his arrival.[22]

The Qur'ān notes, like the Bible before it, that God sent many messengers and prophets. Q Āl 'Imrān 3:81: "[Remember when] God made a covenant with the prophets: 'Whatever I have given you of the Book and wisdom and then a messenger comes to you confirming what is with you, you are to believe in him and help him.'"

This is similar to a famous verse in the Torah, Deuteronomy 18:15: "The Lord your God will raise up for you prophets from among your own people, like myself; you shall heed them."[23]

21. Ibn Sa'd, *Ṭabaqāt*, 1.121–124; Ibn Isḥāq, *Sīrah*, 1.180–182; Barbara Roggema, *The Legend of Sergius Baḥīra: Eastern Christian Apologetics and Apocalyptic in Response to Islam* (Leiden: Brill, 2008); cf. Isa 9:5.

22. Ibn Isḥāq, *Sīrah*, 1.204.

23. The actual reference to prophets here is articulated in the singular (*nāvî*), but the meaning is plural. The Israelites will experience the arrival of more prophets, as Bernard Levinsohn puts it: "*A prophet*, while grammatically singular, is distributive in its meaning: 'I will repeatedly raise up for you a prophet.' More than one prophet is clearly intended." See Adele Berlin and Marc Zvi Brettler (eds.), *The Jewish Study*

The Qur'ān provides many lists of pre-qur'ānic prophets and offers many edifying stories about them. But it also cautions that not all prophet-like persons are actually prophets. There are *kuhhān* and *shuʿarā'*, *sāḥirūn* and *majānīn*—soothsayers and poets, sorcerers and people possessed. These must all be rejected, for they do not speak in the name of God (Q 52:29; 69:41–42; 81:22, etc.)[24] Any of these who claim to speak in God's name are frauds and imposters:

وَمَنْ أَظْلَمُ مِمَّنِ افْتَرَىٰ عَلَى اللَّهِ كَذِبًا أَوْ قَالَ أُوحِيَ إِلَيَّ وَلَمْ يُوحَ إِلَيْهِ شَيْءٌ وَمَنْ قَالَ سَأُنْزِلُ
مِثْلَ مَا أَنْزَلَ اللَّهُ

> And who is more evil than he who forges a lie against God, or says: "It was revealed to me" when nothing was revealed to him; and he who says: "I will bring down the like of what God has brought down?" (Q Anʿam 6:93).

The *mufassirūn*, I should add, typically understood this verse to be referring to the false prophet of Muḥammad's own generation named Musaylimah, who challenged the authority of Muḥammad as the sole and final prophet of God.[25]

It seems clear that the Qur'ān is infused with the problematics of prophecy. It claims repeatedly through exclamation, attestation, narrative, and citation of scriptural prognostication that Muḥammad was God's true prophet. But it also notes that other individuals who were not true prophets claimed the same or similar title or function. And Jews and Christians (not to mention practitioners of traditional Arabian religions) either questioned or outright rejected Muḥammad's prophetic status, and they denied that he was foretold in their own scriptures.

That the Qur'ān is rife with material on the problematic of prophecy parallels similar concerns among Jews and Christians and concerns expressed in their scriptures. The difficulty of proving the truth of Muḥammad's prophetic status lies at the heart of qur'ānic authority and the legitimacy of

---

Bible (New York: Oxford University Press, 2003), 395. Note how the reference is repeated three verses later: "I will raise up prophets for them from among their own people, like yourself: I will put My words in their mouths and they will speak to them all that I command them."

24. The Qur'ān notes how Muḥammad himself was accused of being all of these rather than a true prophet (Q 25:8; 36:69; 52:29; 69:41–42; 81:22).

25. The problem did not plague early Islam alone. A number of Christian prophets surfaced during the first Christian centuries, the best known being Montanus (ca. 200). See Guy G. Stroumsa, "False Prophets of Early Christianity," in *The Making of the Abrahamic Religions in Late Antiquity* (Oxford: Oxford University, 2015), 59–71, and the following footnote.

the new movement that emerged along with it and was legitimized by it. The core of the problem can be summarized simply with the following question: how can one determine whether a person who *claims* to be a prophet is *really* a prophet? A similar anxiety is clear from Jesus' Sermon on the Mount: "Beware of false prophets, who come to you in sheep's clothing but inwardly are ravenous wolves" (Matt 7:15).[26]

Here the Torah is perhaps instructive. Deuteronomy 18 proclaims: "And should you ask yourselves, 'How can we know that the [prophetic] word was not spoken by the Lord?'" It answers,

> אֲשֶׁר יְדַבֵּר הַנָּבִיא בְּשֵׁם יְדֹוָד וְלֹא יִהְיֶה הַדָּבָר וְלֹא יָבוֹא, הוּא הַדָּבָר אֲשֶׁר לֹא דִבְּרוֹ יְדֹוָד
>
> If the prophet speaks something in the name of the Lord that does not come true, that message was not spoken by the Lord.

The verse continues: "The prophet has uttered it presumptuously. Do not stand in dread of him." (Deut 18:21–22).[27]

I should add here that, if you look at the profoundly beautiful and familiar prophecies found in the Hebrew Bible, the poetic and inspiring utterances of Isaiah and Jeremiah and the other biblical prophets, and if you examine the prophetic utterances of the New Testament from the Gospels to Revelation, and if you read the announcements of the approaching End Times with all its cosmic signs found in the Qur'ān, you will find no concrete markers, no indicators that can be used to invalidate them. The prophetic utterances found in all our scriptures are couched in language vague enough so that it is virtually impossible to claim they are wrong, that the time has lapsed and they did not come to pass. But when you observe the description of prophets outside of scripture, in the writings of Flavius Josephus or other historians of Late Antiquity, you will find that those so-called prophets who were destroyed and their movements crushed by the Romans made the fatal flaw of prophesying when the end would come.[28] Here is some helpful advice for

---

26. Cf. John 10:12; Acts 20:29. See also Matt 24:11; 1 Cor 12:27–30; and in the Hebrew Bible, Jer 5:31; 6:13–14; 23:2; Ezek 22:27–28; Mic 3:5–8; Zech 13:2–6.

27. The full citation in 18:21–22 is

וְכִי תֹאמַר בִּלְבָבֶךָ אֵיכָה נֵדַע אֶת הַדָּבָר אֲשֶׁר לֹא דִבְּרוֹ יְדֹוָד: אֲשֶׁר יְדַבֵּר הַנָּבִיא בְּשֵׁם יְדֹוָד וְלֹא יִהְיֶה הַדָּבָר וְלֹא יָבוֹא הוּא הַדָּבָר אֲשֶׁר לֹא דִבְּרוֹ יְדֹוָד בְּזָדוֹן דִּבְּרוֹ הַנָּבִיא לֹא תָגוּר מִמֶּנּוּ:

Elsewhere in Deuteronomy it stipulates that even if the prophecy or oracle comes true, if the prophet calls for the worship of other gods, they must be rejected (Deut 13:2–5).

28. E.g., Josephus, *Antiquities* 20.8.6 and *Jewish War* 6.5.2, in *Josephus: Complete Works* (Grand Rapids: Kregel, 1981), 422, 582.

aspiring prophets: Never give a cut-off date. Remain subtle and mysterious—it may save your life.

This brings us to a very serious problem: what happens when you discover a false prophet? An answer to this question is provided in Deuteronomy: "But any prophet who presumes to speak something in My name that I did not command him to utter, or who speaks in the name of other gods, that prophet shall die (וּמֵת הַנָּבִיא הַהוּא)" (18:20).

This is the very policy carried out by Abū Bakr with the killing of the Arabian false prophet Musaylimah at the Battle of Yamāmah. Musaylimah was a prophetic contender with Muḥammad and actually outlived him. But according to the received interpretation of Q Aḥzāb 33:40, Muḥammad is the last prophet:

مَا كَانَ مُحَمَّدٌ أَبَا أَحَدٍ مِنْ رِجَالِكُمْ وَلَٰكِنْ رَسُولَ اللَّهِ وَخَاتَمَ النَّبِيِّينَ

There can be no prophet after Muḥammad, though David Powers has challenged the assumed meaning of this verse in his recent book, the title of which is the very verse just noted in Arabic, *Muḥammad Is Not the Father of Any of Your Men.*[29] The verse continues: "Rather, he is the Messenger of God and Seal of the Prophets."[30]

Here we observe a very close correspondence between the act of Abū Bakr in ordering the killing of a false prophet and the biblical pronouncement regarding prophetic pretenders. I am not suggesting influence here but rather a shared worldview that results from the problematic of prophecy. Abū Bakr and the Torah arrive at the same conclusion because they are confronted with the same problem and the resultant anxieties to which the problem gives birth.

Prophecy is powerful. Prophecy represents a conduit to the divine will. Nothing is more authoritative than the will and word of God. It is the source of authority for monotheistic religions, and it is also their source of legitimacy. God reveals. That is how the scriptural religions teach what believers must do and how they must function. All monotheistic religions agree on this God-centered core of their being. And all scriptural monotheisms also agree that the core of divine revelation can be recorded and has been recorded—written down, or "scribed"—into scripture.

The scriptural religions all follow the same rules regarding prophets and revelation and scripturalization and canonization, and I include Christianity in this model. God reveals the divine disclosure through prophets, though

29. David S. Powers, *Muḥammad Is Not the Father of Any of Your Men: The Making of the Last Prophet* (Philadelphia: University of Pennsylvania Press, 2011).

30. See Stroumsa, *Making of the Abrahamic Religions*, 59–99, especially Chapter 5, "Seal of the Prophets."

in the case of Christianity the revelation can also be even more direct than prophecy in the appearance of Jesus as God incarnate.[31] But the rules or expectations of divine revelation are virtually the same for all:

(1) God reveals in a variety of ways, but the record is conveyed in words.
(2) Those words are collected and recorded.
(3) The collection becomes scripture when it is formulated into an official text.
(4) It is authenticated through a process of canonization.
(5) All aberrant versions are destroyed.
(6) Henceforth, any new claims for prophecy are patently rejected as false.

The act of scriptural canonization is a declarative act. It declares that, while God can and does continue to reveal the divine glory in multiple ways, once scripture is fixed in its canonical form, there can be no new prophets and no new scripture.

And now we can observe the problem more clearly. The very core authority of monotheistic religion is the authority of God as revealed to the believers and recorded in a timeless scripture that needs no revised edition. To those who revere their scripture, there can be no upgrade, no Bible 2.0, no updates to the Qur'ān.

Fine. But what happens when, after scriptural canonization, a new prophet nevertheless arises?

According to all the scriptural monotheisms, this is impossible. There can be no new prophets. And yet, the annoying truth of the matter is that to many people, it seems to occur nonetheless. New prophets continue to arise.

Established monotheisms reject them.

The rejection of new prophets can be understood in a variety of ways and from a variety of perspectives. From the perspective of established religions (meaning religions that already possess a canonized scripture), new prophets are by definition false prophets. To Judaism, Jesus cannot fulfill the role of prophet or vehicle of the divine word. To Christianity, Muḥammad cannot be a true prophet. And according to Islam, Mīrzā Ḥusayn ʿAlī Nūrī or *Bahā'u'llāh* cannot speak in God's name.

But from the perspective of every emergent prophetic religion, from the viewpoint of every new faith, God sends a new messenger because of enduring and persistent problems that are not being addressed by the established religions.

31. But see Matt 21:11; Acts 3:22; 7:37.

Let's consider this from the perspective of systems theory and the academic study of religion. The emergence of new prophets destabilizes the authority of the establishment by claiming a higher authority. That higher authority is God. Keep in mind that divine authority is the ultimate trump card. It overrules all other authority. God prevails over everything, and that includes any religious establishment. A new divine revelation always corrects, fulfills or supersedes the establishment religions, which are by definition old, flawed, and outmoded—that is... unless the new revelation is not *truly* a *divine* revelation.

Keep in mind that, according to any established religion, whatever the new prophet claims to be the word of God is not the word of God. That is because, from the perspective of established religion, prophecy—*by definition*—has ceased.

This scenario with its resultant tension and conflict is part of what may be called a phenomenology of religious emergence. It is particularly interesting from the standpoint of scriptural studies because the tension and conflict of this phenomenology can be observed within scripture itself. That is because scripture represents the earliest record of religious emergence among scriptural religions. No record preexists scripture because scripture is the core around which religion forms itself.[32] All subsequent writings are informed in one way or another by scripture.

We observe this scenario of tension and conflict in the Qur'ān as well as the earlier revealed texts. Each scripture condemns members of established religions who refuse to accept the new prophecies. Each scripture also ensures that subsequent claims to prophecy must be considered false.

While a few individuals or groups from the scriptural monotheist communities joined up with Muḥammad, the communities as a whole did not voluntarily accept the new prophet. Some tribal communities joined *en masse*, to be sure, including some Christian and Jewish tribes or clans. But the established, organized religions would not, nor could they, accept a new prophet. To do so would be to vote oneself out of business—and nobody votes *themselves* out of business.

When one observes the phenomenon in isolation, one easily arrives at a distorted picture. From the particularist perspective of the Qur'ān and the religion of Islam that grew out of it, the Jews who rejected Muḥammad's

32. Some religious writings can exist contemporaneously with scripture. Examples are apocryphal writings that were rejected from Jewish scripture or extracanonical gospels that were rejected from Christian scripture. These can only be recensions or versions of the scriptural corpus that were rejected from the canon. Their status always remains heretical to the community that rejected them because they were not accepted as part of the canon of that community's scripture.

prophethood were simply subverting and sabotaging God's revelation. But from another particularist perspective, that of the Hebrew Bible and the religions of Judaism and Christianity that grew out of it, rejection of a new claimant for prophecy was a necessary religious act, one of valor and heroism.

I think that the theory of religious emergence I have outlined here provides a valuable perspective. What I'm describing could also be called a phenomenology of prophetic contention. Awareness of the natural tension between scriptural canonization and competing prophetic claims has value for the critical study of the Qur'ān, the very *raison d'être* of this new and wonderful learned society. It can help the Qur'ān scholar to be in touch with our human tendency, even as critical scholars, to misread the data before us because of our own religious history and identity. Bias affects us all, even if we consider ourselves nonbelievers or neutral "children of the world." We all carry with us natural cultural biases, which are informed in part by the religions that infuse the cultures in which we live.

Awareness of this tension can offer perspective and tools to help us make sense of some of the puzzling verses, references, and constructions found in the Qur'ān.

It can also help us detach critical study of the Qur'ān from the low-level tensions that often lie behind cultural, political, and religious issues that infiltrate our daily lives. This mindfulness can help us free ourselves from the omnipresent obstacles, the interference from outside cultural and political distractions that get in the way of engaging in careful and critical study and analysis.

For the scholar, but also for the lay observer and religious believer, understanding the problematics of religious emergence can help us make sense of the often painful and bewildering tensions that have traditionally divided religious communities. Perhaps it can also help us to overcome them.

JIQSA 1 (2016): 23–27

RESPONSE TO REUVEN FIRESTONE'S 2015 IQSA PRESIDENTIAL ADDRESS

EBRAHIM MOOSA

In his presidential keynote, Reuven Firestone has identified multiple features of the problem of prophecy in Islam. He informs us about the ways in which Muḥammad's prophecy was first expected to occur according to reports from some Arabian Jews and how certain features of Muḥammad's prophecy were even noted in Jewish sources. At the same time, he is also cautious and wonders out loud whether these episodes of Jewish notices of Muḥammad's prophecy "could have occurred as depicted or whether something like them happened at all." It is healthy to foster such skepticism. Skepticism allows the historian to explore other possibilities and explanations as to what happened in order to track how these predictions about Muḥammad's prophecy played out, both at the time of their purported occurrence and when these reports were received among Muslim communities and other faith traditions over time.

While Firestone has shared many points of interest with us—and I hope many of you will engage him on some of the valuable points he raised—I will, in turn, only touch on a few issues.

One of the issues Firestone raises is this: Why did the Jews of Medina keep on asking Muḥammad annoying questions? Why were they trying to trip him up, so to speak?

Well, it seems that at least in the eighth century, there was an expectation that someone who claimed to speak on behalf of the supernatural was supposed to know the answers to all questions. Omnipotence and omniscience were viewed as virtues for anyone claiming access to the supernatural, at least among some communities. Yet Muḥammad repeatedly said that he did not know things related to the unseen. And then in a polemical gesture, he said, in the words of the Qur'ān, "If I were to be informed of the unseen and the secrets of things, then I would have excelled in virtue" (*law kuntu aʿlamu al-ghayba la-istakthartu min al-khayri*; Q Aʿrāf 7:188). At the same time, he also said, "Obey God and obey the messenger and those in authority among you" (*aṭīʿū allāha wa-aṭīʿū al-rasūla wa-ūlī al-amri minkum*; Q Nisā' 4:59).

doi: http://dx.doi.org/10.5913/jiqsa.1.2017.a003

I found the recently posthumously published work of Marilyn Robinson Waldman to be very helpful to me. It provides a framework for Muḥammadan prophecy that I found to be extremely productive.[1] Waldman argues that the Prophet Muḥammad's contemporaries held varying criteria of identification and benchmarks for his prophecy. In other words, the problematic of prophecy, as Firestone calls it, did not have just one standard. So one finds that, when skeptics directed a series of questions to the Prophet, on some occasions he provided answers and on other occasions he failed to respond or refused to answer their queries; on other occasions, he provided a reason as to why he was unable to respond.

Waldman argues that none of Muḥammad's contemporaries could quite figure out how to classify him. And in the Qur'ān, there are narratives that indicate the Prophet is repeatedly striving to overcome the skepticism directed at him. So how did the Prophet Muḥammad survive this identification crisis, Waldman asks. How did he fuse gifted speech, opposition, and leadership—all these elements—into a seamless narrative? Her answer to this puzzle is that Muḥammad went beyond the expectations of his immediate audience. He invited comparisons: comparisons of other prophets with himself, or he himself used comparisons to shape his emergent role in a fluid situation. And he seemed to invite such comparisons in both a literal and figurative sense. In other words, he struck the right balance between similarity and difference.

In order to illustrate that Muḥammad did not have unlimited access to knowledge of the unseen but that he only had access to a portion of divine knowledge taught to him, there is clearly a similarity with Moses and Khiḍr. Like Moses, he does not know all the realities of the unseen world. But a different kind of role-player, like Khiḍr, is gifted with a comprehensive understanding of the unseen. In other words, Muḥammad was more like Moses. Biblical scholars are fond of prefiguration, such as those important persons who prefigured the arrival of Jesus. Modern Qur'ān scholarship in the West has yet to configure a narrative register where, say, Moses prefigures Muḥammad. Waldman does not talk about prefiguration, but it is clear she is asking us to think in this direction.

The other element that Firestone introduces is an important one: the phenomenology of religious emergence. What does emergence here mean? Paul Humphreys usefully defines emergence:

> Emergence is, broadly speaking, the fact that there are features of the world—objects, properties, laws, perhaps other things—that are manifested as a result

1. Marilyn Robinson Waldman, *Prophecy and Power: Muhammad and the Qur'an in the Light of Comparison*, ed. Bruce B. Lawrence with Lindsay Jones and Robert M. Baum (Sheffield: Equinox, 2013).

> of the existence of other, usually more basic, entities but that cannot be completely reduced to those other entities. Theories of emergence tend to fall into two basic types: ontological emergence and epistemological emergence—with conceptual emergence serving as a subcategory of the latter, namely, of epistemological emergence.[2]

Well, there are many philosophical accounts of emergence. Usually emergence presents itself in a cluster of features. Some of the features of emergence are that they are irreducible, novel, unpredictable on the basis of any theory, and unexplainable. Most importantly, they must emerge from something.

So how does religion emerge from something, such as an environment or a substrate? How does a religion become known in the world? From what does religion emerge? One element of religion is clearly that which we call prophecy. So in part, prophecy is an ontological phenomenon. It is about becoming, emergence, proceeding in time—and over time, the same religion can take different forms. It becomes historical. Heidegger writes:

> To this aim, we must inspect more carefully in which sense the characterization "historical," which we have just performed, is to be understood. Historical, here means becoming, emergence, proceeding in time, a characterization that befits a reality. Insofar as one remains within the cognitive consideration of the connections among objects, each characterization or use of the sense of "historical" is always determined through this fore-conception of the object. The object is historical; it has the particularity of proceeding in time, of changing.[3]

Epistemological accounts of emergence normally emphasize the unpredictability of phenomena. Taking emergence seriously, one can say following Firestone's conclusion that every scriptural religious tradition has created its own theological language. One novel aspect of religion is that it closes off successor prophecy and deems the previous prophecy to be heresy. However, Islamic prophecy does affirm previous prophecies, but not those prophecies that came after it, that is, going forward. Hence, the challenges to post-Muḥammadan prophecy are legend in Islamic thought.

I was wondering if we could not think of prophecy as a kind of *enframing* in the philosophical sense. (Enframing has nothing to do with frames, or technology, for that matter. Enframing is not a tool or an apparatus; this is the crucial point in Heidegger's argument—the very condition of possibility

---

2. Paul Humphreys, "Emergence," *Encyclopedia of Philosophy*, s.v. (http://www.encyclopedia.com/article-1G2-3446800558/emergence.html).

3. Martin Heidegger, *Studies in Continental Thought: Phenomenology of Religious Life* (Bloomington: Indiana University Press, 2010).

for the truth of the real to be revealed— *poetically*, to humans.) I use the term *enframing*, drawing on Heidegger's idea of *Gestell* in the context of his exploration of technology. Enframing here means "where things gather together in order to reveal." So in this context, I would argue that prophecy is a challenge to human beings to open up, to gather together; it is a challenge to human beings to disclose the real to their own selves, how to reveal the truth. How people engage with prophecy can be infinitely varied.

The reception of prophecy is also very interesting. Muslim philosophers like Muḥammad Iqbal, the prepartition poet-philosopher of the Indian subcontinent, for instance, thought that in the long march of history Islam abrogates all subsequent prophecy. For Iqbal, with the advent of Islam, humanity has reached a certain unspecified maturity and therefore is no longer in need of heavenly instruction.

Modern Muslims hold on to a doctrine of *khatm al-nubuwwah*, the end of prophecy, in the sense that no new leader (and hence no new moral code) can further be expected. But *ilhām*, a form of inspiration, continues. The possibility of a mahdi, a messianic herald, is still active in certain Muslim religious imaginaries; also of a *muḥaddath* (reviver), one in whose being God makes divine truths manifest by way of inspiration, is also a well-attested phenomenon in the literature. The idea that one could be inspired also finds expression in the writings of the Indian poet Mirza Asadullah Ghalib (d. 1869). Ghalib wrote:

> From the unseen (*ghayb*) these themes reach the mind/imagination
> These scratches you hear, O Ghalib, are the sounds made by the pen of the archangel.

> آتے ہیں غیب سے یہ مضامیں خیال میں
> غالبؔ صریرِ خامہ نوائے سروش ہے

For a long time, there has been tension within Islam between poetry and prophecy, because both were viewed as tapping into the same source. Ghalib, just more courageously, others would claim brazenly, acknowledges his inspiration as coming from the mystically unseen realm. Yet, we also know that prophecy is always framed within a theology. It is theology that invests speech in the world, which is a by-product of prophecy. The word of God—or scripture, as we call it—would not be so valorized were it not for the direct role of prophecy in the making of revealed or divine speech.

The question is more acute for modern scriptural traditions: How do they affirm each other when they each have exclusive prophecies, where each is sealed off from the other? Will theology find ways to bridge different prophecies and help us make sense of prophetic traditions across the religious divide? Are we done with the age of prophecy, or are we at the very beginning of this age? These are some of the discursive questions that occur to me, and I am delighted to share them with you. But I want to mostly thank Reuven Firestone for making us think about prophecy again and for sharing his insights on this topic in an engaging and productive manner.

JIQSA 1 (2016): 29–45

THE CURRENT STATE OF QUR'ĀNIC STUDIES: COMMENTARY ON A ROUNDTABLE DISCUSSION*

KAREN BAUER

Abstract

This paper is based on a roundtable discussion held at the 2015 IQSA Annual Meeting about the current state of the field of Qur'ānic Studies and its future, gathering together specialists in different areas from within the academic field of Qur'ānic Studies, as well as from outside it. The panelists were Kecia Ali (Boston University), Herbert Berg (University of North Carolina at Wilmington), Joseph Lumbard (American University in Sharjah), Nicolai Sinai (Oxford University), Devin Stewart (Emory University), and Shawkat Toorawa (Cornell University, now Yale University); Farid Esack (University of Johannesburg) presided. The discussion is here summarized and analyzed by Karen Bauer (the Institute of Ismaili Studies, London). The aim in writing up this discussion is to present a coherent summary and analysis of its major points, so that specialists and non-specialists alike may get a clearer picture of recent trends and changes in the field, as well as of the challenges facing scholars now and in the future.

Introduction

By convening a roundtable discussion on "The Current State of Qur'ānic Studies and its Future" at the IQSA meeting in 2015, Farid Esack and I hoped to initiate a scholarly conversation about the field of Qur'ānic Studies at a time when the very nature of academic study of the Qur'ān is open to debate. The format of a panel discussion with time-limited answers was a conscious attempt to sidestep a typical state-of-the-field literature review, and instead get a series of impressions or "snapshots" from different perspectives. The panel was well attended, with standing room only, and generated much discussion.

* I presented a very early draft of this piece at a Sandpit workshop convened by Rob Gleave, Exeter University, and would like to thank Rob and all of the participants for their helpful feedback.

doi: http://dx.doi.org/10.5913/jiqsa.1.2017.a004

This format enabled the participants to give an overview of the most crucial and important issues facing Qur'ān scholars today. But how to translate this to paper, to be read by people who may not be familiar with the field? I have written this commentary as an attempt to summarize, frame, and situate the lively discussion on that day.[1] I include first a few introductory remarks—my own snapshot of the background to these questions and answers.

Most early scholars of the Qur'ān could be divided into two groups: those who examined the Bible and biblical literature to find the origins of qur'ānic material, and those who broadly adopted the basic assumptions regarding the canonization of the Qur'ān from Islamic histories, which were written hundreds of years after the events in question. The nascent field was populated by non-Muslim Europeans, at a time when the Near East was emerging from the European political control of the colonial and imperial projects. Oriental Studies, as it was known, was not a very popular subject—the sources were difficult to read, find, and access.

By the late 1970s, some scholars, later termed "revisionists," became skeptical of relying on the post-facto accounts of Islamic history that were present in the Islamic sources. John Wansbrough suggested that the Qur'ān had developed along with its interpretation in *Quranic Studies*.[2] With *Hagarism*, Patricia Crone and Michael Cook experimented with discarding Islamic histories altogether, and telling the story of the rise of Islam from contemporary non-Muslim sources.[3] This work proved controversial. Concurrently, Edward Said wrote *Orientalism*, which had an entire section challenging the major premises of Orientalist scholarship as represented by a leader in the field, Bernard Lewis.[4]

Said's work resonated with many because it gave voice to the subalterns, people who were the subjects of both popular and scholarly European literature. Such literature sometimes reflected the biased discourse that had justified colonialism and imperialism. By this time, direct colonialist and imperialist intervention in most Muslim-majority countries had ceased, but its legacy cast a long shadow over the lives of the inhabitants of many Muslim-majority countries. It is possible that Muslim attitudes toward the scholarly discipline of Orientalism were affected by this political legacy. Whatever the reason, many Muslims took exception to the scholarly project of reimagining Islamic history, and particularly the history of the Qur'ān.

1. A full transcript is available on the *JIQSA* website.

2. John Wansbrough, *Qur'anic Studies: Sources and Methods of Scriptural Interpretation* (Oxford: Oxford University Press, 1977).

3. Patricia Crone and Michael Cook, *Hagarism: The Making of the Islamic World* (Cambridge: Cambridge University Press, 1977).

4. Edward Said, *Orientalism* (London: Routledge and Kegan Paul, 1978).

The term "Orientalist" became an accusation, rather than a description of a scholarly method. This combination of factors had a net effect of dampening Qur'ānic Studies. For some time, most scholars avoided studying qur'ānic origins and precursors at all, either through biblical or historical texts. Instead, Qur'ānic Studies became almost synonymous with one of its more interesting subfields—the study of the classical interpretation of the Qur'ān (*tafsīr*). Some would say that this was a period of decline in the field, which was due to scholars' desire to avoid offending Muslim sensibilities. Equally, however, it was a field in need of more sophisticated methodological tools for dealing with the complex text and context of the Qur'ān.

Quietly, inevitably, things began to change, and the nature of this change is at the heart of this roundtable discussion. In recent years, scholars have developed more sophisticated ways of examining the source material. Some focus on the text itself, examining its content, structure, rhetoric, and style (including rhyme). The Bible and biblical literature is no longer studied as the origin of the Qur'ān; yet certain aspects of biblical and other pre-qur'ānic literature (including pagan oral formulae, for instance) have taken an increasingly important place in Qur'ānic Studies. Many scholars now focus their efforts on the late antique milieu of the Qur'ān. "Revisionism" as a label no longer applies to many scholars. However, I would argue that much of the focus on biblical literature, and indeed on the Qur'ān itself as a primary text, could be considered a product of the original revisionist project. There have also been key developments in modern interpretation, and once-niche subfields such as Gender Studies are now well established. One of the most important changes in Qur'ānic Studies was a recurrent theme in this discussion: the issue of confessionalism and non-confessionalism. The demographics of the field have altered radically. We can no longer speak of "Muslim scholarship" and "Western scholarship" as though these were separate enterprises: there are probably as many Muslims studying the Qur'ān in the Western academy today as non-Muslims.

We hoped to get a sense of this zeitgeist through the eyes of experts working in vastly different areas, among them literary approaches to the text, Gender Studies, and recent American Muslim movements, along with tradition-centered approaches and indeed the sort of linguistic study that formed the backbone of medieval Muslim and early Western efforts at understanding the text.[5] The summary below is organized according to the following themes:

5. The panelists were: Kecia Ali (Boston University), Herbert Berg (University of North Carolina at Wilmington), Joseph Lumbard (American University of Sharjah), Nicolai Sinai (Oxford University), Devin Stewart (Emory University), and Shawkat Toorawa (Cornell University, now Yale University). The panel was chaired by Farid Esack (University of Johannesburg).

(1) What is Qur'ānic Studies? (2) Recent developments in the discipline (3) Confessional approaches and scholarly method (4) Political correctness and the study of the Qur'ān (5) What is the future of Qur'ānic Studies?[6]

What Is Qur'ānic Studies?

Today's Qur'ānic Studies is in a sense wide open, and the panelists revealed two main trends in the scholarly study of the Qur'ān: the "big tent" approach and the textual approach. Some participants would not consider themselves experts in the textual-philological discipline of Qur'ānic Studies, because they do not specialize in the textual study of the Qur'ān; yet their work is a perfect illustration of how the big tent approach works in the field. Kecia Ali put it this way: "[I fit here] not by attempting to define what's out of the field but by thinking about what might profitably be considered in [the field]." She suggested that the scholarly study of the Qur'ān might include "the history and redaction of the text, its presence as a material object, its use in communities, both ritual and otherwise. People, especially Muslims but not only Muslims, do an array of things with the written and recited text of the Qur'ān, and I would count scholarship in Qur'ānic Studies to include things like theology, paleography, musicology, art history, anthropology, and of course *fiqh*, Muslim history, Islamic ethics. The study of the Qur'ān includes but is broader than the text and its interpretation."

Herbert Berg suggested "the application of various disciplines, including history, textual criticism, literary criticism, manuscript analysis, philology, anthropology, political science, economics, et cetera, including perhaps most fruitfully interdisciplinarity, to virtually anything that humans have done, said, written, painted, sung, et cetera, that seems somehow connected to the Qur'ān." In another take on what makes a big tent, Joseph Lumbard pointed out that the Western academic study of the Qur'ān is only a small part of what is undertaken globally. Scholars all over the world use various methods

---

6. This organization accords with the main lines of inquiry posed to the panelists. The questions we asked in full were: (1) Can you provide a definition of Qur'ānic Studies? In your area of specialization, given your area of study, what are the most significant strides that you think this field has made in the last two decades? (2) How have the presumptions and methods used in different scholarly approaches to the Qur'ān changed in the last twenty years? Are there methodological differences between descriptive and normative approaches to the text, between revisionism and confessionalism, or are these categorizations worn, tired, simplistic, ill-defined, or no longer of any use? (3) Are contemporary and progressive methods of studying the text less rigorous than the earlier Orientalist text- and language-based study? What do you say about the allegation that the field is increasingly burdened by the baggage of political correctness?

to study the text: those in Indonesia might use different methods than those in Iran or the United Arab Emirates, and all of these use methods other than those commonly found in Western academic discussion. He suggested acknowledging the relativity of different types of approaches, rather than implying that one set of principles or one mode was the "correct" way to study the Qur'ān.

That some of these scholars did not feel that they belonged on a panel about the state of the field is one indication that the scholarly discipline of Qur'ānic Studies has long been somewhat narrowly defined. It is rare for academic organizations to take the big tent approach. Rather than including "anything that humans have sung, read, written, or painted," the academic discipline of Qur'ānic Studies has been focused on historical-critical studies of the Qur'ān and its milieu, and textual studies of a specific body of texts produced by the Muslim scholarly class (*ʿulamāʾ*). This is the point made by Nicolai Sinai when he spoke of a "non-normative, descriptive, non-theological discipline." He distinguished the two main dimensions which I have just mentioned: firstly, a "historical-critical dimension" that is "trying to spell out what the Qur'ān or the texts gathered in the qur'ānic corpus would have meant to their original audience," and secondly, the Qur'ān's reception history.

Reception history would include the genre of works devoted to the Muslim scholarly interpretation of the Qur'ān (*tafsīr*) and other works directly tied to the qur'ānic text, such as variant readings (*qirāʾāt*). This focus on historical-critical studies and reception history means that a certain type of textual study—the non-confessional study of a specific body of texts—has heretofore taken precedent within academe. This is rapidly changing, especially with regard to the inclusion of confessional approaches (the challenges of such a change are discussed further below). Yet it is important to note that even recent confessional approaches undertaken by academics working within the academy are also, to a large extent, based around the same set of texts. Therefore, while the poetry of Hafez is intimately linked with the Qur'ān and could certainly be considered a part of its reception history, I doubt that a scholar of the poetry of Hafez would be able to fit the bill for most job descriptions in Qur'ānic Studies, or indeed Islamic Studies. This academic approach inevitably shapes how we as academics see and understand the qur'ānic text. Some selectivity is a necessary part of creating an academic discipline. The nature of this selectivity might, however, change as the field becomes increasingly populated with scholars championing different disciplinary approaches.

Some might argue that recent academic study has focused too much on milieu and not enough on the text of the Qur'ān itself. Shawkat Toorawa argued for a literary approach to the Qur'ān, lamenting how study of the Qur'ān tends to be "siphoned away from the study of Arabic literature." In his view, the Qur'ān's "literariness" is undeniable, manifesting itself in features such as its "syntax, rhetoric, grammar, rhyme, [and] intentionality." Michael Pregill (Boston University) questioned this approach in the Q & A session at the end of the panel, saying that he did not understand how one could read the Qur'ān as literature without studying origins: "How can we understand the genre of the Qur'ān if we don't understand where it is coming from?" In his response, Toorawa emphasized that certainly someone should be working on paratexts and "where ideas come from." But, he asserted, "if we don't take a literary product as literary and rhetorical, persuasive, intelligent, crafted, and supple also on its own terms alone, we devalue it." For him, the study of the Qur'ān must include the question of why certain lines have been put together and crafted in the way that they have, and what message this conveys. In a somewhat similar vein, qur'ānic rhetoric was key for Devin Stewart, who commented that "rhetorical strategy in the Qur'ān is fundamental." In his view, without studying rhetoric, we are likely to miss the point of many qur'ānic passages.

Some of the panelists cautioned that with renewed interest in situating the Qur'ān in its historical context and in broadening out the field in other ways, we must not lose sight of approaches that were once the norm in the academy. Although the study of *tafsīr* was at one point synonymous with Qur'ānic Studies, the question now is whether *tafsīr*, as a discipline that developed over centuries along many different interpretive and confessional lines, can actually tell us anything about the Qur'ān. Because *tafsīr* must be considered as a part of the Qur'ān's reception history, is it still Qur'ānic Studies? Nicolai Sinai would answer yes. Scholars should be aware of the difference between "the Qur'ān or al-Ṭabarī, but," he added, "I would be uneasy about separating them out too categorically. I think that ultimately a scholar should be conversant with both." Joseph Lumbard agreed with Sinai's view of the importance of what Sinai termed the "dual competence" of Qur'ān and *tafsīr*; Lumbard particularly emphasized the richness of the classical tradition: "The classical tradition is a treasure trove of useful material." He asserted that today's scholars often say things about the text that are "adopted from the [medieval] commentarial tradition, but without acknowledging their dependence on that tradition."

In the Q & A, Emran El-Badawi (University of Houston) questioned Lumbard about his emphasis on traditional sources for understanding the Qur'ān, and whether ignoring the Qur'ān's "conversation partners" in rabbinic and Christian texts might be "ignoring knowledge" as much as ignoring the Muslim commentaries would be. I believe that he was referring to the identity politics that may influence a scholar's choice of text: for Muslim scholars, Muslim texts might be given what he termed "a default position of orthodoxy and *sharʿī* green light." (I would add that for non-Muslim scholars perhaps the opposite has been true. The study of these conversation partners was in a sense reignited for the scholarly world when authors such as Christoph Luxenburg asserted that he had found the Syriac "source" of much of the Qur'ān; such an assertion was viewed by many as driven by polemic.) When replying to El-Badawi's question, Lumbard implied that the study of the Qur'ān's conversation partners, particularly the Syriac sources, may not be as useful as the study of the Muslim tradition. "You can never assume that priority means influence. The point at which you can actually demonstrate influence is often very difficult... But sometimes when we are looking at the milieu we run the risk of bringing in false cognates."

There is another aspect to the identity politics of the use of source material in the discipline. The privileging of the classical Muslim scholarly sources may be partially indicative of a divide in scholarly competence between those who were trained in the classical Muslim sources and those who have a different type of training, for instance in Syriac, Ethiopic, or other languages that might be relevant for situating the Qur'ān in its historical milieu. Yet arguing for competence in the traditional sources in no way negates the view that one could (and should) also have competence in the languages of the Qur'ān's conversation partners. El-Badawi mentioned that he tried to use both types of source in his own work. And Sinai asserted that he believed the next generation of Qur'ān scholars would be better equipped precisely because they would go further in studying languages such as Syriac, which were only of secondary importance in the training of the current generation of scholars in Qur'ānic Studies.

Recent Developments in the Discipline

Any discussion of the nature and definition of Qur'ānic Studies would be incomplete without mentioning some of the recent changes in the field. The mood about Qur'ānic Studies was generally optimistic. Herbert Berg put it this way: "Having presented to virtually empty rooms at the AAR/SBL on topics on the Qur'ān, I now see standing room only. This is fantastic."

Shawkat Toorawa made perhaps the most pertinent comment about the field's development by pointing out that the demographics of the field have changed radically over the past few decades. His anecdotal experience illustrates this: "When I arrived at university thirty-five years ago, there were no Muslims anywhere. I wasn't reading them until I learned Arabic; the scholarship wasn't by Muslims, my teachers weren't Muslims, at conferences there were no Muslims, when I became a professor none of my students were Muslims early on. This has radically changed, in this panel, in the audience, in the wider AAR, and in the field, whatever that means, of Qur'ānic Studies. My answer to the question of how things have changed in the past twenty years, is that now there are Muslims. That does not mean that these Muslims all share the same assumptions. But it is a completely new population, addressing a completely new field."

Other panelists highlighted different types of demographic change. Devin Stewart asserted that there is now a critical mass of scholars who are studying the Qur'ān. Kecia Ali noted that there are women studying the Qur'ān, but that still she was the only woman on the panel. Herbert Berg pointed out that there is room for more narratives in today's study of the Qur'ān, beyond that of "Sunni, Shi'i, Sufi." With new narratives emerging from different actors, such as Muslim women or the Nation of Islam, this opens up space for the recognition that "Islam has always been diverse."

In terms of recent developments in source materials and methods, Joseph Lumbard spoke about the recent work of Behnam Sadeghi in dating Qur'ān codices, which he believes will cause "a paradigm shift."[7] Two panelists highlighted the increased focus on related Jewish and Christian texts. Devin Stewart sought to explain the reason why this had been neglected: starting with Watt, he said, scholars noted that many Muslims became offended by discussions of origins, and so they de-emphasized the Christian and Jewish texts related to the Qur'ān. Instead, scholars studied *tafsīr*. However, now "there is a renewed focus on Jewish and Christian texts, on manuscripts, and some developments in the important field of typology in the Qur'ān." Nicolai Sinai asserted that "we have a much better grasp of the pre-qur'ānic traditions that have informed the text, in particular, Syriac literature." At the same time, he believes that the work on these other traditions has become more sophisticated, and that such work "does not mean to reduce the Qur'ān to just an echo of these traditions. The Qur'ān is doing its own thing with these traditions, it has got its own agenda." Indeed, Toorawa sounded a cautionary note for the study of the Bible as the "origin" of the Qur'ān, or of the Qur'ān as a derivative text. In his words, "the analyses that I've found interesting are those that say 'here is one way that the story has been told, here is another way that this has been told, what can we say about the choices that have been made by the two storytellers?'"

In her summary of recent developments in the study of gender and the Qur'ān, Kecia Ali cited the work of pioneering Muslim feminists such

7. Lumbard later clarified that he was referring specifically to Sadeghi's use of scientific dating methods combined with manuscript analysis to date Qur'ān codices more accurately, and therefore put to rest some of the questions that have lingered in the field over the date of the Qur'ān. He cited the following articles: Behnam Sadeghi and Uwe Bergmann, "The Codex of a Companion of the Prophet and the Qur'ān of the Prophet," *Arabica* 57 (2010): 343–436; Behnam Sadeghi, "The Chronology of the Qur'ān: A Stylometric Research Program," *Arabica* 58 (2011): 210–299.

as amina wadud, Rifaat Hasan, Azizah al-Hibri, and Asma Barlas, who "focused on the Qur'ān itself as much as possible extracted from the grasp of its patriarchal interpreters." More recently, she asserted, scholars such as Sa'adia Shaikh have been looking at interpretation in productive ways, and there has been a recent "flourishing" in the study of women and gender in the Qur'ān, with several works having been published in the last eighteen months "ranging from historical-analytical to theologically constructive."[8]

Finally, panelists who have worked on translating the Qur'ān spoke about the state of translations. Shawkat Toorawa lamented the state of translations as a serious impediment to scholarly advancements. But there were several practical suggestions. Toorawa suggested that translators read works such as Mustansir Mir's *Verbal Idioms of the Qur'ān*.[9] Devin Stewart made another practical suggestion for future Qur'ān translators: "Everybody who does a translation of the Qur'ān needs to study the Qur'ān. Many people who translate the Qur'ān are not specialists in the Qur'ān, many are not native speakers of English or Arabic either. This is a kind of recipe for disaster. They all need to read the *mufradāt* section of the *Mughnī al-labīb* of Ibn Hishām al-Anṣārī which tells you the twenty-seven meanings of *wāw*. If they do that, it will be the biggest step forward." Joseph Lumbard, who worked with a team on *The Study Quran*, added that in other disciplines translation is often a group effort, whereas in Qur'ānic Studies it tends to be an individual effort.[10] His own experience with the group who translated *The Study Quran* was very positive, including the input of the graduate students as well as the faculty leaders of the project.

Confessional Approaches and the Question of Scholarly Methods

The question of the role of confessional perspectives in critical scholarship, for years an elephant in the room of Islamic Studies generally, is at the

8. She referred specifically to the following works: Karen Bauer, *Gender Hierarchy in the Qur'an: Medieval Interpretations, Modern Responses* (Cambridge: Cambridge University Press, 2015); Ayesha Chaudhry, *Domestic Violence and the Islamic Tradition: Ethics, Law, and the Muslim Discourse on Gender* (Oxford: Oxford University Press, 2013); Aisha Geissinger, *Gender and Muslim Constructions of Exegetical Authority: A Rereading of the Classical Genre of the Qur'an Commentary* (IHC 117; Leiden: Brill, 2015); Aysha Hidayatullah, *Feminist Edges of the Qur'an* (Oxford: Oxford University Press, 2014); Jerusha Tanner Lamptey, *Never Wholly Other: A Muslima Theology of Religious Pluralism* (Oxford: Oxford University Press, 2014).

9. Mustansir Mir, *Verbal Idioms of the Qur'ān* (Ann Arbor: The University of Michigan Center for Near Eastern and North African Studies, 1989).

10. Seyyed Hossein Nasr et al. (eds.), *The Study Quran: A New Translation and Commentary* (New York: HarperOne, 2015).

heart of many of the changes and challenges that the panelists describe in Qur'ānic Studies today. It is a topic that is finally being confronted openly.[11] So, while some disciplinary approaches are no longer as tense or polemical as they once were (I am thinking here of the division between revisionism and traditionalism), the question remains whether it is important to make a distinction between academic work that is confessional and that which is non-confessional. The language that scholars use to describe this confessional/non-confessional split is telling. It is often called a distinction between "historical-critical" and "normative" work, and this is how we worded our question to the panelists. But this wording has implications that we did not examine before asking the question: it implies that normative work cannot be historical, whereas actually many scholars who have confessional aims also wish to undertake historically accurate and critical work.

Nicolai Sinai asserted that he finds the distinction between confessional and non-confessional work helpful, because these represent different aims on the part of the scholars. "I don't want to imply that theological or normative work isn't proper scholarly work. The distinction 'normative' versus 'historical' all takes place within the scholarly realm," he said. But for Sinai, drawing the line between these types of approaches is helpful in situating the methods of inquiry that might occur in the work. Similarly, Devin Stewart asked scholars to be honest about their own agenda. In his words, "Some of the progressive work is theological work, and I think it is important for those studies to recognize what they are doing." The sentiment was echoed by Shawkat Toorawa: "Many scholars cannot leave their agenda at the door, and figure out what they can learn, rather than going in with a preconceived idea... I think a lot of scholars go in with an agenda and if they were just trying to make sense of things we would get a lot further."

For Stewart, Sinai, and Toorawa, work with a confessional aim should not necessarily be discarded or ignored by those taking a non-confessional approach. In Stewart's words, "Some of those studies will then tell us something about the Qur'ān... Some of them won't tell us very much about the Qur'ān. They will tell us more about what the person wants to say than about the Qur'ān itself." Building on the point that theological study can tell us something useful about the Qur'ān, Sinai described the classical medieval

11. For instance, a recent issue of *JAAR* is devoted to the question of normativity in Islamic Studies. In it, Elliott Bazzano argues that because of the variety of perspectives, often incompatible with each other, represented in the Muslim sources and the reliance of non-Muslims on those sources for their own perspectives, the distinction between insider and outsider does not matter very much in the field ("Normative Readings of the Qur'ān: From the Premodern Middle East to the Modern West," *JAAR* 84 [2016]: 74–97).

works of exegesis (*tafsīr*) as "an immense reservoir of resources for all of us. While we shouldn't uncritically regurgitate what the medieval *mufassirūn* tell us, there is so much historical, grammatical, and rhetorical analysis in there that I think modern historical-critical scholars are well advised to draw on that." Toorawa said: "I think that the more we attune graduate students to going in for rigorous analysis, then the more these labels will fall by the wayside, because it won't be about confessional and non-confessional boundaries, it will be about rigorous readings and analysis and non-rigorous readings and analysis."

These answers hint at the collapsing boundary between confessional and non-confessional work that I alluded to above. Kecia Ali argued against drawing a firm boundary between these types of work at all: "People shouldn't avoid historical-critical text scholarship because it might somehow threaten Muslim confessional belief. But on the other hand, the idea that Muslims uniformly find this sort of research threatening comes from a place of portraying Muslims as primitive wackos, unable to grapple with the facts of the modern world." For Ali, rather than talk about the differences between descriptive and normative approaches, "I think it is more useful to talk about a range of analytical approaches with different precommitments. It is possible to be both normative and analytical. And normative work is, to some extent, going to happen, because objectivity is not really something that exists. It is possible to strive for a kind of neutrality, for the most possible awareness of one's implicit biases, and I think these are all valuable things, and central to good scholarship wherever it comes from and whatever its claims."

This discussion led Farid Esack to pick up on Toorawa's point, and question directly whether the distinction should be drawn not between confessional and non-confessional work, but between rigorous and sloppy scholarship. Toorawa elaborated, saying that "I think we need to not worry so much about whether it comes out of one camp or another. I think we need to subject it to a standard. We are not all going to have the same standard. That is going to be a difficulty."

Different standards, perhaps stemming from different scholarly aims, were obvious even on the panel itself. Devin Stewart highlighted the importance of studying Arabic; for him, knowledge of the source texts is important over and above the question of scholarly methodology: "I don't think that we are going to make great progress by having arguments over methodology by people who haven't looked at the primary sources enough... Everyone, including myself, should always learn more Arabic. We should study more rhetoric. This is one thing that is missing in the field, all the way through. We are not studying rhetoric, either in English or in Arabic. It is a huge part of the text of the Qur'ān, and people are making all kinds of bad translations and bad assumptions because they are not getting the rhetorical sense of the text." Yet

Kecia Ali pointed out that perhaps different standards are useful in different arenas: "There are other people who have made a case in a variety of ways for the necessity of Muslims, at least, approaching the Qur'ān as it exists in other languages, if indeed the Qur'ān can be said to exist in any other language. I am thinking here of Asma Barlas' 'five theses on the Qur'ān.'"[12]

For all the talk of a collapse of boundaries, Ali's answer seems to expose the tension that still exists between the confessional and non-confessional approaches to the text within the academic realm. While a theological approach to the text does not necessarily require knowledge of Arabic, we can assume that a historical-critical approach does. This is part of the reason that the distinction between theological and non-theological work is, in my view, an important one to maintain, while keeping in mind that scholars with confessional aims may not be writing works of theology and may be engaging in historical-critical or philological scholarship.

It is also important to remember that some non-Muslim scholars now working in Qur'ānic Studies are not primarily scholars of Arabic. Instead, their specialty is in Jewish or Christian texts, and they have come to the Qur'ān through these textual conversation partners. These scholars can add to the discourse on the Qur'ān, particularly since we often have mutually exclusive language and textual competence. My own bias would be towards engagement with primary source texts. To the extent that such scholars do have textual and linguistic competence, they may be able to add profitably to the conversation about the Qur'ān. In some cases, this is true even when their textual and linguistic competence is not Arabic.

While some would argue that the distinction between theological and non-theological work is useful at this time in the field and discipline of Qur'ānic Studies, certain dichotomies that have been used to describe modes or methods of scholarship are no longer useful. Devin Stewart named "the revisionists versus the traditionalists, the skeptics versus the non-skeptics"; these labels, he says, have been "mapped onto good proper scholarship and bad horrible scholarship" without regard for the actual content of what is being said. Similarly, Nicolai Sinai suggested that "we should try to transcend and overcome" the binary between revisionist and traditionalist. Such rigid labels have become something of caricatures, and are no longer meaningful descriptors of scholarly approaches or methods. Herbert Berg pointed out that there are many different types of revisionism. The scholars who have

12. Asma Barlas, "Still Quarrelling over the Qur'an: Five Theses on Interpretation and Authority," presentation from "Redefining Boundaries: Muslim Women and Religious Authority in Practice," Institute for the Study of Islam and the Modern World (Amsterdam, 2007) (http://www.asmabarlas.com/PAPERS/ISIM_Authority_07.pdf).

been labeled as revisionist often offer "mutually exclusive revisions." In his words: "Luxenburg is not compatible with Patricia Crone, for instance. They all have different counter-narratives. I struggle to see what they all share, except for not accepting the normative narrative."

Perhaps the reason that these binaries are unhelpful is that, while they might once have signified something, the different types of scholarship that they once represented have, to a certain extent, collapsed into each other, if they were entirely distinct to begin with. The first wave of revisionist scholarship came out with some radical conclusions, and indeed some of these conclusions were too radical to be plausible. But in my view, the most important effect of revisionism for Qur'ānic Studies is, perhaps, not the conclusions; conclusions about the origins and nature of the Qur'ān will never be shared by all in Qur'ānic Studies. Instead the crucial effect of revisionism has been the method of differentiating between Qur'ān and tradition, and reviving the old Orientalist incorporation of non-Muslim texts for shedding light on Islamic history. Both of these methods have had a profound effect on the discipline as a whole. And while revisionists themselves have relaxed (after *Hagarism*, few experimented with telling Islamic history without Muslim sources), these methods have been adopted, to a greater or lesser extent, across the discipline. Therefore, there has been some melding of what were once profound distinctions between use of sources, methods of analysis, and conclusions being drawn.

It remains to be seen whether there will be a similar collapsing between confessional/theological and non-confessional/non-theological approaches. To the extent that the ultimate aims of such approaches remain distinct, I suspect not; but I could be proven wrong.

Political Correctness and the Study of the Qur'ān

The challenge of revisionism is connected with the question of political correctness: is qur'ānic scholarship constrained by the need to speak in a certain way, to avoid offending the sensibilities of other scholars or the public? As I described in the introduction, many believe that in the wake of the first wave of revisionism, scholarship on the Qur'ān was hampered by political correctness. But things have changed since then. Devin Stewart drew the distinction between the field of today and the field as it was in the previous generation. In the middle of the twentieth century, he said, political correctness had the effect of damping down the discipline, and of preventing certain types of scholarship from being undertaken. Now, however, the field has grown so much bigger that such a stifling effect is impossible.

Shawkat Toorawa pointed out how political correctness had a constructive effect in terms of the way that scholars of the Qur'ān speak about the text. In the 1980s, the way of speaking about the Qur'ān differed between Muslims, who asserted that "God says" (with all that that implies about the Qur'ān as an ahistorical and divine text) and non-Muslims, who asserted that "Muḥammad said" (which seemed to many Muslims like a direct affront to the text's divine origin). Now, everyone describes the words of the Qur'ān as "the Qur'ān says." "And that," he said, "is political correctness. No one [used to say] 'the Qur'ān says,' because of course the Qur'ān can't say anything, not really. But I think that it hasn't impeded scholarship. It hasn't resulted in people saying that they can't think about the Qur'ān in one way or another. It has been an attempt to find a way of referring to qur'ānic passages where everyone can just agree. It's a bit like everyone deciding to say CE instead of AD. It keeps everyone happy." Agreeing on common terms can help scholars with different precommitments (to use Ali's word) engage in dialogue about substantial issues.

Yet another issue was raised with regard to political correctness outside of the academy, because in the public realm we may represent not only ourselves as scholars, but also a whole variety of other actors (including, but not limited to, all Muslims). Herbert Berg put it this way: "I would make a distinction between me as a scholar and me as a public intellectual... In a place like Wilmington, North Carolina, where there aren't a lot of Muslims, the media does not go to Muslims, it comes to me to represent Muslims, which I find very odd. But nevertheless, there I am, burdened by political correctness, but I welcome that burden when I am speaking on behalf of people, particularly given our political climate at this time, I am happy to take on that burden. But focusing more as a scholar, where you have academic political forces, I am not sure that I find [political correctness] a problem." Kecia Ali put it perhaps more directly: "In public discourses about the Qur'ān, so many things are at stake, like the basic idea that Muslims are human beings, that all sorts of other questions pale in comparison." Nicolai Sinai argued that the media can foster a sense of deep divisions in the field. "In a sense, flouting political correctness can be just as unproductive and stereotypical as adhering to the norms of what is perceived to be political correctness. Often that will be fed by the media much more than by scholars because the media are hungry for scholars who are iconoclasts, who refute the Muslim version of history. If you get interviewed by someone like that, there is a real danger of whatever measured, sophisticated evaluation you offer being misquoted or quoted out of context, and you'll end up branded as an iconoclast. I think that we must realize that we as scholars are often not really in control of these discourses."

While there was a general consensus against the notion that political correctness is burdening Qur'ānic Studies, there were also some hints that an effect exists within scholarship, perhaps at times without our own acknowledgment of it. Joseph Lumbard, for instance, said that he did not think that the discipline was burdened by political correctness but admitted that one might need to be sensitive in certain situations, such as the writing of *The Study Quran* for a broad audience. "I can tell you one thing that we did not want to transmit in *The Study Quran*, and that is that there is a lot of pretty bad material about Judaism in [classical *tafsīr*] and we didn't think that was going to be useful, neither here nor there. I don't think it was so much a matter of political correctness, but rather an acknowledgment that the issues that were of concern to the commentators were not of concern in the society which we envision as our audience for *The Study Quran*." Farid Esack questioned this approach: "Joseph, wouldn't you say that you are yielding to immediate political forces, so you have to put this nice, friendly face of Islam forward? I don't mean to be unkind in my question, but who are we to determine what is the need at the moment? Shouldn't we as scholars be saying, "This is it! This is what I find in the text." Lumbard replied: "There are other things in the text that people don't like and people try to get away [from], for example [Q Nisā'] 4:34, *wa'ḍribūhunna* ["then strike them"]. I'm sorry, the Arabic says what it says, and we have to deal with it. And I don't like it, but the interesting thing is that a lot of medieval commentators didn't like it either, so you look at the way that they deal with it... But then [Q Tawbah] 9:5 [the Sword Verse]—we put in some of the stuff that is not very friendly in terms of the interpretive tradition... We are talking about a vast literature, [so] that when any of us are working with it, we are going to make choices. There is no doubt that those choices are going to be in some way fashioned by our contemporary concerns as individuals living within [our] society, and there is going to be an element of political correctness that is going to be at play, in what we think is politically astute. But I don't think it is necessarily burdening the discipline, and constraining it in unnecessary ways."

This exchange was interesting precisely because the nature of political correctness is somewhat vague. By editing out certain aspects of the tradition, even prominent aspects, were the authors of *The Study Quran* sanitizing that tradition, or were they, as Joseph Lumbard suggested, simply cutting unimportant material to make room for more relevant material? These issues were touched upon by Shawkat Toorawa, who mentioned the way in which the spirit of the times might affect the very type of scholarship that is being done on the Qur'ān. It can, however, be hard to see that effect. As he put it, "we are all subject to our own political and social and historical moment."

What Is the Future of Qur'ānic Studies?

The current state of Qur'ānic Studies took up most of our discussion in this roundtable, and that left very little time to discuss the future of the field and discipline. This section is, therefore, much pithier than it might have been, and revolves around key questions asked in the Q & A, most pertinently by Martin Nguyen (Fairfield University). Nguyen asked about the future of the field in practical terms—tenure track positions, journals, and so forth: "In many ways we're trying to map where it's going—what is going to happen structurally in the next ten years?" This question was complemented by another question from the audience about whether Qur'ānic Studies, like Biblical Studies, would become a hyper-specialized field. Both questions ended up raising some of the issues that had come up in the panel: demographics, skill sets, sources, and practical agendas.

Nicolai Sinai predicts a "steep learning curve in the field... I think that the next generation of graduate students is going to be much better equipped than my generation, and I can see that even with my own graduate students. You will have to read proper Syriac... the next generation will have that skill in addition to all of the other skills that have accumulated. The generation that is currently seen as the custodians of the field will quickly become outdated by the next one." Joseph Lumbard cautioned against "a tendency within the Western academy of feeling superior to and having the right to dictate to people who are not in the Western academy" while also urging scholars to "incorporate some of the things that are being done [elsewhere]."

The short answer to whether Qur'anic Studies will become hyper-specialized like Biblical Studies is "no," and the reasons are demographic. According to Devin Stewart, "there are some studies that are specialized, [e.g.] manuscript studies, but we aren't going to have the same kind of specialization, because the history hasn't been as long, there aren't as many people working on it. We are becoming in some ways like Biblical Studies, in other words we are getting a critical mass and there will be some continuity, but there is also going to be a lot of scholarship that you have to wade through to find the decent work," meaning, he clarified, "original studies that truly break new ground."[13]

Kecia Ali broadened the question out, to address the way that positions are funded. "I don't think that we can answer these questions without talking about what's happening to the humanities as a whole in the United States. The question of hyper-specialization in the humanities is not unrelated to how many positions for faculty members to study the Qur'ān there are. If you are at a theological seminary and you have eight positions to teach New Testament, then you are in a position to specialize in that way, versus one position for a Muslim who is going to teach law, Qur'ān, et cetera. What we teach doesn't determine the contours of how we publish, and yet there is a relationship. The other thing that Shawkat brought up about demographics,

13. Clarification by personal email, July 8, 2016.

I'm the only woman here, I'm the woman who is talking about women. I hope that when there is another panel like this in five years, the panel is 30–70% female. Thirty percent is a minimum. The field can do better in these regards, and that takes some doing as a structural agenda item."

There is surely much more to say on the issue of the future of Qur'ānic Studies and the structural changes and challenges facing the university system as a whole which might, incidentally or otherwise, affect the study of the Qur'ān. Perhaps this can be the subject of a future roundtable.

JIQSA 1 (2016): 47–92

FORM CRITICISM OR A ROLLING CORPUS: THE METHODOLOGY OF JOHN WANSBROUGH THROUGH THE LENS OF BIBLICAL STUDIES

MICHAEL GRAVES

Abstract

John Wansbrough's scholarship on the Qur'ān has had a significant impact on Qur'ānic Studies over the last forty years. His ideas continue to stimulate research into historical and literary dimensions of the Qur'ān, even though assessments vary greatly regarding the plausibility of some of his major ideas, and his subtle arguments can be difficult to follow. This essay clarifies and evaluates Wansbrough's thinking about the composition of the Qur'ān by elucidating the models from Biblical Studies that he appropriated. Detailed treatment is given to biblical form criticism and Wansbrough's application of this method to the qur'ānic accounts of the prophet Shu'ayb. It is suggested that Wansbrough's form-critical research yielded positive insights into the Qur'ān, but also left certain questions unanswered. It is then proposed that another model taken from Biblical Studies, the idea of a "rolling corpus" as developed in research on the book of Jeremiah, can sharpen and refine Wansbrough's conclusions.

Introduction

Many important ideas in contemporary Western scholarship on the Qur'ān derive from methods employed in Biblical Studies.[1] A potential benefit

1. Key figures in the nineteenth century who developed foundational critical methods for Qur'ānic Studies in conversation with biblical criticism include Abraham Geiger, "Was hat Mohammed aus dem Judenthume aufgenommen?" (Bonn, 1833); Theodor Nöldeke, "Geschichte des Qorāns" (Göttingen, 1860); and Julius Wellhausen, "Prolegomena zur ältesten Geschichte des Islams" in *Skizzen und Vorarbeiten* (Berlin: Reimer 1899). Geiger (b. 1810) studied as a teenager at Heidelberg, where he was introduced to critical methods in the same milieu as the Jewish biblical scholar Samuel David Luzzatto, and he continued his classical and biblical studies at Bonn. The biblical scholarship of Nöldeke (e.g., *Die Alttestamentliche Literatur, in einer Reihe von*

doi: http://dx.doi.org/10.5913/jiqsa.1.2017.a005

of applying biblical criticism to the Qur'ān is that these approaches have already been worked out and tested on a corpus of literature that is in many ways similar to the Qur'ān. Yet, there are potential problems involved with interpreting the Qur'ān using methods from Biblical Studies. These critical methods were not designed as general reading strategies, but as theories meant to explain how specific texts came together. Thus, source criticism arose out of detailed analysis of the Pentateuch, and the proponents of this theory argued that major sections of the Pentateuch were composed by combining previously independent literary sources. In the end, the legitimacy of source-critical analysis of the Pentateuch depends on the premise that the text was actually composed in that manner.

Traditional form criticism presumed that behind each textual unit stood an oral "form" (*Gattung*) that arose out of a specific communal "life setting" (*Sitz im Leben*). For example, form critics interpreted certain psalms by positing the existence of a New Year's festival in ancient Israel celebrating the kingship of YHWH, at which the Israelites would recite an "Enthronement Psalm."[2] This interpretive approach only makes sense if the theory about the ancient festival and its liturgy is correct. Consequently, when seeking to understand the Qur'ān through methods associated with biblical scholarship, it is essential to ask how likely it is that the conditions that gave rise to the Qur'ān are sufficiently similar to the conditions presumed by the biblical method. In general, the proper application of methods adopted from Biblical Studies is an important question facing modern scholarship on the Qur'ān.

Familiarity with biblical criticism is particularly important for understanding the work of John Wansbrough, especially his *Quranic Studies*.[3] Throughout that work, Wansbrough draws directly from important works of biblical criticism such as Otto Eissfeldt's *Einleitung in das Alte Testament*,

---

Aufsätzen [Leipzig: Quandt and Händel, 1868]) and Wellhausen (e.g., *Prolegomena zur Geschichte Israels* [Berlin: Reimer, 1882]) are well known.

2. It was Sigmund Mowinckel who first proposed that Psalm 93 and other Psalms (e.g., 97–99) originated as liturgical poems from an ancient Israelite New Year's festival celebrating the enthronement of YHWH as king; see *The Psalms in Israel's Worship*, trans. D. R. Ap-Thomas (2 vols.; Nashville: Abingdon, 1962; revised trans. of *Offersang og Sangoffer: Salmediktningen i Bibelen* [Oslo: H. Aschehoug & Co., 1951]), 1.106–192. Mowinckel based his theory on terminology found in these Psalms (especially the phrase יהוה מלך, which Mowinckel translated "YHWH has become king") and also on the model of the Babylonian Akitu festival dedicated to Marduk. Mowinkel's interpretation was widely accepted, but recent scholarship has pointed out uncertainties about the specific liturgical context.

3. John Wansbrough, *Quranic Studies: Sources and Methods of Scriptural Interpretation*, with foreword, translations, and expanded notes by Andrew Rippin (Amherst, NY: Prometheus Books, 2004; revised ed. of Oxford: Oxford University Press, 1977).

James Barr's *Comparative Philology and the Text of the Old Testament*, and Birger Gerhardsson's *Memory and Manuscript: Oral Tradition and Written Transmission in Rabbinic Judaism and Early Christianity*.[4] Perhaps the most significant influence on Wansbrough came through form criticism, because this method gave Wansbrough a model to describe how traditions might evolve over time in response to changing cultural settings. When Wansbrough speaks of "the popular sermon as *Sitz im Leben* of haggadic exegesis," this reflects form-critical analysis as practiced in Biblical Studies.[5] As for his application of the method, Wansbrough was clearly influenced by Klaus Koch, *The Growth of the Biblical Tradition: The Form-Critical Method*, which is cited numerous times in *Quranic Studies*.[6] Form criticism as practiced by Koch played an important role in Wansbrough's methodology.

The issues that Wansbrough raised continue to be widely discussed in academic Qur'ānic Studies.[7] Yet, it is not always easy to grasp the import

---

4. E.g., for Otto Eissfeldt, *Einleitung in das Alte Testament Einleitung* (Tübingen, 1934), see Wansbrough, *Quranic Studies*, 21, 37, 65, 68, 140; for James Barr, *Comparative Philology and the Text of the Old Testament* (Oxford: Clarendon Press 1968), see 100–102, 118, 223, 225; and for Birger Gerhardsson, *Memory and Manuscript: Oral Tradition and Written Transmission in Rabbinic Judaism and Early Christianity* (Uppsala: Uppsala University, 1961), see 47, 49, 54, 63, 79, 156, 174–175, 223. As readers of Wansbrough are aware, references to these and other specific works of biblical criticism occur throughout *Quranic Studies*.

5. Wansbrough, *Quranic Studies*, 145. Note also the term "haggadic," which is appropriated from Jewish Studies.

6. Klaus Koch, *The Growth of the Biblical Tradition: The Form-Critical Method*, trans. S. M. Cupitt (London: Adam & Charles Black, 1969). For example, Wansbrough employs Koch in defining formal elements in qur'ānic discourse such as *corroboratio*, "confirmation" (*Quranic Studies*, 13–15), and *invocatio*, "invocation" (ibid., 18); in discussing a likely *Sitz im Leben* for qur'ānic forms (ibid., 20); and in setting forth his analysis of the stories of the prophet Shuʿayb (ibid., 23).

7. Cf. Fred Donner, "The Historian, the Believer, and the Qur'ān," in Gabriel Said Reynolds (ed.), *New Perspectives on the Qur'ān: The Qur'ān in Its Historical Context 2* (London: Routledge, 2011), 27–29; Harald Motzki, "Alternative Accounts of the Qur'ān's Formation," in Jane Dammen McAuliffe (ed.), *The Cambridge Companion to the Qur'ān* (Cambridge: Cambridge University Press, 2006), 59–75, 60–63; Andrew Rippin, "Foreword," in Wansbrough, *Quranic Studies*, ix–xix, and idem, "Literary Analysis of Qur'ān, Tafsīr, and Sīra: The Methodologies of John Wansbrough," in Richard C. Martin (ed.), *Approaches to Islam in Religious Studies* (Tucson: University of Arizona Press, 1985), 151–163; Daniel Madigan, *The Qur'ân's Self-Image: Writing and Authority in Islam's Scripture* (Princeton: Princeton University Press, 2001), 9–11; and Carlos A. Segovia, "John Wansbrough and the Problem of Islamic Origins in Recent Scholarship: A Farewell to the Traditional Account," in Carlos Segovia and Basil Lourié (eds.), *The Coming of the Comforter: When, Where, and to Whom?* (Piscataway, NJ: Gorgias Press, 2012), xix–xxviii.

of Wansbrough's arguments when they are viewed apart from their context within Biblical Studies. In some cases, Wansbrough merely references a critical method taken from Biblical Studies and presents the results of its application to the Qur'ān, leaving it to the reader to reconstruct how his conclusions were generated from the method in question. This makes it challenging to evaluate Wansbrough's ideas and appreciate what they have to offer.

The goals of this essay are to describe Wansbrough's application of form criticism to the Qur'ān; assess how well this method serves as a template for his main insights; and suggest another model from Biblical Studies to address some of the key issues that he raises. I will first illustrate what biblical form criticism as practiced by Koch sought to accomplish. Then, turning to Wansbrough's *Quranic Studies*, I will explain how understanding form criticism clarifies Wansbrough's methodology, discussing both its strengths and limitations as applied to the Qur'ān. Finally, as a supplement to form criticism, I will propose the idea of a "rolling corpus," developed by William McKane in his research on the book of Jeremiah, as an alternative paradigm for describing the composition of the Qur'ān. As I will explain below, the "rolling corpus" model accounts for many of Wansbrough's best literary observations, accords with possible historical scenarios for the Qur'ān, and has a solid textual basis in the critical comparison of the Masoretic and Septuagint versions of Jeremiah.

Biblical Form Criticism as a Model

The method and potential results of form criticism can be illustrated through Klaus Koch's treatment of a biblical tradition that has been widely recognized as suitable for form-critical analysis, namely, the stories in the book of Genesis in which a patriarch passes his wife off as his sister (Gen 12, 20, 26).[8] Koch identifies the common motif underlying these stories as that of the "Ancestress of Israel in Danger." (In the chart below, significant proper names are given in bold, key redactional elements in chapter 20 are underlined, and those in chapter 26 are italicized.)

8. See Koch, *Growth of the Biblical Tradition*, 111–132. The pioneer of form criticism (*Gattungsforschung*) and the first to treat these stories through this method was Hermann Gunkel, e.g., *Genesis*, trans. Mark E. Biddle (Macon, GA: Mercer University Press, 1997; trans. of Göttingen: Vandenhoeck & Ruprecht, 1901), 223–225. A recent appropriation and development of Gunkel's interpretation of these stories is found in Claus Westermann, *Genesis 12–36: A Continental Commentary*, trans. J. J. Scullion (Minneapolis: Fortress Press, 1995), 161–168, 318–329, 423–430.

The Ancestress of Israel in Danger: Gen 12:10–20, 20:1–18, 26:1–17[a]		
Gen 12 [10] Now there was a famine in the land. So Abram went down to **Egypt** to sojourn there, for the famine was severe in the land. [11] When he was about to enter Egypt, he said to Sarai his wife, "I know that you are a woman beautiful to behold; [12] and when the Egyptians see you, they will say, 'This is his wife'; then they will kill me, but they will let you live. [13] Say you are my sister, that it may go well with me because of you, and that my life may be spared on account of you." [14] When Abram entered Egypt the Egyptians saw that the woman was very beautiful. [15] And when the princes of **Pharaoh** saw her, they praised her to Pharaoh. And the woman was taken into Pharaoh's house. [16] And for her sake he dealt well with Abram; and he had sheep, oxen, he-asses, manservants, maidservants, she-asses, and camels. [17] But the Lord afflicted Pharaoh and his house with great plagues because of Sarai, Abram's wife. [18] So Pharaoh called Abram, and said, "What is this you have done to me? Why did you not tell me that she was your wife?	**Gen 20** [1] From there Abraham journeyed toward the territory of the Negeb, and dwelt between Kadesh and Shur; and he sojourned in **Gerar**. [2] And Abraham said of Sarah his wife, "She is my sister." And **Abimelech king of Gerar** sent and took Sarah. [3] But God came to **Abimelech** in a dream by night, and said to him, "Behold, you are a dead man, because of the woman whom you have taken; for she is a man's wife." [4] Now Abimelech had not approached her; so he said, "Lord, will you slay an innocent people? [5] Did he not himself say to me, 'She is my sister'? And she herself said, 'He is my brother.' In the integrity of my heart and the innocence of my hands I have done this." [6] Then God said to him in the dream, "Yes, I know that you have done this in the integrity of your heart, and it was I who kept you from sinning against me; therefore I did not let you touch her. [7] Now then, restore the man's wife; for he is a prophet, and he will pray for you, and you shall live. But if you do not restore her, know that you shall surely die, you	**Gen 26** [1] Now there was a famine in the land, *besides the former famine that was in the days of Abraham.* And Isaac went to **Gerar,** to **Abimelech king of the Philistines**. [2] And the Lord appeared to him, and said, "Do not go down to Egypt; dwell in the land of which I shall tell you. [3] Sojourn in this land, and *I will be with you, and will bless you; for to you and to your descendants I will give all these lands, and I will fulfill the oath that I swore to Abraham your father.* [4] *I will multiply your descendants as the stars of heaven, and will give to your descendants all these lands; and by your descendants all the nations of the earth shall bless themselves:* [5] because Abraham obeyed my voice and kept my charge, my commandments, my statutes, and my laws." [6] So Isaac dwelt in Gerar. [7] When the men of the place asked him about his wife, he said, "She is my sister"; for he feared to say, "My wife," thinking, "lest the men of the place should kill me for the sake of Rebekah"; because she was fair to look upon. [8] When he had been there a long time, Abimelech king of the Philistines looked out of a window and saw Isaac fondling Rebekah his

19 Why did you say, 'She
is my sister,' so that I took
her for my wife? Now
then, here is your wife,
take her, and be gone."
20 And Pharaoh gave men
orders concerning him;
and they set him on his
way with his wife and all
that he had.

and all that are yours."
8 So Abimelech rose
early in the morning, and
called all his servants,
and told them all these
things; and the men
were very much afraid.
9 Then Abimelech called
Abraham, and said to
him, "What have you
done to us? And how
have I sinned against you,
that you have brought
on me and my kingdom
a great sin? You have
done to me things that
ought not to be done."
10 And Abimelech said
to Abraham, "What
were you thinking of,
that you did this thing?"
11 Abraham said, "I did it
because I thought, 'There
is no fear of God at all
in this place, and they
will kill me because of
my wife.' 12 Besides she
is indeed my sister, the
daughter of my father
but not the daughter
of my mother; and she
became my wife. 13 And
when God caused me to
wander from my father's
house, I said to her, 'This
is the kindness you must
do me: at every place to
which we come, say of
me, "He is my brother."'
14 Then Abimelech took
sheep and oxen, and male
and female slaves, and
gave them to Abraham,
and restored Sarah
his wife to him. 15 And
Abimelech said, "Behold,
my land is before you;

wife. 9 So Abimelech
called Isaac, and said,
"Behold, she is your
wife; how then could
you say, 'She is my
sister'?" Isaac said to
him, "Because I thought,
'Lest I die because of
her.'" 10 Abimelech said,
"What is this you have
done to us? One of
the people might easily
have lain with your wife,
and you would have
brought guilt upon us."
11 So Abimelech warned
all the people, saying,
"Whoever touches this
man or his wife shall be
put to death." 12 And
Isaac sowed in that land,
and reaped in the same
year a hundred-fold. *The
LORD blessed him,* 13 *and
the man became rich, and
gained more and more until he
became very wealthy.* 14 He
had possessions of flocks
and herds, and a great
household, so that the
Philistines envied him.
15 (Now the Philistines
had stopped and filled
with earth all the wells
which his father's servants
had dug in the days of
Abraham his father.)
16 And Abimelech said
to Isaac, "Go away from
us; for you are much
mightier than we." 17 So
Isaac departed from
there, and encamped in
the valley of Gerar and
dwelt there.

	dwell where it pleases you." [16] To Sarah he said, "Behold, I have given your brother a thousand pieces of silver; it is your vindication in the eyes of all who are with you; and before every one you are righted." [17] Then Abraham prayed to God; and God healed Abimelech, and also healed his wife and female slaves so that they bore children. [18] For the Lord had closed all the wombs of the house of Abimelech because of Sarah, Abraham's wife.	

[a] The biblical texts are presented in this chart according to the Revised Standard Version.

According to form critics, Israelite traditions as found in the Hebrew Bible were not assembled from literary sources written by individual authors, as source critics argued. By the late nineteenth century, source criticism had reached a general consensus in its reconstruction of the literary history of the Hebrew Bible, starting with the earliest poems and stories down to the prophetic writings, the Deuteronomic legislation and finally the priestly code. In this scheme, one could reconstruct the history of ideas in ancient Israel by identifying what new concepts emerged in each stage of the literature. Thus, if pure ethical monotheism first appeared in the prophet Amos, then this idea came into being with Amos in the eighth century. Emphasis was placed on the creative spirit of individual literary figures at key moments in Israel's history. However, form criticism, with its emphasis on the anonymous shaping of traditions within communities over time, represented a radical break from this paradigm.[9]

9. On the foundational principles of form criticism, see Herbert F. Hahn, *The Old Testament in Modern Research* (Philadelphia: Fortress, 1966), 119–156; and Gene M. Tucker, *Form Criticism of the Old Testament* (Philadelphia: Fortress, 1971). In recent years, form criticism has moved away from historical reconstructions and focuses instead on genre/form through the lens of literary theory; see Johannes P. Floss, "Form, Source, and Redaction Criticism," in J. W. Rogerson and Judith Lieu (eds.), *The Oxford Handbook of Biblical Studies* (Oxford: Oxford University Press, 2006), 591–603.

According to form criticism, what we have in the Old Testament is the product of various unknown persons within given cultures telling commonly shared stories and reciting familiar poems over a long period of time.[10] The earliest stories and poems were short units that were used in specific settings within the community. These stories and poems were developed and transformed as they were retold. Liturgical material reached relatively fixed form earlier. But popular stories and proverbs, which were created by the people who "cheerfully modified them over and over again," were written down much later.[11] The oral traditions could evolve in a variety of ways through multiple tellings in different contexts. This could result in duplicate accounts of the same story. Eventually, the stories were built up into larger blocks. After the Babylonian exile of Judah (sixth century BCE), these stories were written down into continuous narratives. According to form critics such as Koch, such a process produced the book of Genesis.

In the narrative flow of Genesis, the patriarch travels to Egypt right after his initial divine call and deceives Pharaoh by saying that Sarai, his wife, is his sister (ch. 12). Later, Abraham appears to carry out the same ruse against a certain king Abimelech (ch. 20), and then Isaac uses this deception again on Abimelech king of the Philistines (ch. 26). The fact that the same basic story is told three times suggests to the form critic that we are dealing with a single tradition that has evolved in different ways. Each of the narratives as we find it now constitutes a self-contained literary unit. For example, one could remove Genesis 12:10–20 from its current place in Genesis, and what is left would essentially be a coherent narrative.[12] The "Ancestress of Israel in Danger" stories in Genesis 20 and 26 are also self-contained units, and they also may be seen as intruding on their contexts; this is true despite the fact that Genesis 26:1 introduces the third iteration of this story with a "clumsy" attempt to recognize the existence of an earlier telling: "Now there was a famine in

10. Form-critical research on the Old Testament was greatly influenced by the folklore studies of the brothers Grimm, well known for their collection of children's and household folklore: J. C. L. Grimm and W. C. Grimm, *Kinder- und Hausmärchen* (Leipzig, 1812–1815) ["Grimms' Fairy Tales"]. Gunkel often draws on Grimm and Grimm, *Deutsche Sagen* (Berlin, 1816–1818), e.g., Gunkel, *Genesis*, xix, xlvii–xlviii, 187, 193, 209, 212, 283, 367, 406; and J. C. L. Grimm, *Deutsche Mythologie* (Göttingen: Dieterich'sche Buchhandlung, 1835), e.g., Gunkel, *Genesis*, 13, 343. See also Patricia G. Kirkpatrick, *The Old Testament and Folklore Study* (Sheffield: JSOT Press, 1988), 23–24.

11. Koch, *Growth of the Biblical Tradition*, 84–85.

12. Koch, *Growth of the Biblical Tradition*, 115–116. Thus, Gen 12:9, וַיִּסַּע אַבְרָם הָלוֹךְ וְנָסוֹעַ הַנֶּגְבָּה, is picked up by the reference to the Negeb in Gen 13:1 (וְלוֹט עִמּוֹ- הַנֶּגְבָּה), and the surrounding narrative resumes fully at Gen 13:3, וַיֵּלֶךְ לְמַסָּעָיו מִנֶּגֶב. Koch sees the rest of Gen 13:1–2 as transition clauses that were added by an editor when the story reached the written stage.

the land, *besides the former famine that was in the days of Abraham*."[13] Thus, the "Ancestress of Israel in Danger" story was originally an independent unit, an old oral tradition. Form criticism asks: What did the original story look like? How did it develop? When and why was it told?

The shortest version, Genesis 12, is thought to be closest to the original tale. It has the fewest elaborations, which gives it "an archaic quality."[14] In fact, it leaves a lot of questions unanswered—questions that later tellings attempt to address. In two details, however, Genesis 12 does not reflect the prototype oral story. First, Genesis 20 and 26 tell a story about Abimelech in Gerar taking the patriarch's wife, whereas Genesis 12 has Pharaoh of Egypt do this. It is hard to see why someone in ancient Israel would take a story about Pharaoh and make it into a story about Abimelech; but given the prominent role of Egypt in biblical traditions, it is easy to see why a story about Abimelech would be turned into a story about Pharaoh. Thus, the original story was probably about Abimelech. Second, this same reasoning leads us to suppose that the original story was about Isaac, and was later retold with Abraham, the best-known patriarch, as the protagonist. Otherwise, the simple framework of Genesis 12 is as close as we can get to the original story. This goes to show that even the most primitive form in our text is already an evolved form. In other words, what appears to be the earliest preserved version of this narrative already shows evidence of evolution (Abimelech became Pharaoh, and Isaac became Abraham). Form critics conclude from this that the basic story has a long oral pre-history stretching back behind its first written expression.

The version in Genesis 20 is even more evolved than the one in Genesis 12. References to "integrity of heart" (v. 6), "great sin" (v. 9), and Abraham as a "prophet" (v. 7) all reflect the religious outlook of a later era.[15] Moreover, here problems in the original narrative are addressed: for example, when reading Genesis 12, one might be troubled that Abram lied; in Genesis 20:12, it is explained that, technically speaking, he (now called Abraham) did not lie. Again, when reading Genesis 12, one might wonder if Sarai really had sexual relations with the foreign king; in Genesis 20:6, it is made clear that Sarah was untouched. This increased sensitivity in sexual matters is interpreted as a sign

13. Koch, *Growth of the Biblical Tradition*, 118. What appears to be another attempt to recognize the earlier story occurs at Gen 20:13, where Abraham says to Sarah, "This is the kindness you must do me: at every place to which we come, say of me, 'He is my brother.'" According to a form-critical analysis, this would come from the hand of a literary editor who assembled these stories into the larger narrative after they had essentially reached their present form.

14. Koch, *Growth of the Biblical Tradition*, 123.

15. Ibid.

of later development.[16] It is true, of course, that Genesis 20 has at least one primitive element: in the other two stories, famine is given as a pretext for the journey into the foreign land, where in Genesis 20 no reason is given. In most other matters, however, Genesis 20 is more artistically constructed and has more dialogue, and so reflects a more evolved version of the story.

Genesis 26 represents another development of the story. In Genesis 26, Abimelech in Gerar has become "king of the Philistines" (v. 1), which is anachronistic and thus reflects a later telling.[17] Since Abimelech discovers the patriarch's deception before taking his wife (v. 8), the scandal of the patriarch's wife being in sexual danger is removed entirely. Moreover, the problem in Genesis 12:16 and Genesis 20:14–16, that the patriarch becomes rich through a foreign king, is now resolved: YHWH himself now makes the patriarch wealthy (Gen 26:12–13). The section in Genesis 26:2–5 incorporating the patriarchal blessings is also seen as a later theological addition to the story.[18]

Thus, with the exception of the name changes, the version in Genesis 12 is closest to the original story. Genesis 20 and 26 each represent developments of this story that evolved over time through oral retellings.[19] The elaborations found in Genesis 20 and 26 reflect story-telling tendencies such as the adding of speeches, increased moral scruples, the use of more familiar characters, the introduction of later theological ideas, and decreasing reference to direct divine intervention.[20]

According to form critics, stories such as the "Ancestress of Israel in Danger" narrative arose and gained popularity because they embodied values or addressed concerns that were important to a community within a specific context. A close connection is assumed between the genre (*Gattung*) of the story and the specific "life setting" (*Sitz im Leben*) in which the story was told. The earliest version of the story tells us something about the ancient society that produced it, and the evolution of the story through time offers a window into the evolution of the society as a whole. In this way, form criticism leads to a study of tradition history. From this perspective, what was the *Sitz im Leben* for the original story? And how did it develop?

According to Koch, the original story makes sense for nomadic people living in pre-Israelite times whose wealth was in cattle. These herdsmen felt

---

16. Koch, *Growth of the Biblical Tradition*, 126.

17. See H.J. Katzenstein, "Philistines: History," in David N. Freedman (ed.), *The Anchor Bible Dictionary* (New York: Doubleday, 1992), 5.326.

18. Koch, *Growth of the Biblical Tradition*, 124.

19. The practice of addressing interpretive difficulties in scripture by telling stories is common in haggadic midrash. Samuel Sandmel dealt with the "Ancestress of Israel in Danger" stories in a way similar to Koch in an article called "The Haggada within Scripture," *JBL* 80 (1961): 105–122.

20. Koch, *Growth of the Biblical Tradition*, 126–127.

superior to the people living in established cities, and this tale showed that their own ancestors had been cleverer than the townspeople. Elements of the story such as the willingness of the women to sacrifice their honor to save their husband's lives and the acceptance of marriage between half-brother and sister point to the early conditions under which the story arose.[21] As for the specific context in which the story would have been told, Koch provides this vivid description: "Such a story would perhaps have been related by men before the tents, when it was evening, after the herds had been settled and the children slept."[22] This story was later taken up by prophetic circles, as shown by Genesis 20:7, and also was told at a time when Israel itself lived in cities, as shown by the settled life of Isaac in Genesis 26.[23] Eventually, the story evolved from a simple tale meant to show the cleverness of tribal ancestors to a more complex story that included the developed Israelite theology of patriarchal blessings, with the result that the account became a stage in the "great salvation history (*Heilsgeschichte*) of God."[24]

In this view, the "Ancestress of Israel in Danger" stories came into written form only after centuries of oral transmission. Traditions underwent significant recasting when they were transmitted by word of mouth, obtaining greater fixity only at the final written stage. In addition, the transition from oral to written transmission also involved the linking of individual units together and the composition of introductions and conclusions to connect them to their surroundings.[25] Although the "Ancestress of Israel in Danger" story could be as early as the Late Bronze Age (1400–1200 BCE), the literary versions are thought to have crystalized centuries later and eventually made their way into the Pentateuch through the literary sources that adopted them. Genesis 12 is assigned to the J source, Genesis 20 is from the E source, and

---

21. Koch, *Growth of the Biblical Tradition*, 127.

22. Ibid.

23. Koch, *Growth of the Biblical Tradition*, 128.

24. Koch, *Growth of the Biblical Tradition*, 129. As Koch goes on to say (132), "Against this background we can see that it has been 'preserved for purposes of admonition' (von Rad), and was intended for the ears of those people who were to become the Israelite nation," referring in a note to Gerhard von Rad, *Das erste Buch Mose. Das Alte Testament deutsch* (Göttingen: Vandenhoeck & Ruprecht 1961). For von Rad, the Old Testament comprises the traditions of ancient Israel that had been updated over time for "kerygmatic" purposes, i.e., for the purpose of proclamation, so as to present to each generation a fresh version of their "salvation history" creed; for a brief summary of von Rad's approach, see James Barr, *The Concept of Biblical Theology: An Old Testament Perspective* (Minneapolis, MN: Augsburg Fortress, 1999), 32–37. Von Rad was useful also for Wansbrough in understanding how the evolution of traditions could be theological (e.g., Wansbrough, *Quranic Studies*, 11, 16, 30, 42, 56, 76–77, 103).

25. Koch, *Growth of the Biblical Tradition*, 89–91.

Genesis 26 belongs to another source related to J.[26] For Gunkel and other early form critics, the literary authors of the Pentateuch were merely compilers of ancient oral traditions which they incorporated into their work essentially as they found them. Such critics continued to refer to literary sources such as "J" and "E," perhaps in deference to the source-critical conclusions they inherited, but they failed to clarify what gave these sources their individual identities.[27]

Form Criticism and Wansbrough on the Prophet Shuʿayb

Koch's form-critical analysis serves as a useful model for understanding Wansbrough's conception of how the text of the Qurʾān came to be. In his *Quranic Studies*, Wansbrough provides a treatment of the three main tellings of the story of the prophet Shuʿayb that proceeds along lines very similar to Koch's treatment of the "Ancestress of Israel in Danger" stories in Genesis.

The accounts of Shuʿayb appear in Q Aʿrāf 7:85–93, Hūd 11:84–95 and Shuʿarāʾ 26:176–191. Shuʿayb is also referred to briefly in Q ʿAnkabūt 29:36–37. In Q 7:85, 11:84, and 29:36 it is stated that Shuʿayb was sent to Madyan (usually understood as Midian), and he is identified as their "brother." According to Q 26:176–177, Shuʿayb was sent to the "inhabitants of Aykah." The main contours of Shuʿayb's message as presented in these texts is that people should worship God alone, act justly, prepare for God's day of reckoning, and not hinder those who believe in God. In each account Shuʿayb's hearers reject him, and as a result they are punished. Some Muslim commentators concluded that Shuʿayb was sent on two missions, one to the people of Madyan and another to the "inhabitants of Aykah," but most traditional authorities identified the people of Madyan and the "inhabitants of Aykah" as one and the same people.[28]

---

26. Koch, *Growth of the Biblical Tradition*, 129–131. On the Yahwistic features of Gen 26, see John Skinner, *A Critical and Exegetical Commentary on Genesis* (Edinburgh: T&T Clark, 1910), xlix, 363. These include the use of יְהוָה (vv. 2, 12, 22, 25; even spoken by Abimelech in v. 28), וַיַּשְׁקֵף (v. 8; cf. Gen 18:16, 19:28), and וַיִּקְרָא בְּשֵׁם יְהוָה (v. 25; cf. Gen 4:26; 12:8; 13:4; 21:33).

27. Later practitioners of form criticism, including Gerhard von Rad, ascribed more creative editorial activity to the individual authors of the written pentateuchal sources; see Hahn, *The Old Testament in Modern Research*, 126–127, 152–154.

28. C. E. Bosworth, "The Qurʾānic Prophet Shuʿaib and Ibn Taymiyya's Epistle Concerning Him," *Le Muséon* 87 (1974): 425–440, 426. On the possible location for a region called Aykah (understood to mean "thicket, tanglewood") in northwestern Arabia in proximity to the presumed region of Midian, see idem, "Madyan Shuʿayb in Pre-Islamic and Early Islamic Lore and History," *JSS* 29 (1984): 53–64, 55; and "The Qurʾānic Prophet Shuʿaib," 427.

Modern scholars differ on whether or not the story of Shuʿayb has roots in the biblical tradition. There were many classical Muslim commentators who identified Shuʿayb with the biblical Jethro.[29] But some modern writers argue that the Shuʿayb stories are strictly Arabian in origin, just like the stories about Hūd and Ṣāliḥ.[30] From this perspective, traditional qur'ānic interpretations that connect Jethro and Shuʿayb reflect later exegetical interests and have no basis in the Qur'ān itself.

According to other modern writers, however, the interpretive tradition identifying Shuʿayb as Jethro actually reflects the biblical background of the character Shuʿayb. The two starting points in the Qur'ān for this identification are: (1) the chronology suggested by Q 11:89: Noah, Hūd, Ṣāliḥ, and the people of Lot, who are "not distant from you" (*wa-mā... minkum bi-baʿīd*), followed by Moses in Q 11:96, thus placing Shuʿayb not long after Lot and just prior to Moses; and (2) the association of Shuʿayb with Madyan (= biblical Midian) where Moses lived for a time and encountered the daughters of an aged man at a well (Q Qaṣaṣ 28:23), in a scene reminiscent of Exodus 2:15–22.[31] On the premise that Shuʿayb originally developed out of the figure of Jethro, various theories have been proposed to explain the origin of the name "Shuʿayb." Abraham Geiger located the source of "Shuʿayb" in Jewish traditions saying that Moses received his powerful staff from Jethro, who was "owner of the staff" (*Besitzer des Stabes*), that is "Shuʿayb," since *shuʿbah* means "staff."[32] Alternately, Heinrich Speyer argued that Muḥammad identified Jethro's well in Midian (Exod 2:15) with Beersheba on the basis of Jewish *aggadah* connecting the well encounters of Isaac, Jacob, and Moses,[33] and that Muḥammad correctly understood *bəʾēr* (בְּאֵר) to mean "well," but

29. Bosworth, "The Qur'ānic Prophet Shuʿaib," 428–433.

30. See Robert Tottoli, *Biblical Prophets in the Qur'ān and Muslim Literature* (London & New York: Routledge, 2002), 49–50. At this point, however, it does not seem that the name Shuʿayb occurs anywhere in pre-Islamic Arabic; see Bosworth, "The Qur'ānic Prophet Shuʿaib," 427–428. Josef Horovitz, *Koranische Untersuchungen* (Berlin: Walter de Gruyter, 1926), 119–120 acknowledges that the name "Shuʿayb" does not appear in authentic pre-Islamic Arabic sources but still favors the theory that Shuʿayb was an Arabian figure in the line of Hūd and Ṣāliḥ.

31. Narratives placing Moses in Madyan occur in Q 20:40, 28:22–23, 45, and less clearly in 22:44. Madyan is also mentioned in Q 9:70.

32. Abraham Geiger, *Was hat Mohammed aus dem Judenthume aufgenommen?* (Leipzig: M. W. Kaufmann, 1902; revised ed. of Bonn, 1833), 174. For the Jewish sources, see *Pirqe de-Rabbi Eliezer* 40; *Targum Pseudo-Jonathan*, Exod 2:21, 4:20 (cf. 14:21). On the meaning of *shuʿbah*, see E. W. Lane, *Arabic-English Lexicon* (Edinburgh: Williams & Norgate, 1872), 1556.

33. *Midrash Tanḥuma, Shemot* 10; *Exodus Rabbah* 1.32. See Heinrich Speyer, *Die biblischen Erzählungen im Qoran* (Gräfenhainichen: Schulze, 1931; repr. Hildesheim: Georg Olms, 2013), 252–254.

construed *sheba*ʿ (שֶׁבַע) as a proper name, "Shuʿayb."[34] Overall, I consider it likely that the qurʾānic stories about Shuʿayb go back to the biblical Jethro, even if the origin of the name "Shuʿayb" is not entirely certain. Wansbrough does not suggest that the biblical Jethro stands behind the Shuʿayb narratives, but the possibility of such an antecedent will be significant later in discussing how one might adopt Wansbrough's reading of these stories into a different framework from what he proposed.

I will now turn to Wansbrough's discussion of the three major qurʾānic accounts of the prophet Shuʿayb as found in Q 7:85–93, 11:84–95, and 26:176–191.

Shuʿayb the Prophet: Q 7:85–93, 11:84–93, 26:177–188[a]		
Q 26 **I.** . . .	**Q 7** **I.** [85] **And to Midian their brother Shuʿayb.**	**Q 11** **I.** [84] **And to Midian their brother Shuʿayb.**
II. [178] (Shuʿayb said) I am a messenger entrusted to you.	**II.** [87] (He said) if some of you believe in that with which I have been sent, and others of you do not, then have patience until God judges between us, for He is the best of judges.	**II.** [88] (He said) My people, do you not see that I bear a sign from my Lord, Who has provided well for me. I do not wish to oppose you in that which I forbid, but only to put things right so far as I can. And my success lies with God upon Whom I rely and towards Whom I turn.

34. Speyer proposed that the phrase "the inhabitants of Aykah (the thicket)" in Q 26:176 goes back to the tamarisk plant (אֵשֶׁל) that Abraham planted at Beersheba in Gen 21:33 (cf. *Genesis Rabbah* 54.6). Shuʿayb is also connected to the midrashic Jethro in that Jethro already knew the true religion before the Mosaic revelation (= one view expressed in *Leviticus Rabbah* 9.6). Finally, Speyer cited Deut 25:13–15 and Prov 11:1 as background for Shuʿayb's call for just weights and measures.

III. [177] Thus said Shuʿayb to them: Will you not fear? [179] Fear God and obey (me). [180] For that I ask of you no reward. I have no reward but with the Lord of the universe. [181] Give full measure, and be not of those who cause loss. [182] Weigh in straightforward equity. [183] And do not cheat your fellows of their property, nor work evil in the land.	**III.** [85] My people, worship God, for you have no other than Him. And a sign has come to you from your Lord. Give full measure and weight, and do not cheat your fellows of their property, nor work evil in the land, now that matters have been put right. There will be benefit to you if you have faith. [86a] So occupy not any path, seeking to make it devious, and threatening and barring from the way of God him who believes.	**III.** [84] *My people, worship God, for you have no other than Him.* Give not short measure and weight, for I see you in wealth and fear for you the punishment of the last day. [85] My people, *give full measure and weight in equity, and do not cheat your fellows of their property, nor work evil in the land.* [86] That which abides with God will be a benefit to you, if you have faith. For I cannot preserve you.
IV. [184] And fear Him Who created you and those who went before.	**IV.** [86b] But remember that you were few and He increased you, and consider the destiny of those who work evil.	**IV.** [89] My people, let not rejection of me make you guilty, *lest that afflict you which afflicted the people of Noah or of Hūd or of Ṣāliḥ, nor are the people of Lot irrelevant.*
V. [185] They replied: You are one of the possessed. [186] And are only a mortal like ourselves, and we think you a liar. [187] But if you speak the truth, then let some part of heaven fall upon us.	**V.** [88a] And the assembly of those of his people who regarded themselves as authorities said: We will expel you from our midst, Shuʿayb, and those who believe with you, unless you return to our law.	**V.** [87] They replied: Shuʿayb, does your prayer command that we abandon that which our fathers worshipped or that we (do not) conduct our affairs as we wish? But are you not clement and righteous?

VI. . . .	**VI.** [88b] He replied: And if we do not wish to? [89] We should be guilty of denying God were we to return to your law after He delivered us. It is not for us to return unless our Lord God wishes it. His wisdom comprehends all things, upon God do we rely. Lord, judge in truth between our people and ourselves, for You are the best of judges.	**VI.** [90] (He said) Ask forgiveness of your Lord and turn towards Him. My Lord is merciful (and) loving. [92] He said: My people, is my family dearer to you than God, for you have cast Him behind you. My Lord understands that which you do.
VII. . . .	**VII.** [90] And the assembly of those of his people who did not accept said: If you follow Shuʿayb then you are lost.	**VII.** [91] They replied: Shuʿayb, we do not understand much of what you say and regard you as without support. Were it not for your family, we would stone you, for you have no power over us.
VIII. [176] The men of the copse rejected the messengers. [189] Thus they rejected him, and the punishment of the last day, a momentous day, overtook them. [190] In that there is a sign, but most of them have no faith.	**VIII.** [91] So disaster overtook them and they were left prostrate in their place. [92] Those who rejected Shuʿayb were as though they had not been, those who rejected Shuʿayb were indeed lost.	**VIII.** [94] And when Our decree was uttered We delivered Shuʿayb and those who had faith with him, as a mercy from Us. *And disaster overtook those who had done wrong and they were left prostrate in their place.* [95] As though they had not been, **Midian** perished **as Thamūd had perished**.
IX. [188] He said: My Lord knows best what you have done.	**IX.** [93] And he turned away from them saying: My people, I brought you messages from my Lord and advised you, so how shall I have pity on a people who does not accept?	**IX.** [93] (He said) My people, do in your position (as) I do. You will know him to whom a grievous punishment comes, and who it is who lies. And watch, for I watch with you.

[a] The translation is that of Wansbrough, *Quranic Studies*, 21–23.

The appearance of what seems to be the same essential prophetic report three times in different locations in the Qur'ān suggests that form-critical analysis may yield insights into the development of this tradition. Wansbrough's first task is to identify the "form" (*Gattung*, "genre") of these texts. Whereas Klaus Koch in Genesis dealt with an "ethnological saga," Wansbrough organizes these reports according to the outline of a prophetic "messenger's speech" (*Botenwort*), which he explicitly derives from Claus Westermann's *Grundformen prophetischer Rede*, appropriating Westermann's specific terminology.[35] Wansbrough identifies his texts as "prophetical" and so he bases his interpretation on a prophetic form known from the Hebrew Bible.

Wansbrough regards the version in Q 26 as the most "primitive" (i.e., earliest), as it is shortest and least coherent.[36] In other words, Wansbrough believes that the story was elaborated and made more coherent over time. The primitive nature of the Q 26 version is also suggested by the absence of the "formula of commission" (*Beauftragung*): "And to Midian their brother Shuʿayb." In place of this formula, the Q 26 version is introduced merely with the phrase *idh qāla* ("thus he said," or "when he said") in 26:177. In Sūrah 7 and 11, the commissioning formula is thus seen as an "editorial interpolation."[37] Wansbrough regards element II, the "messenger formula" (*Botenformel*), as nearest its original position in Q 26, where "I am a messenger entrusted to you" leads directly into the substance of the message, element III (*Anklage*, "accusation").[38] Finally, the counter-arguments found at elements VI and VII are absent from Q 26, and are therefore regarded as elaborations added later in Sūrah 7 and 11.

The story of Q 7 bears some marks of evolution. The position of element IX, the "epilogue" or "final assessment," is said to be logical only in Q 7, which presumes either that it was made more coherent vis-à-vis Q 26 or that it was added independently in each account, and most coherently in Q 7. Wansbrough sees the version in Q 7 as more evolved than the story of Q 26, but not yet the most developed telling of the tale.

35. Koch, *Growth of the Biblical Tradition*, 120; Wansbrough, *Quranic Studies*, 23–24. See Claus Westermann, *Grundformen prophetischer Rede* (5th ed.; Munich: Chr. Kaiser, 1978), 79–80, translated into English as *Basic Forms of Prophetic Speech*, trans. H. C. White (Louisville, KY: Westminster/John Knox, 1991). According to Wansbrough, the scheme by which he organizes these texts is "widely attested in the literature of prophetic expression" (*Quranic Studies*, 23).

36. Wansbrough, *Quranic Studies*, 23–24.

37. Ibid., 24.

38. Ibid. Wansbrough labels element III as either *Scheltwort* ("diatribe") or *Anklage*, but Westermann strongly favored the term *Anklage* for this component (Westermann, *Grundformen*, 46–49).

According to Wansbrough, the story of Shuʿayb in Q 11 is the latest version. The simple "a messenger entrusted" (*rasūlun amīn*) in element II of Q 26, which in Q 7 is "in that with which I have been sent" (*bi'lladhī ursiltu bi-hi*), has become in Q 11 "a sign from my Lord" (*bayyinah min rabbī*), this last phrase being taken to reflect the most developed terminology. In Sūrah 26 and 7, element III ("accusation") is directly followed by element IV ("announcement of disaster," *Unheilsankündigung*), which Wansbrough considers to be the natural and original sequence.[39] This indicates to him that Q 11 reflects a later reordering of these elements. Significantly, the addition of Noah, Lot, Hūd and Ṣāliḥ (IV) in Q 11 further suggests to Wansbrough that Q 11 is closest to "the final shape of the tradition."[40]

In Wansbrough's analysis, a biblical subtext can be found for this tradition even in its earliest known stage, as seen in the admonition to justice with reference to weights and measures (element III in all versions), which is common in the Pentateuch.[41] Wansbrough does not suggest that the story of Shuʿayb itself belongs to the biblical subtext, only the motif of honest weights and measures. According to Wansbrough, this connection to the biblical tradition is taken further by the addition of element I in Sūrah 7 and 11, since he understands the references to Midian as belonging to the Mosaic tradition.[42] The specific naming of prophets in element IV of Q 11, including the prophets Noah and Lot, adds to the Shuʿayb story another direct link to the biblical heritage. Wansbrough sees the development of the Shuʿayb tradition as representing a gradual movement toward greater contact with the biblical framework. Within the broader context of *Quranic Studies*, this analysis suggests that the story evolved over time in contexts that involved increasing interactions with Jews or Christians, culminating in the canonical text of the Qur'ān in the early ninth century.[43]

In sum, Wansbrough thinks each of these versions developed through its own separate process out of a single prototype original. In a manner

39. Wansbrough, *Quranic Studies*, 24. Wansbrough labels this either *Drohwort* ("threat") or *Unheilsankündigung*, but Westermann, *Grundformen*, 46–49, argues for *Unheilsankündigung* and regards *Drohwort* as unsuitable.

40. Ibid.

41. Ibid., 25. Wansbrough refers to Lev 19:35–36, Deut 25:13–16, and also Amos 8:5, Micah 6:11.

42. Ibid.

43. Wansbrough, *Quranic Studies*, 44, 47–52, 144–146, 202, 225–227; cf. ibid., *The Sectarian Milieu* (Oxford: Oxford University Press, 1978), 29, 49, 58, 138–139. Wansbrough is skeptical about evidence for significant Jewish influence in the Hijaz during the sixth and seventh centuries, preferring Mesopotamia in the period leading up to the ninth century as a more likely environment for the growth of these traditions in the midst of sectarian disputes (see *Quranic Studies*, 50–51).

reminiscent of Koch, the Qur'ān is seen as a composite text made up of originally independent units that evolved orally over a long period of time. Wansbrough refers to these originally separate units as "prophetical *logia*."[44] The term *logia* (λόγια, plural of λόγιον, "oracle") was used in New Testament form criticism for presumed early sayings of Jesus that were transmitted, shaped, and elaborated in the decades following the life of Jesus, leading up to their eventual use in the writing of gospels.[45] This specific use of *logia* further illustrates Wansbrough's debt to form criticism, showing the picture he imagines of originally distinct prophetic units that evolved in the process of oral transmission.

Form Criticism: Genesis and the Qur'ān

How should Wansbrough's application of biblical form criticism to the Qur'ān be evaluated? Is form criticism itself methodologically sound? Could the Shuʿayb accounts in the Qur'ān have evolved in a way similar to what Klaus Koch proposed for the "Ancestress of Israel in Danger" stories in Genesis?

As for Koch's interpretation of Genesis, his basic understanding of the relationship between the different tellings of the "Ancestress of Israel in Danger" story is convincing.[46] Moreover, given the potentially early origins

44. Ibid., 47; cf. 48–52.

45. The use of *logia* for the early "sayings" of Jesus is based on a Papias fragment in Eusebius, *Historia ecclesiastica* 3.39.16. It was once believed that Papias was referring to an early collection of such sayings, but contemporary Gospel criticism no longer favors this interpretation of the Papias fragment, and now uses Q to designate the early "sayings" source; see J. M. Robinson, P. Hoffmann, and J. S. Kloppenborg (eds.), *The Critical Edition of Q* (Minneapolis, MN: Fortress, 2000), xix–xxxiii. For the conceptual framework of Wansbrough's appropriation of gospel criticism, see Rudolf Bultmann, *The History of the Synoptic Tradition*, trans. John Marsh (New York: Harper & Row, 1963). Bultmann emphasized the adaptability of the traditions of Jesus' teaching in light of early Christian proclamation (*kerygma*). For recent discussions of Jesus' sayings and orality, see Henry Wansbrough (ed.), *Jesus and the Oral Gospel Tradition* (Sheffield: Sheffield Academic Press, 1991); and James D. G. Dunn, *The Oral Gospel Tradition* (Grand Rapids, MI: Eerdmans, 2013). Although Wansbrough frequently borrows concepts from Gerhardsson, *Memory and Manuscript*, his approach to the preservation of oral traditions is closer to Bultmann than to Gerhardsson. For current evaluations of Gerhardsson's work, see Werner H. Kelber and Samuel Byrskog (eds.), *Jesus in Memory: Traditions in Oral and Scribal Perspectives* (Waco, TX: Baylor University Press, 2009).

46. Even if one were to accept the historicity of the Patriarchs, the narratives in Gen 12, 20, and 26 report an occurrence that is intrinsically unlikely to have happened three times; cf. Umberto Cassuto, *A Commentary on the Book of Genesis, Part 2: From Noah to Abraham*, trans. Israel Abrahams (Jerusalem: Magnes Press, 1964), 337–344.

of the patriarchal narratives and the late date of our evidence for the text of Genesis (third century BCE, based on the Septuagint and Qumran), a long period of development for the accounts in Genesis 12, 20, and 26 is possible.[47]

Nevertheless, Koch's form-critical interpretation of Genesis can also be challenged on a few points. First, form criticism assumes that composition took place primarily through a process of oral transmission.[48] It is not impossible that these stories were preserved through oral means, but this is far from certain. The transmission history of ancient Near Eastern texts such as the *Epic of Gilgamesh* demonstrates that some narratives were transmitted and evolved as literature.[49] Further, recent research suggests that in many cultures

47. On the early setting of the patriarchal stories, Koch, *Growth of the Biblical Tradition*, 128, states: "To begin with, it must be recognized that the saga is wholly imbued with the atmosphere of the period it describes, and therefore must certainly belong to the period before the settlement of the later Israelite tribes." For a well-documented argument that the patriarchal stories fit plausibly within the general cultural milieu of the Bronze Age, see Kenneth A. Kitchen, *On the Reliability of the Old Testament* (Grand Rapids, MI: Eerdmans, 2003), 313–372. On the current state of research on evidence for ancient Israel, see Susan Niditch (ed.), *The Wiley Blackwell Companion to Ancient Israel* (West Sussex, UK: Wiley, 2016). On the textual evidence for Old Testament books, see Emanuel Tov, *Textual Criticism of the Hebrew Bible* (3rd ed.; Minneapolis, MN: Fortress, 2012).

48. The study of ancient literature through the lens of orality received its foundations from works by Milman Parry; see Adam Parry (ed.), *The Making of Homeric Verse: The Collected Papers of Milman Parry* (Oxford: Oxford University Press, 1971), based on studies in the 1930s, and Albert B. Lord, *The Singer of Tales* (2nd ed.; Cambridge, MA: Harvard University Press, 2000 [1960]), who investigated the oral composition practices of South Slavic singers. In this context, key traits of oral composition include the use of specific meters, formulaic language, and the completion of thought units at the end of a line. Milman and Parry successfully demonstrated the relevance of this material to the *Iliad* and the *Odyssey*, but biblical scholarship still lacks clear evidence to show what oral composition would look like for biblical literature; for discussion, see Susan Niditch, *Oral World and Written Word: Ancient Israelite Literature* (Louisville, KY: Westminster John Knox, 1996); and idem, "Hebrew Bible and Oral Literature: Misconceptions and New Directions," in Robert B. Coote and Annette Weissenrieder (eds.), *The Interface of Orality and Writing: Speaking, Seeing, Writing in the Shape of New Genres* (Tübingen: Mohr Siebeck, 2010), 3–18.

49. See David M. Carr, *The Formation of the Hebrew Bible: A New Reconstruction* (Oxford: Oxford University Press, 2011), 37–56; and Jeffrey H. Tigay (ed.), *Empirical Models for Biblical Criticism* (Philadelphia: University of Pennsylvania Press, 1985), 21–52. On literacy in Israel, see Baruch Halpern, "Jerusalem and the Lineages in the Seventh Century BCE: Kinship and the Rise of Individual Moral Liability," in Baruch Halpern and Deborah W. Hobson (eds.), *Law and Ideology in Monarchic Israel* (Sheffield: JSOT, 1991), 79–91, and Christopher A. Rollston, *Writing and Literacy in the World of Ancient Israel* (Atlanta: SBL, 2010), 95–113, who identifies from epigraphic

oral and written modes of composition and transmission worked in tandem.[50] Thus, it may not be valid to assume that the "Ancestress of Israel in Danger" stories took shape primarily by oral tellings.

Second, a long period of time may not have been necessary for the kinds of developments in the story that Koch describes. John Van Seters sees Genesis 12 as the oldest version, Genesis 20 as a literary embellishment of Genesis 12 (e.g., the shift of focus away from the hero to Abimelech in Gen 20 does not reflect the oral storyteller's art), and Genesis 26 as a rewriting of Genesis 20. According to Van Seters, all of this took place roughly during the exilic period.[51] Whether the stories are early or late, it may be acknowledged that the evolution of this story could have taken place in much less time than Koch envisioned. Still, theories about time and process have implications for what we should expect in terms of literary coherence. In classical form criticism, the final editors of Genesis were merely collectors who assembled traditions essentially as they found them. Such a process would leave incongruities in the narrative. For Van Seters, however, the writer of Genesis was a historian who should be regarded as the single author of the book.[52] By placing greater emphasis on the role of a single writer in determining the shape of the text, this model leads us to expect greater overall coherence in the narrative.[53] In other words, a shorter time frame with a single author should result in a more coherent text.

---

materials such consistency in scribal practices within given time periods as to suggest formal training of scribes already in the early eighth century BCE.

50. E.g., Martin Jaffee, *Torah in the Mouth: Writing and Oral Tradition in Palestinian Judaism 200 BCE–400 CE* (Oxford: Oxford University Press, 2001); Elizabeth Shanks Alexander, *Transmitting Mishnah: The Shaping Influence of Oral Tradition* (Cambridge: Cambridge University Press, 2006); Weissenrieder and Coote, *The Interface of Orality and Writing*; and Carr, *The Formation of the Hebrew Bible*, 3–9, 98–101.

51. John Van Seters, *Abraham in History and Tradition* (New Haven, CT: Yale University Press, 1975), 167–191.

52. See John Van Seters, *The Edited Bible: The Curious History of the "Editor" in Biblical Criticism* (Winona Lake, IN: Eisenbrauns, 2006), 399–401. Cf. idem, *Prologue to History: The Yahwist as Historian in Genesis* (Louisville: Westminster John Knox, 1992), and idem, *The Life of Moses: The Yahwist as Historian in Exodus-Numbers* (Louisville: Westminster John Knox, 1994).

53. Van Seters, of course, recognizes that there are incongruities in the narrative, but his overall reading of the Pentateuch perceives more coherence than classical form criticism suggested. Robert Alter, *The Art of Biblical Narrative* (New York: Basic Book, 1981), and Shimon Bar-Efrat, *Narrative Art in the Bible* (Sheffield: Almond Press, 1989) both argue for strong elements of compositional coherence in the Pentateuch, although Alter is clear that textual difficulties exist that cannot be harmonized as part of the literary artistry of the writer (Alter, *Art of Biblical Narrative*, 20).

Third, it must be acknowledged that Koch was forced to rely considerably on his imagination in reconstructing a precise *Sitz im Leben* for the original version of this story ("related by men before the tents, when it was evening…").[54] His attempts to describe the new settings in which the story developed were also by necessity vague. In general, we do not have as much information as we would like about the social settings of ancient Israel. Contemporary form critics are more cautious regarding their reconstruction of the *Sitz im Leben* of a text.[55]

Understanding the insights and limitations of classical form criticism as applied to the Hebrew Bible helps to clarify some of the key issues surrounding Wansbrough's treatment of the Shuʿayb accounts. I will begin with three points where I think the form-critical model serves Wansbrough's analysis well.

First, Wansbrough's perception that prophetic stories from the Qurʾān can be described using formal genre classifications is beneficial. In fact, his specific application of Westermann's biblical prophetic categories to the Qurʾān was generally successful. Components such as the "formula of commission," "messenger formula," "accusation," "counter-arguments," and "announcement of judgment" seem to operate in the Qurʾān in ways similar to how they work in biblical texts such as Amos 7:10–17, 1 Kings 21:17–26, and 2 Kings 1:3–4.[56] The similarities could reflect parallel cultural developments, but more likely they indicate the Qurʾān's awareness of the biblical prophetic tradition.[57] Of course, the Shuʿayb accounts do not simply reduplicate biblical patterns. The form-critical insights that Wansbrough brought to the Qurʾān would be improved by more precise descriptions of the

54. Koch, *Growth of the Biblical Tradition*, 127.

55. "Texts are indeed composed by authors, whose outlooks and techniques are influenced by their respective sociohistorical context. Nevertheless, the hypothetical nature of such reconstructions has undermined confidence in the ability of modern scholars to carry out such work with precision. Despite these difficulties, many form-critical researchers will continue their efforts at reconstruction, but there will be a more candid recognition of the tentative nature of such argumentation; that is, they will realize that they put forward theories, not assured facts" (Marvin A. Sweeney and Ehud Ben Zvi, "Introduction," in idem (eds.) *The Changing Face of Form Criticism for the Twenty-First Century* [Grand Rapids, MI: Eerdmans, 2003], 10).

56. Cf. Westermann, *Grundformen prophetischer Rede*, 92–94.

57. On the possibility of prophet-like intermediaries arising independently in different societies with similar social conditions, see Robert Wilson, *Prophecy and Society in Ancient Israel* (Philadelphia: Fortress, 1980), 89–90. Still, according to Jaakko Hämeen-Anttila, "Arabian Prophecy," in Martti Nissinen (ed.), *Prophecy in Its Ancient Near Eastern Context: Mesopotamian, Biblical, and Arabian Perspectives* (Atlanta: SBL, 2000), 115–146, prophecy in Arabia adopted specifically biblical characteristics in its transition from pre-Islamic to Islamic expressions.

Qur'ān's own "forms," such as has been carried out by Angelika Neuwirth.[58] Neuwirth's research has focused on the Meccan *sūrahs*, identifying types of compositional units out of which the Meccan *sūrahs* were constructed.[59] Examples of unit types noted by Neuwirth include the "eschatological unit," the "confirmation of revelation," "encouragement to the prophet," and "punishment stories."[60] Research along these lines showing the internal structure of particular qur'ānic units based on models throughout the Qur'ān would improve the results that Wansbrough obtained through his biblically-rooted form-critical analysis.[61]

Second, in view of the shared material between the Shuʿayb accounts (e.g., elements I, III, and VIII), Wansbrough was justified to conclude that these three texts represent three variants of a single story. Moreover, the logical relationships between the accounts make plausible the idea that we can identify material that was added in the development of a version (e.g., Q 11, element IV) or that a feature in one version is earlier than the corresponding features of the other versions (e.g., Q 26, element II). Whether we are imagining a lost "original" for which we have three separate renditions (cf. Koch), or texts whose authors were directly using the other texts (cf. Van Seters), the basic concept of the compositional inter-relationship of these narratives constitutes the strongest aspect of Wansbrough's reading.

Third, form criticism gave Wansbrough a useful model for considering the social settings that likely gave rise to the accounts one finds in the Qur'ān, including, but not limited to, the Shuʿayb narratives. Because Wansbrough did not accept the historicity of the *sīrah* literature, and little otherwise can be said about a specific social setting for the Shuʿayb pericope, Wansbrough did not attempt to describe a specific *Sitz im Leben*. Yet, in the context of his study of the Qur'ān as a whole, Wansbrough saw literary forms, terminology, motifs, and argumentation that broadly imply a social context, namely, disputes among those who are in conflict over the proper interpretation of

58. See Angelika Neuwirth, "Form and Structure of the Qur'ān," *EQ*, s.v. and eadem, *Studien zur Komposition der mekkanischen Suren* (2nd ed.; Berlin: de Gruyter, 2007).

59. Neuwirth employs the term *Gesätz* in *Studien zur Komposition* to describe such a unit, and she also uses the French *enjeu* (stake) in "Form and Structure of the Qur'ān."

60. Neuwirth, *Studien zur Komposition*, 124–136.

61. Neuwirth, *Studien zur Komposition*, 277, provides the following outline of the Shuʿayb account in Q 26 as part of a broader description of the construction of the whole *sūrah*: verses 176–180, Shuʿayb's speech to his people; 181–182, positive summons; 183–184, negative summons; 185–187, call for the people to fear God; 188–189, warning and punishment; 190–191, refrain.

the biblical monotheistic heritage.[62] This is an insightful theory that flows from form-critical thinking.[63]

At the same time, I see at least two problems that arise from Wansbrough's application of form criticism to the Qur'ān.

First, Koch described a scenario where the basic "Ancestress of Israel in Danger" tale circulated freely in various renditions for hundreds of years before crystalizing into written versions. In like manner, Wansbrough imagined a somewhat long process for the development of the Qur'ān, stretching from early seventh century Arabia to the ninth century outside of Arabia.[64] Yet, although a centuries-long process may be feasible for the patriarchal narratives, the idea of a long process of textual fluidity extending into the early ninth century is problematic for the Qur'ān. Manuscript evidence for the Qur'ān makes it almost certain that something close to the canonical version of the Qur'ān existed in writing by the end of the seventh century CE.[65] Therefore, if one were to view the early seventh century as

62. See Wansbrough, *Quranic Studies*, 118. For more recent arguments favoring the idea that the Qur'ān's polemic is directed not at pagan polytheists but at Abrahamic monotheists, see Gerald Hawting, "Qur'ānic Exegesis and History," in Jane Dammen McAuliffe, Barry D. Walfish, and Joseph W. Goering (eds.), *With Reverence for the Word: Medieval Scriptural Exegesis in Judaism, Christianity, and Islam* (Oxford: Oxford University Press, 2010), 412–418; and idem, *The Idea of Idolatry and the Emergence of Islam: From Polemic to History* (Cambridge: Cambridge University Press, 1999).

63. Fred Donner, "The Historian, the Believer, and the Qur'ān," 29, evaluates Wansbrough's sectarian milieu theory in this way: "That the Qur'ān crystallized in an environment of monotheistic debate, not in a pagan environment... This seems to be true. But the location of this monotheistic sectarian milieu is still far from clear."

64. See the passages from Wansbrough cited in n. 43. For example, arguing against the notion of an early fixed text of the Qur'ān based on masoretic literature, Wansbrough states: "The chronology of the literature indicates a period of approximately two centuries during which the text of scripture was anything but stable" (*Quranic Studies*, 225–226). For Wansbrough, these two centuries stretch from the early seventh to the early ninth centuries. It is true that Wansbrough believes that the "imagery and lexicon of Muslim scripture" suggest or presuppose "some contact with literary precursors" (*Quranic Studies*, 48). But Wansbrough does not seem to view these precursors as organically part of the composition of qur'ānic pericopes, but rather considers them resources utilized in the composition of these pericopes, which apparently take shape as units in the early seventh century. On the beginnings of Islamic literature in Mesopotamia, see *Sectarian Milieu*, 49.

65. François Déroche, *Qur'ans of the Umayyads: A First Overview* (Leiden: Brill, 2014), 34–35, dates Codex Parisino-petropolitanus to the third quarter of the seventh century. Behnam Sadeghi and Uwe Bergmann, "The Codex of a Companion of the Prophet and the Qur'ān of the Prophet," *Arabica* 57 (2010): 343–436, show the high probability that the Ṣan'ā' palimpsest gives a qur'ānic text close to the canonical version from the mid- or late seventh century. For other evidence pointing to a recognizable Qur'ān

the decisive starting point for the development of qur'ānic literary units, the process as a whole could not have taken as long as Wansbrough proposed.

Second, it is questionable whether form criticism's emphasis on oral transmission as the primary vehicle for composition is suitable to the Qur'ān. The relative uniformity of early qur'ānic codices on certain minor elements of language suggests that writing had a more integral role in the compositional process.[66] Furthermore, the Qur'ān contains what appear to be lengthy interpolations that intrude on the surrounding context, such as Q Muddaththir 74:31, which was likely added to explain the obscure phrase *ʿalayhā tisʿata ʿashara* ("over it are nineteen") in Q 74:30.[67] Interpolations of this kind are best explained as the work of a literary editor. These observations do not rule out the possibility that orally composed material made its way into the Qur'ān. As noted above, orality and literacy can coexist as modes of transmission.[68] But as with the book of Genesis, so also with the Qur'ān, classical form criticism assigned too extensive a role to oral composition.

As for these two problems, I can see two possible ways to address them. First, one could agree with Wansbrough that at least some qur'ānic passages underwent a relatively long period of development, but with the understanding that these passages originated prior to the seventh century. According to this way of thinking, not only did the Qur'ān make use of inherited images and vocabulary, but certain concrete units of qur'ānic material originated in the fifth or sixth century CE, or before. Both oral composition and the use of written sources could come into play. In such a situation, we would expect strong connections with prophetic and other relevant traditions from Late

---

in writing in the seventh century, see Déroche, "Written Transmission," in Andrew Rippin (ed.), *The Blackwell Companion to the Qur'ān* (Malden, MA: Blackwell, 2006), 173–176; Beatrice Gruendler, *The Development of the Arabic Scripts: From the Nabatean Era to the First Islamic Century according to Dated Texts* (Atlanta: Scholars Press, 1993), 135, 138–139; Keith E. Small, *Textual Criticism and Qur'ān Manuscripts* (Lanham, MD: Lexington Books, 2011), 174–175; and Fred Leemhuis, "From Palm Leaves to the Internet," in McAuliffe (ed.), *The Cambridge Companion to the Qur'ān*, 147–149.

66. See Sadeghi and Bergmann, "The Codex of a Companion of the Prophet," 344–345, on the combined role of orality and writing in view of early manuscripts of the Qur'ān.

67. Theodor Nöldeke, Friedrich Schwally, Gotthelf Bergsträßer and Otto Prezl, *The History of the Qur'ān*, trans. and ed. Wolfgang H. Behn (Leiden: Brill, 2013; revised ed. and trans. of *Geschichte des Qorāns* [Göttingen: Dieterich, 1860]), 73, suggests that the conclusion of this explanatory comment, *wa-mā hiya illā dhikrā li'l-bashar*, "it is nothing but a reminder to humankind" might be the original continuation of verse 30.

68. See the studies cited in n. 50. For example, people may write down and edit material composed orally, and texts may be used as mnemonic aids for further oral performances.

Antiquity, including biblical traditions.[69] To apply this to the Shuʿayb accounts, one could imagine that stories about this prophetic figure circulated in the regions around Arabia for perhaps a century or two prior to the stabilization of the qur'ānic text in the seventh century. This would fit, but does not require, that the prophet Shuʿayb was based on Jewish traditions about the biblical Jethro. Overall, I think this approach has merit for describing the pre-history of at least some units of text within the Qur'ān.

As a second way to address the above concerns, one could posit a compositional process for the Qur'ān whereby interpretive developments took place relatively quickly, for example, from the early to the mid-seventh century. This faster process would make best sense in a situation that includes written texts. On one level, a shorter time frame would fit better with traditional accounts of the Qur'ān that are rooted in the biography of Muḥammad.[70] One matter to consider, however, is the relationship between time frame, compositional process, and textual coherence.

As noted above when discussing Van Seters' work on Genesis, if the text came together in a short time under a single authorial enterprise, we would expect a greater degree of literary coherence. The Qur'ān, by way of contrast, exhibits

> abrupt changes of rhyme… the intrusion of an extraneous subject into a passage otherwise homogeneous; a differing treatment of the same subject in neighboring verses… breaks in grammatical construction… abrupt changes in the length of verses; sudden changes of the dramatic situation, with changes of pronoun from singular to plural, from second to third person, and so on; the juxtaposition of apparently contrary statements,[71]

and features of this kind that do not suggest a text created according to a deliberate plan. Moreover, the Qur'ān can offer a variety of perspectives on a given topic, as with the various passages dealing with wine.[72] Classical

69. Examples of the Qur'ān's interface with biblical traditions can be found in Gabriel Said Reynolds, *The Qur'ān and Its Biblical Subtext* (London: Routledge, 2010).

70. For example, Nicolai Sinai interprets the Abraham section of Q 37 as a rereading of the Abraham section in Q 51 which in his view took place in just a few years during Muḥammad's activity in Mecca; see Nicolai Sinai, "The Qur'ān as Process," in Angelika Neuwirth, Nicolai Sinai, and Michael Marx (eds.), *The Qur'ān in Context: Historical and Literary Investigations into the Qur'ānic Milieu* (Leiden: Brill, 2011), 407–439.

71. W. Montgomery Watt, *Bell's Introduction to the Qur'ān* (Edinburgh: Edinburgh University Press, 1970), 93; for examples, see 93–101.

72. Q 12:41; 16:67; 47:15; 56:18; 2:219; 4:43; 5:90–91. On the traditional ordering of these verses chronologically so as to interpret them as reflecting an evolving viewpoint, see Nöldeke, *The History of the Qur'ān*, 161.

form criticism was meant to explain how a text characterized by incongruities came into being. If, together with shortening the time frame, composition of the final form is centralized, then one no longer has a theory that explains how such a diverse text was created. Therefore, if at some stage the text of the Qur'ān developed through editorial work in a short span of time, a different model is necessary to account for the elements of disunity that remain.

The Rolling Corpus: A Different Model

Alongside form criticism, Biblical Studies can provide another model for understanding the composition of the Qur'ān, a model that is grounded in preserved textual evidence for a book that shares certain features in common with the Qur'ān. The model I will suggest for comparison is the idea of a "rolling corpus" developed by William McKane in his commentary on the book of Jeremiah.[73]

The starting point for scholarship on Jeremiah is the fact that the book of Jeremiah is preserved in two different versions. One version, represented by the Masoretic Text (MT), is the familiar one known in modern English Bibles. It is a longer text with numerous reduplicated passages and apparent glossing. The second edition, represented by the Septuagint (LXX) and two fragments from Qumran (4QJer[b], [d]), is one-sixth shorter in overall length than MT, with many missing passages vis-à-vis MT (e.g., MT Jer 11:7–8, 29:16–20, and 33:14–26), and lacking reduplication where this is found in MT (e.g., MT Jer 6:13–15 is repeated at MT 8:10b–12, but not in the LXX).[74] Furthermore, the oracles against the nations, found in chapters 46–51 in MT, are located in the LXX right after the "Cup of God's Wrath" section in Jeremiah 25:13a, with the oracles given in a slightly different order.[75] The virtually unanimous opinion of modern scholarship is that the text represented by the LXX is earlier than that represented by MT.[76]

---

73. William McKane, *A Critical and Exegetical Commentary on Jeremiah* (2 vols.; Edinburgh: T&T Clark, vol. 1, 1986; vol. 2, 2000). McKane (d. 2004) was professor of Hebrew and Oriental Languages at the University of St. Andrews.

74. Not only does the LXX sometimes lack verses found in MT, but frequently throughout the book, short phrases present in MT are absent from the LXX; e.g., MT often adds the phrase נְאֻם יְהוָה ("says the Lord") where it is lacking in the LXX.

75. LXX: Elam, Egypt, Babylon, Philistines, Edom, Ammon, Kedar, Damascus, Moab. MT: Egypt, Philistines, Moab, Ammon, Edom, Damascus, Kedar, Elam, Babylon. Whereas the LXX ends with Moab, MT has been edited so that it ends with Babylon.

76. See Tov, *Textual Criticism of the Hebrew Bible*, 286–294; idem, "Some Aspects of the Textual and Literary History of the Book of Jeremiah," in P.-M. Bogaert (ed.), *Le livre de Jérémie: le prophète et son milieu, les oracles et leur transmission* (Leuven: Peeters, 1997):

McKane's theory of Jeremiah as a rolling corpus is an attempt to combine the textual evidence of the LXX and MT versions: on the one hand, with literary-critical insights, and on the other hand, to form a picture of how the book was built up by stages. The logic behind the idea of a rolling corpus is as follows. We start by comparing the LXX and MT of specific passages, taking the LXX to be the earlier form (in most cases), and MT to be an expanded form. Looking at the differences between the two, we can see what kinds of literary additions were made between the "Septuagint" stage and the "Masoretic" stage of the text. Jeremiah 10:1–6 may serve as an illustration of such a textual starting-point. Textual material that is shared between the two versions but is ordered differently is indicated in bold and italics.

Jeremiah 10:1–16[a]	
LXX: [1] Hear a word of the Lord that he spoke to you, O house of Israel. [2] This is what the Lord says: Do not learn according to the ways of the nations, and do not be afraid of the signs of the sky, because they are afraid of them to their faces, [3] because the precepts of the nations are vain: there is a tree from the forest, cut down, a work of a craftsman, and a molten image. [4] They have been beautified with silver and gold; they fastened them with hammers and nails, and they shall not be moved. [5a] **Wrought silver it is—they will not walk.** [(9)] *Beaten silver will come from Tharsis, gold of Mophas and a hand of goldsmiths—works of craftsmen all; they will clothe them in blue and purple.*	**MT:** [1] Hear the word which the Lord speaks to you, O house of Israel. [2] Thus says the Lord: "Learn not the way of the nations, nor be dismayed at the signs of the heavens because the nations are dismayed at them, [3] for the customs of the peoples are false. A tree from the forest is cut down, and worked with an axe by the hands of a craftsman. [4] Men decorate it with silver and gold; they fasten it with hammer and nails so that it cannot move. [5] **Their idols are like scarecrows in a cucumber field, and they cannot speak;**

145–167; P.-M. Bogaert, "De Baruch à Jérémie: les deux rédactions conservées du livre de Jérémie," in *Le livre de Jérémie*, 168–173; idem, "Le vetus latina de Jérémie: texte très court, témoin de la plus ancienne Septante et d'une forme plus ancienne de l'hébreu (Jer 39 et 52)," in Adrian Schenker (ed.), *The Earliest Text of the Hebrew Bible: The Relationship between the Masoretic Text and the Hebrew Base of the Septuagint Reconsidered* (Atlanta: SBL, 2003), 51–82; and J. Gerald Janzen, *Studies in the Text of Jeremiah* (Cambridge, MA: Harvard University Press, 1973).

5b **Raised they will be carried, because they will not walk. Do not be afraid of them, because they shall not do evil, and there is no good in them.**	**they have to be carried, for they cannot walk. Be not afraid of them, for they cannot do evil, neither is it in them to do good."**
[Verses 6–8, 10 are lacking in the LXX]	6 There is none like you, O Lord; you are great, and your name is great in might. 7 Who would not fear you, O King of the nations? For this is your due; for among all the wise ones of the nations and in all their kingdoms there is none like you. 8 They are both stupid and foolish; the instruction of idols is but wood! 9 *Beaten silver is brought from Tarshish, and gold from Uphaz. They are the work of the craftsman and of the hands of the goldsmith; their clothing is violet and purple; they are all the work of skilled men.* 10 But the Lord is the true God; he is the living God and the everlasting King. At his wrath the earth quakes, and the nations cannot endure his indignation.
11 Thus shall you say to them: Let gods who did not make the sky and the earth perish from the earth and from under this sky. 16 Such a portion is not Jacob's; because he who formed all things, he is his inheritance; the Lord is his name.	11 Thus shall you say to them: "The gods who did not make the heavens and the earth shall perish from the earth and from under the heavens." 16 Not like these is he who is the portion of Jacob, for he is the one who formed all things, and Israel is the tribe of his inheritance; the Lord of hosts is his name.

[a] In this and the following charts, MT is presented according to the Revised Standard Version and the LXX is given according to A. Pietersma and B. G. Wright (eds.), *New English Translation of the Septuagint* (Oxford: Oxford University Press, 2007). See McKane, *A Critical and Exegetical Commentary on Jeremiah*, 1.216–228.

For this segment, the scope of the LXX is limited to verses 1–5, 9 (within MT v. 5), and 11–16. Verses 6–8 and 10 are later expansions that appear only in MT. One can see in this example both the addition of new material in MT and also the reordering of material (e.g., v. 9). By examining many passages in this way, we can develop a sense of the process by which the text was built up. Since there is no reason to assume that the LXX represents the original version, we can then consider further how the text presumed by the LXX might also have been built up by a similar process.[77] This allows us to get back to the earliest possible form of the text. The earliest core of a given passage is the "kernel." This may or may not represent actual words of Jeremiah; that is impossible to know. But the gradual augmentation of the kernel over time by expansions added by a series of scribes is described as the growth of a rolling corpus.

McKane does not think that the book of Jeremiah underwent a coherent, ideological redaction as, for example, at the hands of Deuteronomists. Rather, he argues that material was added to the text here and there throughout the book by various scribes in response to isolated problems or prompts perceived in kernel units. The problem or prompt in the kernel is called a "trigger."[78] The trigger generates further text, often borrowed from or based on material elsewhere in the book.

I will present two examples that show how this process of building-up by "triggering" works. First, Jeremiah 5:20–25:

---

77. "I am guided by the experience gained from A.1(c), [i.e., the growth of the Hebrew text by comparing MT with the LXX] and alerted to the possibility that a similar pattern of secondary expansion was already present in the Hebrew *Vorlage* of Sept., so that no process of textual comparison as between MT and Sept. will disclose it. These results rest on nothing more than my judgment and critical acumen; on my nose for secondary processes of expansion which have been superimposed on a shorter, more original, Hebrew text" (McKane, *A Critical and Exegetical Commentary on Jeremiah*, li).

78. McKane, *A Critical and Exegetical Commentary on Jeremiah*, lxii–lxxxiii.

Jeremiah 5:20–25	
Kernel (McKane): {[20] Declare this in the house of Jacob, proclaim it in Judah:} [21] "Hear this, O [You] foolish and senseless people, who have eyes, but see not, who have ears, but hear not. [22] Do you not fear me? says the Lord. Do you not tremble before me? I placed the sand as the boundary for the sea, a perpetual barrier which it cannot pass; though the waves toss, they cannot prevail; though they roar, they cannot pass over it.	**MT:** [20] Declare this in the house of Jacob, proclaim it in Judah: [21] "Hear this, O [You] foolish and senseless people, who have eyes, but see not, who have ears, but hear not. [22] Do you not fear me? says the Lord; Do you not tremble before me? I placed the sand as the boundary for the sea, a perpetual barrier which it cannot pass; though the waves toss, they cannot prevail; though they roar, they cannot pass over it. [23] But ***this people*** has a stubborn and rebellious heart; ***they*** have turned aside and gone away. [24] ***They*** do not say in ***their*** hearts, 'Let us fear the Lord our God, who gives the rain in its season, the autumn rain and the spring rain, and keeps for us the weeks appointed for the harvest.' [25] Your iniquities have turned these away, and your sins have kept good from you.

According to McKane, this passage does not fit within the general context of chapter five, "which is occupied with enemy invasion and its disastrous consequences."[79] The kernel of this passage is essentially verses 20–22 (part of v. 21 may be editorial). Verses 23–25 were generated by a glossing scribe, who used the language of the previous two verses. Verses 21–22 address Judah directly, whereas 23–24 speak of Judah in the third person, this shift in person showing the secondary character of 23–24. Verse 25 returns to second-person direct address, indicating that it was not added at the same moment as 23–24. Thus, McKane postulates three stages of development for the passage: (1) a kernel (a brief commission plus vv. 21–22); (2) a gloss in the third person (vv. 23–24); and (3) a comment applying this oracle of condemnation to a present experience of drought (v. 25).

Our second example is Jeremiah 3:1–13. (The first stage of expansion in MT [vv. 6–11] is underlined, and the second stage [v. 12a] is indicated with italics.)

79. McKane, *A Critical and Exegetical Commentary on Jeremiah*, 128.

Jeremiah 3:1–13	
Kernel (McKane): [1] "If a man divorces his wife and she goes from him and becomes another man's wife, will he return to her? Would not that land be greatly polluted? You have played the harlot with many lovers; and would you return to me? says the Lord. [2] Lift up your eyes to the bare heights, and see! Where have you not been lain with? By the waysides you have sat awaiting lovers like an Arab in the wilderness. You have polluted the land with your vile harlotry. [3] Therefore the showers have been withheld, and the spring rain has not come; yet you have a harlot's brow; you refuse to be ashamed. [4] Have you not just now called to me, 'My father, thou art the friend of my youth—[5] will he be angry forever, will he be indignant to the end?' Behold, you have spoken, but you have done all the evil that you could."	**MT:** [1] "If a man divorces his wife and she goes from him and becomes another man's wife, will he return to her? Would not that land be greatly polluted? You have played the harlot with many lovers; and would you return to me? says the Lord. [2] Lift up your eyes to the bare heights, and see! Where have you not been lain with? By the waysides you have sat awaiting lovers like an Arab in the wilderness. You have polluted the land with your vile harlotry. [3] Therefore the showers have been withheld, and the spring rain has not come; yet you have a harlot's brow, you refuse to be ashamed. [4] Have you not just now called to me, 'My father, thou art the friend of my youth—[5] will he be angry forever, will he be indignant to the end?' Behold, you have spoken, but you have done all the evil that you could." [6] The Lord said to me in the days of King Josiah: "Have you seen what she did, that faithless one, Israel, how she went up on every high hill and under every green tree, and there played the harlot? [7] And I thought, 'After she has done all this she will return to me;' but she did not return, and her false sister Judah saw it. [8] She saw that for all the adulteries of that faithless one, Israel, I had sent her away with a decree of divorce; yet her false sister Judah did not fear, but she too went and played the harlot. [9] Because harlotry was so light to her, she polluted the land, committing adultery with stone and tree. [10] Yet for all this her false sister Judah did not return to me with her whole heart, but in pretense, says the Lord." [11] And the Lord said to me, "Faithless Israel has shown herself more righteous than false Judah. [12] *Go, and proclaim these words toward the north, and say,*

12b "Return, faithless **Israel**, says the Lord. I will not look on you in anger, for I am merciful, says the Lord; I will not be angry forever. 13 Only acknowledge your guilt, that you rebelled against the Lord your God and scattered your favors among strangers under every green tree, and that you have not obeyed my voice, says the Lord.	"Return, faithless **Israel**, says the Lord. I will not look on you in anger, for I am merciful, says the Lord; I will not be angry forever. 13 Only acknowledge your guilt, that you rebelled against the Lord your God and scattered your favors among strangers under every green tree, and that you have not obeyed my voice, says the Lord.

The kernel is verses 1–5 and 12b–13. Verses 6–11 are a secondary exegetical development based on the kernel.[80] According to McKane, verses 1–5 and 12b–13 were originally meant to describe the sins of Judah. The reference to "Israel" in verse 12b was not meant literally but as a theological term for Judah. Yet, a scribe misunderstood these verses, wrongly concluding that 1–5 were talking about the Northern Kingdom of Israel, since the Northern Kingdom had been sent away and thus needed to "return." If this were so, however, then the connection with Jeremiah's context in Judah is not clear. Therefore, the scribe responded to this "trigger"—in this case, a misunderstanding—by adding verses 6–11, which makes the fate of Israel into an object lesson for Judah. The reference to the "north" in verse 12a ("Go, and proclaim these words toward the north, and say") is a later scribal attempt to join the oracle in verses 6–11 to 12b–13. As a result of this final addition in 12a, the text now clearly offers reconciliation to the Northern Kingdom on the basis of their lesser guilt. No more than a generation of scribal activity would be necessary for a process such as this to occur; but if McKane is correct, enough distance existed between the original prophetic saying and the later scribe/editor that this individual failed to understand an early oracle that he received.

Three points are worthy of further comment regarding the historical circumstances that McKane imagines for this process. First, the concept of a rolling corpus focuses on textual development at the literary level. Oral traditions may have played a role in creating the text in the first place, and for a period of time texts may have been copied and preserved as aids for oral recitation, but the theory of a rolling corpus picks up at a stage where a written version of what became the book of Jeremiah already existed.[81]

Second, this is not a theory involving a unified redaction of the book as a whole. On the contrary, the idea of a rolling corpus envisions a somewhat haphazard process of textual growth. Scribes added material and made

80. McKane, *A Critical and Exegetical Commentary on Jeremiah*, lxii.

81. On writing in the book of Jeremiah, see Jer 25:13; 30:2; 36:32; 51:59–64.

alterations because they had new traditions to incorporate, perceived that clarification was necessary, or simply wanted to amplify the meaning. For the most part, this is seen as a matter of localized exegesis, that is, compositional activity on discrete units based on specific observations made by individual scribes, and not a comprehensive program of redaction meant to give the book a consistent ideology. McKane's theory may be contrasted with other views of the composition of Jeremiah that postulate a comprehensive redaction of the book during or after the exile by "Deuteronomists" who added many of the so-called "prose sermons" of the book, such as the Sabbath violation charge in Jeremiah 17:19–27.[82] As McKane observes, the book of Jeremiah does not exhibit the kind of literary and ideological coherence one would expect if it were the product of such a unified, purposeful editorial endeavor. In general, the rolling corpus model envisions scribes who are actively engaged in expanding the text but who operate with no grand literary design and without an overall agenda.

Third, in this model, the scribal authors who worked on the book of Jeremiah would have held the Jeremiah traditions in high standing, but they still regarded the prophet's literary heritage as unfixed. As a point of comparison, the *Epic of Gilgamesh* was apparently still subject to literary growth even after it had achieved a kind of canonical status.[83] The *Tanḥuma*

82. According to Ernest W. Nicholson, *Preaching to the Exiles: A Study in the Prose Tradition in the Book of Jeremiah* (New York: Schocken, 1971), 65, 110, the prose sermons in Jeremiah were composed in Babylon during the exilic period by members of the "Deuteronomistic" school, who were using Deuteronomy's homiletical form to admonish and encourage the Babylonian exiles. On shared language and ideology between Deuteronomy and Jeremiah, see James Philip Hyatt, "The Deuteronomic Edition of Jeremiah," in Leo Perdue and Brian Kovacs (eds.), *A Prophet to the Nations* (Winona Lake, IN: Eisenbrauns, 1984), 252–253. The complexity of identifying Deuteronomic influence in Jeremiah is discussed in Carolyn J. Sharp, *Prophecy and Ideology in Jeremiah: Struggles for Authority in the Deutero-Jeremianic Prose* (London: T&T Clark, 2003), 13–27. Nicholson's view bears some similarity to Wansbrough's proposal that the text of the Qur'ān was built up through popular preaching (*Quranic Studies*, 145–148, 175–176). Yet elsewhere, Wansbrough indicates that he does not suspect that later material (such as preaching) was worked into the Qur'ān through centralized redaction but through a more random process: "Particularly in the exempla of salvation history, characterized by variant traditions, but also in passages of exclusively paraenetic or eschatological content, ellipsis and repetition are such as to suggest not the carefully executed project of one or of many men, but rather the product of an organic development from originally independent traditions during a long period of transmission" (Wansbrough, *Quranic Studies*, 47).

83. The *Epic of Gilgamesh* was known throughout the Near East in the middle of the second millennium in a form that was broadly consistent but still fluid. The Standard Version came into being near the end of the second millennium, although this did not prevent the addition of a new (twelfth) tablet in the first millennium; see

midrashim provide another instructive parallel. The textual witnesses show enough continuity to suggest that they embodied a recognized midrashic tradition, but the evolution from earlier to later versions demonstrates that the *Tanḥuma* material continued to be malleable into the early Middle Ages.[84] Evidence from the Dead Sea Scrolls and from variant traditions between biblical texts suggests that prior to stabilization, biblical works were subject to scribal elaboration even by scribes who regarded them as authoritative in some sense.[85] Thus, the idea of a rolling corpus presumes the existence of a text seen as important enough to preserve with diligence but still fluid enough to modify. Of course, a fully fixed text could emerge from this process as cultural perceptions about the text changed.

The Qur'ān as a Rolling Corpus

In contrast with the book of Jeremiah, the Qur'ān has not been transmitted in two different versions. In fact, few variant readings are preserved in qur'ānic codices. But this is to be expected, because after the text was standardized, the only variant readings preserved were those regarded as useful for *tafsīr* and compatible with orthodoxy.[86] Yet, hints in the transmission history of the

William Moran, "The Gilgamesh Epic: A Masterpiece from Ancient Mesopotamia," in Jack M. Sasson (ed.), *Civilizations of the Ancient Near East* (New York: Scribner, 1995), 4:2330; and Benjamin R. Foster, "Gilgamesh," in William W. Hallo and K. Lawson Younger, Jr. (eds.), *The Context of Scripture, Volume 1: Canonical Compositions from the Biblical World* (Leiden: Brill, 2003), 458.

84. The Tanḥuma literature includes a composite homily from circa the fifth century CE (known from a Geniza fragment), four families of manuscripts from circa the late seventh century CE that appear to be precursors to what became the printed version of Tanḥuma-Yelammedenu, and various textual witnesses for Tanḥuma (Buber edition) stemming from the early Middle Ages; see Marc Bregmann, *The Tanḥuma-Yelammedenu Literature: Studies in the Evolution of the Versions* (Piscataway, NJ: Gorgias Press, 2003), 2–5.

85. For variant traditions between biblical texts and within the Qumran *Community Rule*, see Carr, *Formation of the Hebrew Bible*, 57–98. On early scribal practices as suggested by many Qumran texts, Emanuel Tov summarizes: "The earlier scribes were involved not only in the copying of texts, but to a limited extent also in the creative shaping of the last stage of their content. Expressed differently, at one time scribes often took the liberty of changing the content, adding and omitting elements, sometimes on a small scale, but often substantially… The nature of this creative scribal activity requires us to conceive of the persons involved as scribes-editors, who were not only active in the transmission of the texts, but also in the final stage of their creative edition" (Emanuel Tov, *Scribal Practices and Approaches Reflected in the Texts Found in the Judean Desert* [Leiden: Brill, 2004], 24–25).

86. See Arthur Jeffery, *Materials for the History of the Text of the Qur'ān: The Old*

Qur'ān suggest a period of textual fluidity that may reflect the kind of gradual development envisioned by the rolling corpus model. For example, traces of phrase length variants are still preserved in some manuscripts.[87] The qur'ānic quotations inscribed within the Dome of the Rock also point to a measure of fluidity in the wording of certain passages.[88] David Powers discusses an instance where a textual variation in a qur'ānic manuscript appears to be a scribal effort to clarify the text in response to a specific problem, in a manner comparable to McKane's treatment of Jeremiah.[89] On a larger scale, and perhaps stretching back to an even earlier period, are reports of different ways to configure *sūrahs* and verses.[90] All of this evidence for textual fluidity could be explained through the model of a rolling corpus.

Moreover, there are numerous short passages in the Qur'ān that appear to be glosses because of their style and content, and these passages can be

---

Codices (Leiden: Brill, 1937), 9–10. Variant reading traditions preserved in exegetical literature are likely to be interpretive in origin and not actually based on manuscripts; see Wansbrough, *Quranic Studies*, 203; and Reynolds, *The Qur'ān and Its Biblical Subtext*, 208–214.

87. See Small, *Textual Criticism and Qur'ān Manuscripts*, 125.

88. On this inscription, see David S. Powers, *Muḥammad Is Not the Father of Any of Your Men: The Making of the Last Prophet* (Philadelphia: University of Pennsylvania Press, 2009), 292, n. 48; and Oleg Grabar, *The Dome of the Rock* (Cambridge, MA: Harvard University Press, 2006), 90–92.

89. As Powers explains, in the early Qur'ān manuscript BNF 328a, the word *kalālah* in Q 4:12b, traditionally interpreted as "collateral relatives," was originally the word *kallah*, "daughter-in-law" (known from other Semitic languages), but this word was changed by a scribe into *kalālah* so as to revise the legal principle in question. Based on the date of the manuscript and of the scribal activity, this revision would have taken place near the end of the seventh century. See Powers, *Muḥammad Is Not the Father of Any of Your Men*, 169–182. Moreover, the exemplar upon which BNF 328a was based appears to have lacked the final verse of Sūrah 4 (176), which reformulates the issue addressed in Q 4:12b (Powers, *Muḥammad Is Not the Father of Any of Your Men*, 184–193).

90. E.g., John of Damascus mentions *On Woman* [sic] (Q 4), *The Table* (Q 5), and *The Heifer* (Q 2) as books written by Muḥammad, as well as a certain *The Camel of God* (cf. 11:64; 26:155; 54:27; 91:13); see *Saint John of Damascus: Writings*, trans. F. H. Chase (New York: Fathers of the Church, 1958), 157–159. A Syriac text dating perhaps to the early eighth century CE mentions Sūrat al-Baqarah (Q 2) as a work distinct from the Qur'ān (Robert G. Hoyland, *Seeing Islam As Others Saw It* [Princeton, NJ: Darwin Press, 1997], 471). Wansbrough, *Qur'ānic Studies*, 137, refers to a manuscript of the exegetical work of Sufyān al-Thawrī (d. 161/777–778?) in which the sequence of verses within *sūrahs* is not the same as the canonical sequence. If these eighth-century works relate to the manuscript tradition of the Qur'ān, they would be preserving early categorizations and arrangements of qur'ānic material that did not survive in qur'ānic manuscripts.

explained cogently through the rolling corpus theory. For example, the phrase *mā adrāka mā*, "what will make you know what...," can be interpreted as a later scribe introducing an explanatory gloss, particularly when this formula follows an unusual term or expression, as in Q Qāriʿah 101:9–11: *fa-ummuhu hāwiyah / wa-mā adrāka mā hiya / nārun ḥāmiyah* ("Then his mother is *hāwiyah*—and what will make you know what she/it is? A scorching fire!").[91] Q Tīn 95:6 appears to be a gloss by a later hand in that it abruptly qualifies the preceding statement with a longer, formulaic sentence within a *sūrah* otherwise made up of short, rhyming verses.[92] In Q Raḥman 55:8–9, we find two verses of moral admonition dealing with justice in scales and weights, which appear to have been inserted into a passage otherwise devoted to praising God (vv. 1–7, 10–24). Q 55:7 reads: "The sky—He raised it, and He laid down to scale." The reference to "scale" in this hymnic reflection on God's greatness "triggered" the moral injunction in verses 8–9, which interrupts the flow of thought.[93] The Qur'ān contains many apparent glosses such as these that seem to respond to an immediate textual prompt and intrude on the surrounding context. This indicates a process of textual development similar to what McKane described for the book of Jeremiah.

Although this paradigm shares elements in common with other theories about qur'ānic origins, the rolling corpus idea as applied to the Qur'ān entails its own set of premises and issues. First, this model attempts to explain the growth of the text apart from the framework suggested by traditional accounts of Muḥammad's life. In this way, the rolling corpus model remains in continuity with Wansbrough and differs from approaches to the Qur'ān

91. Wansbrough, *Quranic Studies*, 28. Cf. Q 74:27; 77:14; 82:17–18; 83:8; 83:19; 97:2; 104:4–5. Translations of the Qur'ān in this section will be taken from A. J. Droge, *The Qur'ān: A New Annotated Translation* (Sheffield: Equinox, 2013). On the meaning of the unusual term *hāwiyah* in Q 101:9, proposals include (1) "childless," as in "his mother will be childless," i.e., "will come to ruin;" or (2) "ruin," based on the Hebrew הֹוָה, "ruin, disaster" (Isa 47:11; Ezek 7:26); see Rudi Paret, *Der Koran: Kommentar und Konkordanz* (8th ed.; Stuttgart: Kohlhammer, 2012), 518–519.

92. Q 95:5–6: "(5) Then We return him to the lowest of the low—(6) except for those who believe and do righteous deeds. For them (there is) a reward without end." The precise language of Q 95:6 occurs also in Q 84:25. Perhaps verse 5 originally described the infirmity of old age, but verse 6 reinterpreted it as a reference to afterlife punishment (see Paret, *Der Koran*, 514). Cuypers, *The Composition of the Qur'ān*, 85, acknowledges that verse 6 might be an interpolation but still attempts to read it as the central segment of a "concentric composition." Yet verse 6 is not structurally at the center of the *sūrah*, and the "extreme members" do not actually match ("humanity" and "God"), which make this literary reading unconvincing.

93. Neal Robinson, *Discovering the Qur'ān* (2nd ed.; Washington, DC: Georgetown University Press, 2003), 135, outlines this part of the *sūrah* as follows: "vv. 1–7 Hymnic signs list; vv. 8–9 Ethical inference; vv. 10–24 Hymnic signs list."

that follow Nöldeke's chronology.[94] Second, the rolling corpus idea posits the existence of primitive kernel units that were built up through scribal activity, but it does not address how these kernels came into being. Any combination of written sources, oral traditions, or new compositions might have been used in creating kernel texts. Third, this model assumes that the author or authors of individual "kernels" generally composed coherent textual units with recognizable conventions in mind, such as consistent line length, theme, and sometimes rhyme. Scribal interventions in the text can be identified because the scribes did not concern themselves with matching the style of the kernel text or preserving the flow of thought, but were primarily interested in clarifying the topic discussed by the text.[95] Fourth, in this model, the viewpoints reflected in textual expansions are those of individual scribes, not

---

94. Nöldeke was skeptical about much traditional biographical information on Muḥammad (e.g., *The History of the Qur'ān*, 56), but he frequently attempted to identify a "grain of truth" or "historical core" in traditional reports (e.g., ibid., 11, 13, 43, 47, 84, 230), especially in regard to public events or reports that cast Muḥammad or his family in a negative light (ibid., 342). For an example of the latter, Nöldeke accepted the reliability of a story involving gossip about 'Ā'ishah as the background for Q 24:11–20 (ibid., 171). Most importantly, Nöldeke outlined his three Meccan periods of revelation on the basis of biographical traditions associated with passages from the Qur'ān: Q 53 is taken as referring to the flight to Abyssinia (615 CE), Sūrah 20 is dated to just before Umar's conversion (616 CE), and revelations between these events are ascribed to the second Meccan period; everything before this, i.e., from 610–614 CE, is the first Meccan period, and all of Muḥammad's time in Mecca after this, i.e., 617–622 CE, is the third Meccan period (ibid., 58–59). Angelika Neuwirth, *Scripture, Poetry and the Making of a Community: Reading the Qur'ān as a Literary Text* (Oxford: Oxford University Press, 2014), 16, accepts the "basic data" about Muḥammad derived from traditional sources, i.e., "the lifetime of the Prophet, the places of his activity, the hijrah, the community's cohabitation with Jewish groups and its military activities in Medina." In fact, Neuwirth's dependence on later biographical tradition is even more extensive than this through her use of Nöldeke's chronology (e.g., *Scripture, Poetry and the Making of a Community*, 26–27, 49, 277–303).

95. This suggests that the individuals who added material to the kernel were not the original authors of the kernel. This model differs from theories that ascribe all or most textual insertions to Muḥammad (e.g., Carl Ernst, *How to Read the Qur'ān: A New Guide, with Select Translations* [Chapel Hill: UNC Press, 2011], 98). Neuwirth envisions updating during Muḥammad's lifetime (e.g., *Scripture, Poetry and the Making of a Community*, 26, 156), but she also recognizes redaction after Muḥammad's death (e.g., ibid., 18, 22–23). For Neuwirth, oral recitation was the primary medium of communication both for Muḥammad and his followers (ibid., 22), so that oral forms were instrumental in shaping the Qur'ān (e.g., ibid., 153–155). The rolling corpus model, by contrast, pictures the growth of the tradition primarily through written means, i.e., scribes glossing a text.

a community or an official body.[96] Finally, the rolling corpus theory operates on the basis that scribes typically made additions for identifiable reasons. Therefore, along with attention to style and flow of thought, an essential step in working backward to the kernel is asking the question: "Why would a scribe have added this?" Each of these ideas is part of the overall picture that the rolling corpus model implies, but of course none of them is unique to this model.

I will now offer two illustrations of how specific qur'ānic texts might be explained according to the theory of a rolling corpus.

The first example is Q 85, Sūrat al-Burūj. In the chart below I give a translation of the canonical form of the text in the right column, and in the left column I give a proposal for what the kernel form of this text might have been before it was expanded through scribal elaboration. According to this proposal, the kernel text began with a series of conjurations (vv. 1–3); was followed by an imprecation against those who mistreated the believers (vv. 4–7, 12); continued with a reminder that God also restores and forgives (vv. 13–15); and concluded with a reference to previous examples of divine punishment as known through a glorious Qur'ān (vv. 16–22). This reading posits that verses 8–11 are expansions, probably added in two stages.

Q 85:1–22	
Proposed Kernel: [In the Name of God, the Merciful, the Compassionate] 1 By the sky full of constellations, 2 by the promised Day, 3 by a witness and what is witnessed! 4 May the companions of the pit perish 5—the fire full of fuel—6 when they are sitting over it, 7 and they (themselves) are witnesses of what they have done to the believers.	**Canonical Text:** [In the Name of God, the Merciful, the Compassionate] 1 By the sky full of constellations, 2 by the promised Day, 3 by a witness and what is witnessed! 4 May the companions of the pit perish 5—the fire full of fuel—6 when they are sitting over it, 7 and they (themselves) are witnesses of what they have done to the believers.

96. Neuwirth emphasizes the role of the community in shaping the Qur'ān, such that the canonical version expresses the consensus of the community (e.g., *Scripture, Poetry and the Making of a Community*, xxiv, xxxiii, 15, 18, 36). With the rolling corpus model, revisions are primarily driven not by a community's response to recitations but by copyists' responses to issues in the text.

	8 They took vengeance on them only because they believed in God, the Mighty, the Praiseworthy, 9 the One who—to Him (belongs) the kingdom of the heavens and the earth. God is a witness over everything. 10 Surely those who persecute the believing men and the believing women, (and) then have not turned (in repentance) - for them (there is) the punishment of Gehenna, and for them (there is) the punishment of the burning (fire). 11 Surely those who believe and do righteous deeds—for them (there are) Gardens through which rivers flow. That is the great triumph!
12 Surely your Lord's attack is harsh indeed. 13 Surely He—He brings about (the creation) and restores (it). 14 He is the Forgiving, the Loving, 15 Holder of the throne, the Glorious, 16 Doer of what He intends. 17 Has the story of the forces come to you, 18 of Pharaoh and Thamūd? 19 No! But those who disbelieve persist in calling (it) a lie. 20 Yet God surrounds them from behind. 21 Yes! It is a glorious Qur'ān, 22 in a guarded tablet.	12 Surely your Lord's attack is harsh indeed. 13 Surely He—He brings about (the creation) and restores (it). 14 He is the Forgiving, the Loving, 15 Holder of the throne, the Glorious, 16 Doer of what He intends. 17 Has the story of the forces come to you, 18 of Pharaoh and Thamūd? 19 No! But those who disbelieve persist in calling (it) a lie. 20 Yet God surrounds them from behind. 21 Yes! It is a glorious Qur'ān, 22 in a guarded tablet.

After the first verse (*burūj*), the core verses in the kernel rhyme either with *-ūd* (vv. 2–7, 14, 17–18) or *-īd* (vv. 12–13, 15, 16), with some variation at the end (*-īb* in v. 19; *-īṭ* in v. 20; *-īd* in v. 21; *-ūẓ* in v. 22). All the verses in the kernel are brief. Within the short *-ūd*/*-īd* body of verses in the kernel (vv. 2–7, 12–18), verses 8–11 are out place in terms of length, and verses 10–11 are out of place in terms of rhyme (*-īq* in v. 10; *-īr* in v. 11).[97] It may be suggested, therefore, that verses 8–9 were added first by a scribe who still endeavored to maintain the rhyme scheme, and verses 10–11 were inserted even later.

The expansion in verses 8–9 may be taken as clarification for the words in verse 7, "what they have done to the believers."[98] In verse 7, those identified

97. Cf. Nöldeke, *The History of the Qur'ān*, 80–81, who proposes that verses 8–11 were probably added later, "possibly by Muḥammad himself."

98. *mā yafalūna bi'l-mu'minīna*. The language of verse 8 may have been borrowed from elsewhere, cf. Q 5:59; 7:126; 60:1.

as "companions of the pit" (*aṣḥāb al-ukhdūd*, v. 4) will be punished because of the harm they did to the believers. But one could ask: "What did the believers do to provoke this? Did they perpetrate some misdeed that caused these 'companions of the pit' to harm them?" Verses 8–9 answer unequivocally that the companions of the pit took vengeance on the believers for no other reason except that the believers put their faith in God. No crime or wrongdoing can be attributed to the believers that would justify mistreating them. The sole basis for the persecution they suffer is their belief in the Deity.

The addition of verses 10–11 might be explained as follows: verses 8–9 contain elements of doxology ("the Mighty, the Praiseworthy... to Him (belongs) the kingdom of the heavens and the earth"). This material, suitable for peroration but now situated in the middle of the *sūrah*, may have seemed disjointed next to the terse severity of verse 12: "Surely your Lord's attack is harsh indeed" (*inna baṭsha rabbika la-shadīd*).[99] Of course, the kernel itself moves from harshness (vv. 4–7, 12) to the possibility of restoration (vv. 13–15) but with the addition of verses 8–9, we now have a doxology in the body of the *sūrah* before the segment on harshness is concluded. This juxtaposition of praise to God and divine judgment causes a scribe to add verses 10–11, which explain that it is only those who refuse to repent who will experience the Fire. For those who do repent, there will be gardens with rivers flowing through them. This is a proper picture to accompany the doxological material in verses 8–9, and the fact that forgiveness is possible for the penitent offers theological justification for the Lord's harsh attack mentioned in verse 12.

The second example comes from Q 52, *Sūrat al-Ṭūr*. The proposed kernel opens with invocations (vv. 1–6) and an affirmation of punishment (vv. 7–8). What follows is a section describing a Day of Judgment involving fire against those who called the message a lie (*mukadhdhibīna*, vv. 11, 14) and said it was "magic" (*siḥr*, v. 15). This section consists of verses 9–15 and at least part of verse 16. The unit made up of verses 17–20, 22–28 constitutes a scribal addition, which has itself been subject to interpolation at verse 21. I will discuss these initial parts of the *sūrah* first.

99. The term *baṭsha*, "attack," has the sense of a "violent grip or clutch," related to *b-ṭ-sh* + *bi-*, "to grip with violence" (Arne A. Ambros with S. Procházka, *A Concise Dictionary of Koranic Arabic* [Wiesbaden: Reichert, 2004], 40).

Q 52:1–28	
Proposed Kernel: 1 By the mountain 2 and a Book written 3 on parchment unrolled! 4 By the inhabited house! 5 By the roof raised up 6 and the sea surging! 7 Surely the punishment of your Lord is indeed going to fall! 8 (There is) no one to repel it. 9 On the Day when the sky will shake, 10 and the mountains fly away, 11 woe that Day to the one who called (the message) a lie, 12 who—they were playing around in their banter. 13 On the Day when they will be shoved forcefully into the fire of Gehenna: 14 'This is the fire which you called a lie! 15 Is this magic or do you not see? 16 Bear it patiently or do not bear it patiently—(it is) the same for you.'	**Canonical Text:** 1 By the mountain 2 and a Book written 3 on parchment unrolled! 4 By the inhabited house! 5 By the roof raised up 6 and the sea surging! 7 Surely the punishment of your Lord is indeed going to fall! 8 (There is) no one to repel it. 9 On the Day when the sky will shake, 10 and the mountains fly away, 11 woe that Day to the one who called (the message) a lie, 12 who—they were playing around in their banter. 13 On the Day when they will be shoved forcefully into the fire of Gehenna: 14 'This is the fire which you called a lie! 15 Is this magic or do you not see? 16 **Burn in it!** Bear it patiently or do not bear it patiently—(it is) the same for you. **You are only being repaid for what you have done.**' 17 Surely the ones who guard (themselves) will be in gardens and bliss, 18 rejoicing in what their Lord has given them, and (because) their Lord has guarded them against the punishment of the furnace. 19 'Eat and drink with satisfaction, (in return) for what you have done.' 20 (There they will be) reclining on couches lined up, and we shall marry them to (maidens) with dark, wide eyes. 21 (For) those who believe, and whose descendants followed them in belief, We shall join their descendants with them, and We shall not deprive them of any of their deeds. Each person (is held) in pledge for what he has earned. 22 We shall increase them with fruits and meat of whatever (kind) they desire. 23 There they will pass (around) a cup to each other in which there is no frivolous or sinful talk, 24 and among them will circulate boys of their own, as if they were hidden pearls. 25 And they will approach each other asking questions.

	[26] They will say, 'Surely we were fearful among our family before, [27] but God has bestowed favor on us, and guarded us against the punishment of the scorching (fire). [28] Surely we used to call on Him before. Surely He—He is the Beneficent, the Compassionate.'

The first sixteen verses exhibit an identifiable progression of thought. The text opens with invocations, an affirmation of punishment, and then a statement against those who will be punished. Verse 16 is unusually long, and may have been subject to some rewriting. It is not certain what the original kernel of verse 16 would have been, but I have given: "Bear it patiently or do not bear it patiently—(it is) the same for you" as a reasonable suggestion. The sense of the passage as a whole is: "Although you deny the message, you will indeed suffer punishment by fire, and when this happens it will not matter whether you bear it patiently or not—it will be miserable."

The phrase that likely gave rise to scribal activity is what I have suggested as the kernel of verse 16: "Bear it patiently or do not bear it patiently—(it is) the same for you." Typically, patience is a characteristic associated with the righteous.[100] Could these disobedient people really bear the fire patiently? And is there no difference in fate between those who endure with patience and those who do not? These questions may have generated two scribal responses. First, the remainder of verse 16, "You are only being repaid for what you have done," could have been added to clarify that the deniers should not be seen as people who bear trouble patiently (a noble quality) but as wrongdoers who are justly punished for their misdeeds. Second, verses 17–20, 22–28 were inserted as a unit to make it clear that there will be blessing for the righteous; in other words, the fate of the patient is not the same (*sawā'un*, v. 16) as the fate of the wicked. Within this unit, verse 21 appears to be an even later interpolation, because of its greater length and because it interrupts the surrounding description of the Garden with general encouragement toward belief and good deeds. It may be that this pious insertion at verse 21 was

100. Words derived from the root *ṣ-b-r*, "patient" occur over one hundred times in the Qur'ān, and the overwhelming majority of occurrences describe those who trust God and receive God's favor, e.g., examples in the perfect and imperfect forms: Q 3:120, 125, 186; 4:25; 11:11; 12:90; 13:22, 24; 14:12; 16:42, 96; 23:111; 25:20, 75; 28:54; 29:59; 32:24; 42:43; 76:12. An example where patience is not construed positively is found at Q 41:24. But in general, God is said to be with the patient (e.g., Q 2:153, 249; 3:146; 8:46, 66).

triggered by the seemingly sensual reference to fair, wide-eyed (maidens) at the end of verse 20.[101]

If the beginning of the kernel is made up of verses 1–15 and part of verse 16, what is the rest of the kernel?[102] I propose that verses 29–49 comprise four units: (A) 29–34 defending the authenticity of the Messenger;[103] (B) 35–43, a unit that extols God above the unrighteous and ends with a doxology ("Glory to God..."); (C) 44–47, which revisit the topic of a Judgment Day; and (D) 48–49, which offer encouragement and instruction to the prophetic speaker.[104] The final two verses (unit D) of the canonical form of the *sūrah* are the most distinctive in content and so are unlikely to be the original continuation of the kernel. Although it is impossible to form definite conclusions, I think that verses 44–47 (unit C) probably represent the original concluding verses to the kernel (vv. 1–16). After the conjurations and affirmation of punishment, the text describes a Day of Judgment when the sky will shake (v. 9). This is picked up in verses 44–47 with the assertion that, even if they see the sky fall, they will nevertheless deny the Day. If so, then the original kernel of Q 52 might have been verses 1–15, part of 16, and 44–47, with perhaps other material as well.[105] The rest of the *sūrah* would have developed through scribal elaboration. The process of textual growth is clearer in verses 17–28 and is more difficult to reconstruct for verses 29–49.

101. On the interpretation of verse 20, "and we shall marry them to (maidens) with dark, wide eyes," see Stefan Wild, "Lost in Philology? The Virgins of Paradise and the Luxenberg Hypothesis," in Neuwirth et al. (eds.), *The Qur'ān in Context*, 625–647; and Oliver Leaman, "Houris," in Oliver Leaman (ed.), *The Qur'ān: An Encyclopedia* (London: Routledge, 2006), 269–271.

102. Nöldeke considered verses 29–49 to be secondary because they contain what he regarded as later diction, such as *subḥāna li'llah 'ammā*, "Glory to God beyond what..." and the verb *sharaka*, "to associate" in verse 43, and also the phraseology of verses 48–49 (*The History of the Qur'ān*, 86–87). He points to a source by one Ibn 'Abd al-Kāfī (citing ms. Leiden Codex 674, on which see 52, n. 23) as well as Suyūṭī (d. 911/1505), *al-Itqān fī 'ulūm al-Qur'ān* ("The Perfection in the Science of the Qur'ān"), to justify that this language is "Medinan" (79–80). Yet, these sources are not chronologically close enough to the composition of the Qur'ān to be relied on for this purpose.

103. *fa-dhakkir*, "so remind!" at the beginning of verse 29 could be an editorial link.

104. The predominant rhyme in verses 29–47 is *-ūn*, occurring at the end of 29–30, 32–33, 35–37, 39–43, and 45–47. Intermingled is also *-īn* (vv. 31, 34, 38) and *-ūm* (v. 44).

105. The defense of the messenger in verses 29–34 (unit A) picks up the theme in verses 11–15 of denying the message, although 29–34 use different terms. Perhaps some of this material was part of the kernel, or it may have been added because of this thematic connection.

To sum up, the idea of a rolling corpus as applied to the Qur'ān envisions it as made up of units that came to exist in written yet unfinished form prior to the mid-seventh century, and posits scribal elaboration in response to perceived issues in the text as the primary means by which the Qur'ān reached its present form.

Conclusion

Biblical form criticism had a positive impact on John Wansbrough's work on the Qur'ān in that it encouraged reflection on the genre and structure of qur'ānic texts and provided useful paradigms for describing how traditions might evolve. The multiple versions of the Shuʿayb story in the Qur'ān appear to be well suited to form-critical analysis. Wansbrough's application of this method to these accounts yielded valuable insights, especially regarding the interrelationships between the different versions.

At the same time, at least two dimensions of classical form criticism are probably not applicable to the Qur'ān in quite the way Wansbrough imagined. First, classical form criticism presumes that stories and sayings evolved into their canonical form primarily through oral transmission, and that these units were assembled at the end of the process with little creative input from the final redactors. As I argued above, however, the canonical Qur'ān reflects textual editing beyond what this model would suggest. Second, Wansbrough conjectured that qur'ānic material crystallized into canonical form only at the end of the eighth or beginning of the ninth century. As mentioned above, this late date for the canonical text seems untenable based on the manuscript evidence, although it is entirely possible that certain units in the Qur'ān did evolve for a long period of time, starting before the seventh century. All in all, although some of the tools of form criticism enhanced Wansbrough's analysis of the Qur'ān, classical form criticism is not a perfect model for explaining how the canonical text of the Qur'ān came into being.

The idea of a rolling corpus is another model from Biblical Studies that may illuminate the process by which the Qur'ān was written. This model focuses on textual evolution leading up to the final form; it allows for textual evolution to take place relatively quickly; it accounts well for the phenomenon of interpolations; and it can explain why incongruities remain in the text. Some stylistic irregularities in the Qur'ān, which Wansbrough saw as the result of stitching together a body of originally independent units, might be better explained through the rolling corpus paradigm as arising through scribal elaborations on a collection or collections of kernel texts. Still, since the rolling corpus idea presupposes kernel units and does not rule out oral tradition as a source upon which scribes drew, certain aspects of Wansbrough's version of form criticism could be combined with the rolling corpus model.

The two ways of thinking about the composition of the Qur'ān can and probably should be seen as complementary.

As a theory meant to describe the history behind the preserved text, the rolling corpus model obviously cannot be proven. The literary judgments involved in separating the kernel from later additions entail a measure of subjectivity. It is also a matter of critical conjecture to determine what issue in the kernel might have generated a scribal comment. Nevertheless, the rolling corpus model has the virtue of being founded on real textual data, namely, the Masoretic and Septuagint versions of the book of Jeremiah. Although the rolling corpus idea certainly shares features in common with other theories about the composition of the Qur'ān, it has the potential to make a significant contribution to our understanding of how the Qur'ān reached its canonical form.

JIQSA 1 (2016): 93–125

DID ḤAFṢAH EDIT THE QUR'ĀN? A RESPONSE WITH NOTES ON THE CODICES OF THE PROPHET'S WIVES

SEAN W. ANTHONY AND CATHERINE L. BRONSON

Abstract

This article revisits, assesses, and critiques the recent claim made by Ruqayya Khan that Ḥafṣah bt. ʿUmar, a wife of the Prophet Muḥammad, played a significant editorial role in the early establishment of the text of the Qur'ān but that her prominent editorial role in this enterprise has been suppressed by androcentric scholarship. In the course of our critique, we also attempt to offer insight into what role the Qur'ān codices owned by the Prophet's wives played in early Muslim narratives of the ʿUthmānic codex, as well as how modern historical-critical and feminist readings of the early source material can, and must, mutually inform one another.

In a recent issue of the *Journal of the American Academy of Religion*, Ruqayya Khan published a promising and somewhat provocative article entitled "Did a Woman Edit the Qur'ān? Hafṣa [sic] and Her Famed 'Codex.'"[1] Khan's article puts forward bold historical claims and a trenchant critique of the androcentrism endemic to scholarship on the Qur'ān and its codification. Khan's article, however, is not merely a critique. She also aims to ameliorate the ailing state of Qur'ānic Studies by exploring how feminist criticism might shed light on an important historical case study: the role of Ḥafṣah bt. ʿUmar's *muṣḥaf* (or written copy of the Qur'ān) in the codification of the Qur'ān under the caliph ʿUthmān b. ʿAffān (r. 644–656). Most, if not all, of Khan's general criticisms about the neglect of women's history and agency in scholarship

1. Ruqayya Khan, "Did a Woman Edit the Qur'ān? Hafṣa [sic] and Her Famed 'Codex,'" *JAAR* 84 (2014): 174–216. Page citations will appear in parentheses in references to Khan's article below. Note that another article has appeared since the publication of Khan's that presents a virtually identical thesis and makes many of the same methodological missteps: see Sharon Silzell, "Ḥafṣa and al-Muṣḥaf: Women and the Written Qur'ān in the Early Centuries of Islam," *Hawwa* 13 (2015): 25–50. The relationship of Silzell's work to Khan's is unclear.

doi: http://dx.doi.org/10.5913/jiqsa.1.2017.a006

on the Qurʾān and early Islam are fully justified. Yet, however profoundly sympathetic we may be with Khan's criticism of the androcentricism rife in the study of early Islam and with her advocacy for feminist critique, we have rather strong objections to her historical methodology.

Our objections to Khan's essay are not against the general project but rather its execution. Although Khan's targets merit critique, she assumes a posture of moral superiority in order to indict the field of Qurʾānic Studies in the name of feminist criticism. However, she then proceeds with her critique while neglecting not only some of the most seminal Western scholarship on the Qurʾān but also some of the most germane and important discussions of the putative object of her analysis: Ḥafṣah's role in the codification of the Qurʾān. Most alarmingly, Khan limits her analysis to scholarship written in English, as though any analysis of Western scholarship could possibly neglect the contributions of francophone and germanophone scholars (175). Unintentionally perhaps, Khan thus blithely dismisses the most seminal and recent discussions of Ḥafṣah's codex. These include not only the epoch-making *Geschichte des Qorâns* of Theodor Nöldeke and his successors,[2] but also the recent research of francophone scholars such as the late Alfred-Louis de Prémare and especially Viviane Comerro.[3] Khan's neglect of these last two scholars comes across as an especially egregious case of selection bias given that their research in particular has added important new insights into the formation and dissemination of the traditions about Ḥafṣah's codex.

Moreover, Khan's discussion of the English secondary literature is often skewed. While she criticizes Jeffery's and Burton's discussions of Ḥafṣah's codex as hopelessly blind to gender—hardly surprising for scholars of their era—she extols Asma Afsaruddin as a paragon of feminist scholarship merely for a passing mention of the existence of Ḥafṣah's codex. One gets the distinct sense here, as elsewhere in her essay, that Khan is playing favorites.

Beyond the charge that Western Qurʾān scholarship has been remiss in its discussion of gender, Khan takes aim at the depictions of Ḥafṣah's role in the traditional Muslim narrative of the Qurʾān's collection. In this narrative—most likely first promulgated by the Medinan scholar Ibn Shihāb al-Zuhrī (d. 124/742) in the late Umayyad period—Ḥafṣah inherits an early copy of the Qurʾān from her father, the caliph ʿUmar b. al-Khaṭṭāb (r. 634–644), which he

2. Theodor Nöldeke, Friedrich Schwally, Gotthelf Bergsträßer, and Otto Pretzl, *Geschichte des Qorâns* (3 vols.; Leipzig: Dieterich, 1909–1938), 2.47ff. *et passim* [English: *History of the Qurʾān*, ed. and trans. W. H. Behn (Leiden: Brill, 2013), 251ff. *et passim*]; hereafter abbreviated as *GdQ*.

3. Alfred-Louis de Prémare, *Les fondations de l'Islam: Entre écriture et histoire* (Paris: Éditions du Seuil, 2002), 290–292, 452–456; Viviane Comerro, *Les traditions sur la constitution du muṣḥaf de ʿUthmān* (Beiruter Texte und Studien 134; Beirut: Ergon, 2012), 56–59 *et passim*.

ordered compiled in consultation with the first caliph Abū Bakr (r. 632–634).[4] When the third caliph, ʿUthmān, sets about to establish a definitive copy of the Qurʾān, the committee appointed by ʿUthmān and led by the Medinan Companion Zayd b. Thābit relies on the codex Ḥafṣah had inherited from her father as the template for their project. This account came to be the consensus account in traditional Sunnī scholarship, even if its historicity has been seriously challenged since at least the early twentieth century.[5]

Like the early pioneers of Western scholarship on the Qur'ān, Khan also aims to challenge the Sunni consensus narrative first articulated by Zuhrī; however, she undertakes her distinctive project to demonstrate what a 'feminist reading' of the story might contribute to our current understanding of the tradition. She writes:

> A feminist reading would counter with the following question: Could the historicity of "the first 'collection' under Abū-Bakr" be challenged on the basis of an obscuring of Hafṣa's [sic] possible role in the preparation of a written Qur'ān? In other words, the Hadīth [sic] account of "the first 'collection' under Abū-Bakr" may have been fabricated for many reasons, among them not only to suppress Hafṣa's role in establishing an 'official' text given that she was a woman, but also because she, too, came to be shrouded in some controversy due to the stigma of divorce (206).

Albeit couched in guarded language, Khan's argument pushes the reader to an easily discernable conclusion: the narratives of Abū Bakr's collection of the Qur'ān into a written codex (*muṣḥaf*)—as well as how he bequeathed the codex to ʿUmar, and how ʿUmar subsequently bequeathed the same codex to his daughter Ḥafṣah—purposefully obscure Ḥafṣah's editorial role in the establishment of the standard qur'ānic text. The animus behind the narrators' conspiracy to obscure Ḥafṣah's importance, Khan argues, arise from their attitudes toward gender more generally and their anxieties about the stigma Ḥafṣah incurred by her divorce from the Prophet more specifically—attitudes ripe to be exposed by feminist readings of the accounts.

---

4. Harald Motzki, "The Collection of the Qur'ān: A Reconsideration of Western Views in Light of Recent Methodological Developments," *Der Islam* 78 (2001): 1–34. See also G. H. A. Juynboll, *Encyclopedia of Canonical Ḥadīth* (Leiden: Brill, 2007), 695–697.

5. Cf. the helpful summary in Motzki, "Collection of the Qur'ān," 6–15 and the recent defense of the historicity of the traditional account in Gregor Schoeler, "The Codification of the Qur'an: A Comment on the Hypotheses of Burton and Wansbrough," in Angelika Neuwirth, Nicolai Sinai, and Michael Marx (eds.), *The Qur'ān in Context: Historical and Literary Investigations into the Qur'ānic Milieu* (Leiden: Brill, 2010), 779–794.

Alas, although the study sets out with salutary aims, Khan's execution falls short of its avowed goals. As a work of feminist criticism, Khan's 'feminist reading' of Ḥafṣah's marriage to the Prophet and the stigma she claims tarnished Ḥafṣah's reputation suffers from interpretations of the source material that are either poorly substantiated or too credulous; surprisingly, these poorly substantiated and often overly credulous readings also undermine her avowed aim to offer a feminist critique of the traditional narrative. Khan's essay wavers, on the one hand, between uncritically accepting accounts deeply entrenched in androcentric currents in the Islamic tradition and, on the other, reading into early accounts conspiracies that are mostly the product of her own guesswork. Lastly, as a work of historical analysis, her methods for adducing new evidence for Ḥafṣah's editorial activities are insufficient and often unsound; her arguments too often rely on readings of the early Arabic source material that are tendentious and ahistorical.

In what follows, we revisit two issues raised by Khan's essay by way of three specific lines of inquiry. The first asks what a 'feminist reading' of Ḥafṣah's life, and particularly her marriage to Muḥammad, might look like—especially if informed by historical-critical methods and decoupled from a straightforward, credulous reading of the *sīrah* and *ḥadīth* literature. The second asks what evidence actually exists for Ḥafṣah's knowledge of the Qur'ān and for her alleged editorial involvement in establishing the definitive text of the Qur'ān. To these two questions, we intervene with a third question of our own which Khan does not address: what light might the narratives of the codices of the Prophet's wives cast upon the early codification of the Qur'ān?

Ḥafṣah's Marriage to Muḥammad: A Feminist Reading?

Traditional scholarship dates Muḥammad's marriage to Ḥafṣah to the month of Shaʿbān in year 3 after the hijrah (January–February 625 CE), when she was eighteen years of age.[6] According to one account, her marriage ceremony to Muḥammad was quite the affair, occasioned by such a generous dower and bountiful banquet that Ḥafṣah would boast that her wedding's grandeur even outstripped her co-wife ʿĀ'ishah's.[7] Ḥafṣah's marriage to Muḥammad

6. Muḥammad b. Saʿd (d. 230/845), *Al-Ṭabaqāt al-kubrā* (Beirut: Dār Ṣādir, 1957), 8.81; ʿAlī b. ʿAbd Allāh Samhūdī (d. 911/1506), *Wafā' al-wafā bi-akhbār dār al-Muṣṭafā*, ed. Qasim al-Samarrai (London: Mu'assasat al-Furqān, 2001), 1.497. For an early tradition that places Ḥafṣah's marriage to the Prophet in 2 AH, see Ibn Abī Khaythamah (d. 279/892), *Al-Tārīkh*, ed. Ṣalāḥ b. Fatḥī Halal (Cairo: al-Fārūq al-Ḥadīthah, 2003), 2.5.

7. Ibn Zabālah (d. after 199/814), *Al-Muntakhab min kitāb azwāj al-Nabī bi-riwāyat*

was not her first. Most accounts claim that the young Ḥafṣah was already a widow at the time of her marriage to the Prophet. Her previous husband was Khunays b. Ḥudhāfah al-Sahmī, one of the earliest Meccan converts to Islam. Fleeing persecution in Mecca, Ḥafṣah emigrated to Abyssinia with Khunays *ca.* 617, when she was ten years of age, and they returned to the Hijaz after Muḥammad's hijrah to Medina in 622.[8]

On other matters relating to Ḥafṣah's marriage, our sources offer less of a consensus. Most authorities assert that Ḥafṣah's first husband, Khunays, joined Muḥammad in Medina just prior to the Battle of Badr in March 624 but quickly fell ill. Too ill to fight at Badr, Khunays died before the battle's end and was buried in Medina soon thereafter.[9] Three additional stories of Khunays' death circulated as well. According to one, Khunays died in Mecca during his return journey from Abyssinia and never reached Medina.[10] Another claims that Khunays lived long enough to fight at Uḥud in Shawwāl 3/March–April 625 but that he perished soon thereafter from a fatal wound received during the battle.[11] Yet another places his death in Sassanid Ctesiphon after the Prophet sent him as an emissary to Khusro's court.[12]

Khan playfully calls Ḥafṣah "the least favorite" wife of the Prophet, citing a famous story in which the Prophet purportedly divorced her (188). However, Khan's comments potentially undermine her aim of providing a feminist reading of Ḥafṣah's biography, likely because of her overestimation of the historicity of the accounts of Ḥafṣah's divorce. This is an unfortunate misstep, as her argument depends on demonstrating that the Prophet's divorce of Ḥafṣah stigmatized her and thus led to the suppression of her

---

al-Zubayr ibn Bakkar, ed. Akram Ḍiyā' al-ʿUmarī (Medina: Maṭbaʿat al-Jāmiʿah al-Islāmiyyah, 1981), 45.

8. Ibn Saʿd, *Ṭabaqāt*, 4.392; Aḥmad b. Yaḥyā al-Balādhurī (d. 279/872), *Ansāb al-ashrāf*, vol. 1/2, ed. Yūsuf al-Marʿashlī (Wiesbaden: Klaus Schwarz, 2008), 1053f.; idem, *Ansāb al-ashrāf: Sā'ir furūʿ Quraysh*, vol. 5, ed. Iḥsān ʿAbbās (Stuttgart: Franz Steiner, 1996), 334.

9. Ibn Saʿd, *Ṭabaqāt*, 4.392; Balādhurī, *Ansāb*, 1/2.1054 and 5.334.

10. Muṣʿab al-Zubayrī (d. 236/851), *Nasab Quraysh*, ed. E. Lévi-Provençal (Cairo: Dār al-Maʿārif, n.d.), 352.

11. Ibn Ḥajar al-ʿAsqalānī (d. 852/1449), *Al-Iṣābah fī tamyīz al-ṣaḥābah*, ed. Khalīl Ma'mūn Shayḥā (Beirut: Dār al-Maʿrifah, 2004), 1.519.

12. Abū Nuʿaym al-Iṣfahānī (d. 430/1038), *Maʿrifat al-ṣaḥābah*, ed. ʿĀdil b. Yūsuf al-ʿAzāzī (Riyadh: Dār al-Waṭan, 1998), 6.3205 and Ibn ʿAsākir (d. 571/1176), *Tārīkh madīnat Dimashq*, ed. ʿUmar b. Gharāmah al-ʿAmrawī (Beirut: Dār al-Fikr, 1995–2000), 3.173. These two accounts likely conflate Khunays' story with that of his brother, ʿAbd Allāh b. Ḥudhāfah, whom the Prophet purportedly sent to Khusro II Parvēz with his famous letter; cf. Balādhurī, *Ansāb*, 5.334f. Scholars who placed Khunays' death *after* Uḥud and, therefore, also after Ḥafṣah's marriage to the Prophet speculated that perhaps Khunays had divorced Ḥafṣah prior to Uḥud. See Samhūdī, *Wafā'*, 3.279f.

extensive editorial involvement in the Qur'ān's codification (206, 209). Khan also overlooks how embedded the Ḥafṣah divorce story (as well as its many variants) is in early exegesis of the Qur'ān, leading her to poorly measure her standing among the Prophet's wives during the divorce episode.

Few stories of Ḥafṣah's allegedly rocky marital relationship with Muḥammad survive that do not derive from qur'ānic exegesis. Ḥafṣah's purported divorce appears as a centerpiece narrative in the exegetes' treatment of the marital dispute between the Prophet and his wives recounted in Q Taḥrīm 66:1–5. According to the most seminal exegetical readings of these verses, the marital strife arising between Ḥafṣah and Muḥammad is set in motion when Ḥafṣah witnesses her husband in her quarters having sexual relations with his slave-girl (*jāriyah*)—sometimes identified with Māriyah the Copt[13] and other times with a young, Ethiopian slave-girl (*juwayriyah ḥabashiyyah*) named Ḥuṣn.[14] Ḥafṣah upbraids the Prophet for having so humiliated her, and to show his contrition, Muḥammad foreswears any future sexual relations with the slave-girl. Having thus appeased Ḥafṣah, Muḥammad stipulates to Ḥafṣah that she must not inform anyone else of the incident—especially her co-wife ʿĀʾishah. When Ḥafṣah fails to uphold her side of the agreement by informing ʿĀʾishah about what had transpired, a marital dispute ensues that ultimately is resolved by divine revelation—namely, Q 66:1–5.

Q 66:1–5 provides the exegetes with narrative elements which they then expand, albeit in manifold ways, into the longer narratives preserved in the *tafsīr* and *ḥadīth* literature. Because of the importance of the qur'ānic pericope to these narratives, and arguably because the exegesis of these verses may even account for the existence of these narratives in the first place, the relevant verses are worth quoting in full:

---

13. Muqātil b. Sulaymān (d. 150/767), *Al-Tafsīr*, ed. ʿAbd Allāh Maḥmūd al-Shiḥātah (Cairo: al-Hay'ah al-Miṣriyyah al-ʿĀmmah li'l-Kitāb, 1989), 4.375; Abū Jaʿfar Muḥammad b. Jarīr al-Ṭabarī (d. 311/923), *Jāmiʿ al-bayān ʿan taʾwīl āy al-Qurʾān*, ed. ʿAbd Allāh b. ʿAbd al-Muḥsin al-Turkī (Cairo: Dār Hajar, 2001), 23.83; Hūd b. Muḥakkam al-Hawwārī (d. *ca.* 280/893) *Tafsīr kitāb Allāh al-ʿazīz*, ed. Balḥājj b. Saʿīd Sharīfī (Beirut: Dār al-Gharb al-Islāmī, 1990), 4.378; ʿAlī b. Ibrāhīm al-Qummī (d. 307/919), *Al-Tafsīr* (Beirut: Mu'assasat al-Aʿlamī, 2007), 710–711. On the figure of Māriyah and the sexual scandals surrounding her, see now Uri Rubin, "The Seal of the Prophets and the Finality of Prophecy: On the Interpretation of the Qur'ānic Sūrat al-Aḥzāb (33)," *ZDMG* 164 (2014): 65–96, 76–79. For a recent study that calls the very historicity of Māriyah into question, see Christian Cannuyer, "Māriya, la concubine copte de Muḥammad, réalité ou mythe," *Acta Orientalia Belgica* 21 (2008): 251–264.

14. Abū Isḥāq al-Thaʿlabī (d. 427/1025), *Al-Kashf wa'l-bayān*, ed. Abū Muḥammad Ibn ʿĀshūr and Naẓīr al-Sāʿidī (Beirut: Dār Iḥyā' al-Turāth al-ʿArabī, 2002), 9.343.

66:1 O Prophet, why do you forbid that which God has declared lawful for you while seeking to please your wives? God is forgiving, merciful.

66:2 God has already ordained a means for you believers to release yourselves from your oaths.[15] God is your protector, knowing and wise.

66:3 Recall how the Prophet confided in one of his wives and how she divulged what he said—God exposed it to him. He made it known in part and concealed it in part. When he told it to her, she said, "Who told you this?" "He who knows and sees all informed me," he said.

66:4 If only you two were to repent before God, for your two hearts are twisted.[16] Were you two to seek to overcome him, God would surely protect him, as would Gabriel, the righteous of the believers, and the angels after that.

66:5 If he divorces you women, perhaps his Lord will give him better wives than you in exchange—women who are submissive, pious, obedient, worshipful, and fasting[17]—whether previously married or virgins.

The events behind these verses are tantalizingly elusive when reading the qur'ānic pericope on its own. What did the Prophet forbid himself, and why would his doing so please his wives? What oath must be broken, and why did this oath displease God? What secret did the Prophet confide to his wife, and to which wife? To whom did she divulge the secret of 'what he said' (*ḥadīth*) in verse 3? Who are 'the two' with twisted hearts called upon to repent in verse 4? How did these two seek to overcome the Prophet? What is the rationale behind the warning that God will replace the Prophet's wives with better women in verse 5?

Equally as curious as modern readers, the early exegetes filled in the gaps. Each did so in their own way, of course, but a reasonably stable consensus position—probably emerging in Medina and itself accommodating internal diversity—came to dominate the interpretation of these verses from at least as early as the mid-eighth century. At the risk of oversimplification, this consensus position may be summarized as follows:

Verse 1 (*why do you forbid that which God has declared lawful for you…*) admonishes the Prophet against a previous action: he had declared forbidden to himself what God declared permissible in order to placate his wives. In the

---

15. *taḥillat aymānikum*; *v.l.* "expiation for your oaths" (*kaffārat aymānikum*). The means to release oneself from an oath referenced here appears in Q Mā'idah 5:89.

16. *ṣaghat qulūbukumā*; *v.l.* "both your hearts have gone astray" (*zāghat qulūbukumā*).

17. *sā'iḥāt*; perhaps "traveling" and thus having abandoned their homes for the sake of God. Cf. Q Tawbah 9:112. All of these qualities reference the hypothetical wives' attitudes toward God and not necessarily toward their spouse.

mainstream interpretation of the exegetes, the Prophet declared his slave-girl forbidden to himself once Ḥafṣah discovered him having relations with her, saying, "She is now forbidden to me (*hiya ʿalayya ḥarām*)!"[18]

Verse 2 (*God has already ordained a means for you believers to release yourselves from your oaths...*) expands upon the content of what precedes it: an oath must now be broken in accord with the ordinances prescribed in Q Māʾidah 5:89. The exegetical literature specifies that the verse refers to Muḥammad's oath not to have relations with his slave-girl, for his concession contravened God's decree. The revelation thus dictates that the Prophet's oath must be rescinded in the manner ordained in a previous revelation.[19]

Verse 3 (*Recall how the Prophet confided in one of his wives and how she divulged what he said...*) mentions a conversation (*ḥadīth*) that the Prophet requested one of his wives not to divulge, but when she acts contrary to his wishes, God reveals her misdeed to the Prophet, who confronts her. The exegetical literature specifies this 'conversation' to have been the Prophet's command to Ḥafṣah not to spread word of the incident involving the slave-girl—either commanding her, "Keep quiet and mention this to no one" (*uskutī lā tadhkurī hādhā li-aḥad*)[20] or "Hide this matter for me, and do not tell ʿĀʾishah what you saw" (*uktumī ʿalayya wa-lā tadhkurī li-ʿĀʾishah mā raʾayti*)![21] Acting contrary to his wishes, Ḥafṣah informs ʿĀʾishah of the matter in secret, but God exposes Ḥafṣah's misdeed to the Prophet.

Verse 4 (*If only you two were to repent before God...*) singles out two individuals and calls them to repent of their misdeeds. The exegetical tradition unanimously identifies the two persons as Ḥafṣah and ʿĀʾishah, who together conspire to sow discord between the Prophet and the rest of his wives because of the incident involving the slave-girl.[22] The verse affirms God's support of his Prophet against their designs.

Verse 5 (*If he divorces you women...*) contains the divine rebuke and a threat against the Prophet's wives as a collective: if they oppose the Prophet any further, God will replace them with better wives who are more pious and tractable than they. The exegetical tradition thus expands these verses by emphasizing the seriousness of the Prophet's divinely sanctioned threat to

18. ʿAbd al-Razzāq b. Hammām al-Ṣanʿānī (d. 211/827), *Tafsīr al-Qurʾān*, ed. Muṣṭafā Muslim Muḥammad (Riyadh: Maktabat al-Rushd, 1983), 2.301; Ṭabarī, *Jāmiʿ*, 23.85.

19. Ṭabarī, *Jāmiʿ*, 23.90.

20. Balādhurī, *Ansāb*, 1/2.1055; Ṭabarī, *Jāmiʿ*, 23.85.

21. Ṭabarī, *Jāmiʿ*, 23.85.

22. Tradition often portrays the two as being of one mind. Ḥafṣah and ʿĀʾishah purportedly lived in neighboring quarters during the Prophet's lifetime and continued to live in neighboring homes after their husband's death. Samhūdī, *Wafāʾ*, 2.299 and 3.46.

divorce them, as well as to divorce Ḥafṣah in particular. Ḥafṣah's divorce sometimes appears as an actualization of this threat, although Gabriel prevents the divorce by divine fiat. What must be emphasized, however, is that the tradition frequently asserts that the Prophet divorced not only Ḥafṣah but *all* of his wives, arousing angelic, and thus divine, intervention to affect reconciliation in the Prophet's household.[23] This last point is key, because Khan would have her readers believe that these events uniquely stigmatized Ḥafṣah to the exclusion of the Prophet's other wives.

Certainly *this* is the story that needs feminist intervention. As the exegetes would have it, Q Taḥrīm 66:1–5 admonishes the Prophet against placing self-imposed limits on his sexual access to the women of his household, wedded or enslaved, and rebukes any of his wives who object and assert their own agency and desires. This interpretive stream, dominant as it may be, is a clear example of an androcentric scriptural reading.

Yet the Muslim exegetical tradition is nothing if not multivocal, and Muslim exegetes offer alternative interpretations for this passage. The alternatives differ over what exactly the Prophet had declared to be forbidden to himself in order to placate his wives and seem to have proliferated among the *ḥadīth* folk more broadly that it did among the Qur'ān exegetes. Among the *ḥadīth* scholars—such as Muḥammad b. Ismāʿīl al-Bukhārī (d. 256/870) and Muslim b. al-Ḥajjāj (d. 261/875)—the issues discussed in the opening passages of Q 66 relate to a scandal over the Prophet's love of enjoying honey with Zaynab bt. Jaḥsh, a wife whose beauty inspired jealousy among his other wives. Bukhārī's version of the story is narrated by ʿĀ'ishah:[24]

> The Messenger of God used to sip honey in Zaynab bt. Jaḥsh's chambers and would spend a long time there, so I made an agreement with Ḥafṣah, "Whichever one of us he comes to next, she will say, 'Did you eat *maghāfīr*?[25] I swear I can smell the stench of *maghāfīr* on your breath!'" The Prophet replied, "No, but I was sipping honey in the chambers of Zaynab bt. Jaḥsh. I shan't do it again!"

---

23. Aḥmad Ibn Ḥanbal (d. 241/855), *Al-Musnad*, ed. Shuʿayb al-Arna'ūṭ et al. (Beirut: Mu'assasat al-Risālah, 1993–), 1.348–349 (from Ibn Shihāb al-Zuhrī); cf. Balādhurī, *Ansāb*, 1/2.1059–1062 and Ṭabarī, *Jāmiʿ*, 23.94–96.

24. Muḥammad b. Ismāʿīl al-Bukhārī, *Al-Ṣaḥīḥ, kitāb al-tafsīr* (Stuttgart: TraDigital, 2000), 2.1023, no. 3961. Cf. ibid., *kitāb al-ṭalāq*, 3.1102–1103; Muslim b. al-Ḥajjāj, *Al-Ṣaḥīḥ, kitāb al-ṭalāq* (Stuttgart: TraDigital, 2000), 1.613–616; Balādhurī, *Ansāb*, 1/2.1057–1059; Ibn Ḥanbal, *Musnad*, 43.41. The exegetes know the story as well, of course, and some favor it; e.g., see ʿAbd al-Razzāq, *Tafsīr*, 2.301–302 (from Ibn al-Zubayr) and Abū'l-Ḥasan ʿAlī b. Aḥmad al-Wāḥidī (d. 468/1076), *Al-Tafsīr al-basīṭ*, ed. Muḥammad b. Ṣāliḥ b. ʿAbd Allāh al-Fawzān (25 vols.; Riyadh: Jāmiʿat al-Imām Muḥammad b. Saʿūd al-Islāmiyyah, 2010), 22.5–6.

25. Gum from the Urfuṭ tree known for its pungent smell.

And I made Ḥafṣah swear not to tell anyone of this.

Hence, this tradition and its kindred variants replace the scandal of the slave-girl story with a minor plot among the Prophet's wives to put an end to his lengthy visits to sip honey with one wife to the neglect of the others.

Modern scholars have been inclined to regard the more scandalous story involving the slave girl as the earlier one given that it appears in the earliest sources, and despite the fact that the honey story has a superior pedigree in the eyes of the *ḥadīth* scholars. These modern scholars reason that, if the story of Ḥafṣah's jealousy after seeing the Prophet with his slave-girl predates the honey story, then exegetes likely contrived the honey narrative at a later date in order to provide an alternative to the unflattering portrayal of the Prophet and his wives in the former story.[26] Furthermore, while the honey story may provide a somewhat plausible explanation for Q 66:1–2, its explanatory force greatly diminishes when applied to the remainder of the pericope. The gravity of Q 66:5–6, which threatens divorce as a penalty for plotting against the Prophet, makes a poor match for the trifles of the honey story.[27]

In addition to the above alternative, there is the sectarian Shi'ite reading of the passage. In this reading, Ḥafṣah and 'Ā'ishah walk in together on Muḥammad and both find him with Māriyah the Copt. To placate Ḥafṣah, the Prophet reveals a secret to her that she subsequently divulged to 'Ā'ishah—namely, that Abū Bakr and 'Umar will succeed him as the community's leaders. Inasmuch as this story aims to abnegate the merits of Abū Bakr and 'Umar as well as their daughters, the divulgence of this secret stirs up the political ambitions of the four and inspires them to plot against the Prophet in order to poison him and hasten his death and thus their rise to power.[28]

---

26. See *GdQ*, 1.217 (trans. Behn, 175f.) where it is argued that the story was invented to mitigate the scandal of the story of Ḥafṣah and the slave-girl. Cf. G.H.A. Juynboll, *Encyclopedia of Canonical Ḥadīth* (Leiden: Brill, 2007), 155, 675–676. Such arguments do run the risk of using anachronistic assessments of what early Muslims did, or did not, find scandalous to determine the historicity of the tradition. In at least this case, however, it is clear that early Muslims did indeed find such intrigues by the Prophet's wives scandalous—a fact that is attested, for example, by comments on the Zaynab-Zayd scandal in the late seventh-century *Kitāb al-Irjā'* of Ḥasan b. Muḥammad b. al-Ḥanafiyyah. See J. van Ess, "Das *Kitāb al-Irǧā'* des Ḥasan b. Muḥammad b. al-Ḥanafiyya," *Arabica* 21 (1974): 20–52, 37–38. Cf. 'Abd al-Razzāq, *Tafsīr*, 2.117; Ṭabarī, *Jāmi'*, 19.115–117.

27. Muslim scholars put forward a juridical rationale for rejecting the honey story, too. According to the exegete Wāḥidī (*Basīṭ*, 22.11), for example, al-Shāfi'ī argued that if the Prophet had merely forbade himself honey, or any other food or drink, then the prescribed expiation (*kaffārah*) would have been entirely unnecessary.

28. Qummī, *Tafsīr*, 710–711; cf. Me'ir Bar-Asher, *Scripture and Exegesis in Early Imāmī-Shiism* (Leiden: Brill, 1999), 44–45. The claim that the secret told to Ḥafṣah

Regardless of the plurality of these stories, one important point deserves to be emphasized: outside of the divorce anecdotes, there is little reason to suppose that Ḥafṣah was particularly disliked among the Prophet's wives. Even if, for example, her father purportedly once admonished her to never contradict the Prophet's wishes since she lacked Zaynab's beauty and 'Ā'ishah's favored position, such fatherly admonitions hardly indicate actual antipathy towards Ḥafṣah.[29] Furthermore, although Khan is keen to play up the stigma attached to Ḥafṣah after her divorce, she adduces no evidence that Ḥafṣah had been stigmatized by the nascent community in the years following. The story of Gabriel convincing the Prophet to remain married to Ḥafṣah is less likely to be a source of stigma against Ḥafṣah than it is an explanation of how God intervened on her behalf to restore her to the Prophet. Hence, many accounts claim that the Prophet declared divorce against her merely one of the three times required for the divorce to be binding (*tallaqa ḥafṣah taṭlīqatan*); others flatly deny that the Prophet divorced Ḥafṣah at all, claiming he had merely resolved to do so (*hamma bi-ṭalāq ḥafṣah*).[30]

The stigma touted by Khan is hard to find anywhere outside these stories. This is especially true when one compares her to her co-wives. For instance, in the course of her life, Ḥafṣah clearly experiences nothing tantamount to 'Ā'ishah's humiliation from rumors spread about her alleged adulterous tryst with Ṣafwān b. al-Mu'aṭṭal,[31] or her estrangement after leading the opposition to 'Alī b. Abī Ṭālib alongside her co-conspirators, Ṭalhah and al-Zubayr, into catastrophe at the Battle of the Camel.[32]

Hence, even a straightforward, credulous reading of the *sīrah* literature does not lead one to conclude that Ḥafṣah was any more disliked than any of the other wives—and certainly no more than any of the wives whom the

---

that she conveyed to 'Ā'ishah was that Abū Bakr and then 'Umar would become the community's leaders appears in non-Shi'ite sources, too (see Balādhurī, *Ansāb*, 1/2. 1056 and n. 4 thereto); however, the murder plot is absent.

29. Balādhurī, *Ansāb*, 1/2.1063, *laysa laki jamāl zaynab wa-lā ḥuẓwat 'ā'ishah.* The *ḥadīth* folk record a long account of the disagreement between the Prophet and his wives narrated by 'Umar in which he says to his daughter Ḥafṣah, "By God, I know that God's Messenger does not love you—were it not for me, the Messenger of God would divorce you" (*law lā anā la-ṭallaqaki*). Yet even in this story the rumor that prods 'Umar to confront his daughter (as well as 'Ā'ishah) is that the Prophet had divorced *all* of his wives, not merely Ḥafṣah. See, e.g., Muslim, *Ṣaḥīḥ*, *kitāb al-ṭalāq*, 1.616–621; Ibn Ḥanbal, *Musnad*, 1.346–350; Abū Ya'lā al-Mawṣilī (d. 307/919), *Al-Musnad*, ed. Ḥusayn Salīm Asad (Beirut: Dār al-Ma'mūn, 1989), 1.149–153.

30. Ibn Sa'd, *Ṭabaqāt*, 8.84–85; Balādhurī, *Ansāb*, 1/2.1061.

31. Ma'mar b. Rāshid (d. 153/770), *The Expeditions (Kitāb al-Maghāzī)*, ed. and trans. Sean W. Anthony (New York: NYU Press, 2014), 148–159.

32. Cf. Denise A. Spellberg, *Politics, Gender, and the Islamic Past: The Legacy of 'A'ishah bint Abi Bakr* (New York: Columbia, 1994), 107–149.

ḥadīth scholars report Muḥammad actually divorced. These wives include Ghuzayyah bt. Dūdān (divorced for old age),[33] Rayḥānah bt. Shamʿūn al-Quraẓiyyah (divorced temporarily),[34] al-ʿĀliyah bt. Ẓabyān (divorced for freely going about outside the house, *al-taṭalluʿ*),[35] ʿAmrah bt. Yazīd al-Kilābiyyah (divorced because the Prophet found a disconcerting flaw on her skin, a white mark at her waist),[36] Asmāʾ bt. Qays al-Kindiyyah (divorced allegedly because she refused to come at the Prophet's beckoning),[37] or the wife whom Muḥammad divorced after she cruelly mocked the death of his infant son Ibrāhīm.[38] On the other hand, one need not adopt a credulous reading of any of the above stories nor even of the story of Ḥafṣah's divorce. If one reads, in particular, the narratives of Ḥafṣah's scandal as evolving out of efforts to interpret Q 66:1–5, then Ḥafṣah's divorce and the stories of her contentious relationship with the Prophet might conceivably be regarded as a concoction of the exegetes.

Ḥafṣah and the Commitment of the Qurʾān to Writing

Central to Khan's thesis as well is that Ḥafṣah "memorized, recited, and *edited* the Qurʾānic materials" (190, emphasis ours). That Ḥafṣah would have memorized and recited the Qurʾān (at least in part) is a given, since the quotidian practice of Islamic ritual necessitates the memorization and

33. Balādhurī, *Ansāb*, 1/2.1052f. (citing al-Kalbī), *raʾā... bi-ghuzayyah kibratan fa-ṭallaqahā*; cf. Ibn Ḥabīb (d. 245/860), *Al-Muḥabbar*, ed. Ilse Lichtenstädter (Hyderabad: Dāʾirat al-Maʿārif al-ʿUthmāniyyah, 1942), 81 and Abū Jaʿfar al-Ṭabarī, *Tārīkh al-rusul wa'l-mulūk*, ed. M.J. de Goeje et al. (Leiden: Brill, 1879–1901), 1.1776.

34. Ibn Saʿd, *Ṭabaqāt*, 8.129f.; Balādhurī, *Ansāb*, 1/2.1120f.

35. Balādhurī, *Ansāb*, 1/2.1123f.; cf. Ibn Saʿd, *Ṭabaqāt*, 8.142: Ibn Abī Zayd al-Qayrawānī, *Al-Jāmiʿ*, ed. ʿAbd al-Majīd Turkī (Beirut: Dār al-Gharb al-Islāmī, 1990), 163; and Abū Bakr al-Bayhaqī, *Dalāʾil al-nubuwwah wa-maʿrifat aḥwāl ṣāḥib al-sharīʿah*, ed. ʿAbd al-Muʿṭī Amīn Qalʿajī (Beirut: Dār al-Kutub al-ʿIlmiyyah, 1985), 7.286.

36. Balādhurī, *Ansāb*, 1/2.1124, *raʾā bi-kashḥihā bayāḍan fa-ṭallaqahā*; cf. Ibn Ḥabīb, *Muḥabbar*, 96; Ibn Saʿd, *Ṭabaqāt*, 8.143; and Ibn ʿAsākir, *Dimashq*, 3.164. The likely implication here is that she showed signs of leprosy; see M. W. Dols, "Djudhām," *EI*[2], s.v.

37. Balādhurī, *Ansāb*, 1/2.1125.

38. Bayhaqī, *Dalāʾil*, 8.289. After Ibrāhīm's death, the wife purportedly commented, "Were he truly a prophet, then the one dearest to him would not have died (*law kāna nabiyyan mā māta aḥabb al-nās ilayhi*)." Though the story is relatively widespread in the tradition, there is no consensus regarding the name of the wife who uttered these words. See, e.g., Ṭabarī, *Tārīkh*, 1.1774 (where the name is given as Shanbāʾ bt. ʿAmr al-Ghifāriyyah); Ibn ʿAsākir, *Dimashq*, 3.164 (Shanbāʾ bt. ʿAmr al-Ghifāriyyah); and Muḥammad b. Yaʿqūb al-Kulaynī, *al-Kāfī*, ed. ʿAlī Akbar al-Ghaffārī (Tehran: Dār al-Kutub al-Islāmiyyah, 1968–1971), 5.421 (Bint Abī'l-Jawn al-Kindiyyah).

recitation of at least part of the Qur'ān. Since the first two feats are banalities, it suffices to focus on Khan's third assertion: that Ḥafṣah edited the Qur'ān. What evidence does Khan adduce for her readers?

The first evidence Khan puts forward is a tradition attributed to the Medinan scholar ʿUrwah b. al-Zubayr (d. *ca* . 94/713) preserved in the *Jāmi*ʿ of the Egyptian scholar ʿAbd Allāh b. Wahb al-Miṣrī (d. 197/812). Citing the tradition on the authority of Abū'l-Aswad (d. 131/748 or later), ʿUrwah's orphan ward, Ibn Wahb's account reads as follows:

ʿUrwah b. al-Zubayr said:

> People disagreed over how to read, "Those of the People of Book and the Pagans who disbelieved..." (Q Bayyinah 98:1), so ʿUmar went with a strip of leather (*adīm*) to see [his daughter] Ḥafṣah. He said, "When the Messenger of God comes to see you, ask him to teach you "Those of the People of Book and the Pagans who disbelieved...," then tell him to write the verses down for you on this strip of leather. She did so, and the Prophet wrote them down for her and that became the generally accepted reading (*al-qirā'ah al-ʿāmmah*).[39]

Commenting on this tradition, Khan avers that, "'Umar is shown as asking Hafṣah [sic] to edit the Qur'ān on the basis of Muḥammad 'teaching' her the correct recitation and writing of the said verse" (191–192). But Khan's reading is tendentious. Ḥafṣah does not even transcribe, let alone edit, the Qur'ān in this anecdote; rather, she asks the *Prophet* to write it down for her.

The tradition is certainly a curious one, not so much because it casts Ḥafṣah in the role of an editor (which it does not) but rather because it portrays the Prophet as capable of writing the Qur'ān down himself. That the Prophet was illiterate and could neither read nor write is, of course, a staple of Sunni prophetology, but the dogmatic insistence on his illiteracy is a later development. The earliest strata of the tradition speak without hesitation of the Prophet as capable of reading and writing.[40] "Hafṣa's [sic] edited version of the verse is then presumably orally disseminated," Khan further argues, but her presumption of editing goes too far. It rests too precariously on the idea that Ḥafṣah actually edited anything, an assertion for which this tradition provides zero evidence. The Prophet's personal record of the ninety-eighth *sūrah* establishes the consensus reading (*al-qirā'ah al-ʿāmmah*), and Ḥafṣah is certainly, to use Khan's words, "a significant 'go-between'" (192) on her

39. ʿAbd Allāh b. Wahb al-Miṣrī, *Al-Jāmi*ʿ, ed. Miklos Muranyi (Beirut: Dār al-Gharb al-Islāmī, 2003), 3.62. On the disputed reading referenced here, see *GdQ*, 1.241–242 (trans. Behn, 194–195).

40. Alan Jones, "The Word Made Visible: Arabic Script and the Committing of the Qur'ān to Writing," in Chase F. Robinson (ed.), *Texts, Documents, and Artefacts: Islamic Studies in Honour of D.S. Richards* (Leiden: Brill, 2003), 1–16, 6ff.

father's behalf, but she is not an editor. To assert that Ḥafṣah acts as an editor of the Qur'ān in this tradition, or plays any editorial role whatsoever here, is, alas, ultimately untenable.

Khan's second, and surprisingly last, piece of evidence for her claims regarding Ḥafṣah's editorial activity hearkens back to a tradition of the Medinan scholar Ibn Shihāb al-Zuhrī that is preserved in the *Jāmi*ʿ of Zuhrī's student, the Basran scholar Maʿmar b. Rāshid (d. 153/770), as well as the *Muṣannaf* of Maʿmar's student ʿAbd al-Razzāq al-Ṣanʿānī (d. 211/827). This account reads:

> Zuhrī said:
>
> Ḥafṣah brought the Prophet a piece of writing from the stories of Joseph on a shoulder blade (*kitāb min qiṣaṣ yūsuf fī katfin*), and she began reading it to him. The Prophet's countenance suddenly changed, and he said, "By Him in whose hand my soul resides! Were Joseph to come to you while I remained in your midst and were you then to follow him and abandon me, you would surely go astray (*law atākum yūsuf wa-anā baynakum fa-ttabaʿtumūhu wa-taraktumūnī la-ḍalaltum*)![41]

Noting that the text displays "Hafṣa's [sic] literacy, intellectual curiosity, and recitation skills," Khan cites this tradition as further proof that Ḥafṣah "read, recited, collected, and/or wrote scriptural writings" (192).

Khan's insight into Ḥafṣah's literacy and intellectual curiosity is certainly correct and deserves commendation—indeed, the Islamic tradition notes with striking regularity the prevalence of literacy among ʿUmar's female kin. In accounts of ʿUmar's conversion to Islam, what leads him to embrace the faith is, at least in part, his remorse for having brutally beaten his sister Umm Jamīl Fāṭimah bt. al-Khaṭṭāb with the very shoulder blade from which she had been reading verses of the Qur'ān.[42] Ḥafṣah herself learned writing and incantations to mend wounds (*ruqyat al-namlah*) from another woman of her clan, the Qurashī Companion al-Shifā' bt. ʿAbd Allāh al-ʿAdawī.[43] However,

41. ʿAbd al-Razzāq al-Ṣanʿānī, *Al-Muṣannaf*, ed. Ḥabīb al-Raḥmān al-Aʿẓamī (Beirut: al-Majlis al-ʿIlmī, 1972), 6.113f. and 11.110.

42. Maʿmar, *Expeditions*, 18–21; Ibn Hishām, *Al-Sīrah al-nabawiyyah*, ed. Muṣṭafā al-Saqqā, Ibrāhīm al-Ibyārī, and ʿAbd al-Ḥafīẓ Shalabī (Beirut: Dār al-Fikr, n.d.), 1.344.

43. Ibn Saʿd, *Ṭabaqāt*, 8.84; Ibn Abī Khaythamah, *Tārīkh*, 2.82; Ibn Ḥanbal, *Musnad*, 44.43–45. Iṣfahānī (*Maʿrifat*, 6.3371–3372) records the text of this incantation and notes that she would utter over a stick of turmeric (*ʿūd kurkum*) seven times and, after placing the stick on a clean spot, rub it with acidic vinegar (*khall khamr thaqīf*) and then apply it to the wounds. On the use of incantations and enchantments in the medicinal practices of the Prophet and his circle, see Toufic Fahd, "Ruḳya," *EI²*, s.v. and Uri Rubin, "Muḥammad the Exorcist: Aspects of Islamic-Jewish Polemics," *JSAI*

Khan goes further by asserting that this tradition also displays Ḥafṣah's fluency in several scriptural traditions and, hence, underscores Ḥafṣah as an editor of the text of the Qur'ān.

A careful reading of the tradition hardly vindicates Khan's interpretation. What, for example, are 'the stories of Joseph (*qiṣaṣ yūsuf*)' written on the shoulder blade? And why would Ḥafṣah's reading of these stories so perturb Muḥammad? The 'stories of Joseph' are certainly not identical with Yūsuf, the twelfth *sūrah* of the Qur'ān. Ḥafṣah's reading of this *sūrah* of the Qur'ān would hardly have provoked such marked displeasure in Muḥammad—"[the Prophet's] face changed color (*yatalawwin wajhuh*)," as the tradition words it. Although somewhat obscure if read in isolation, the meaning of the tradition, within the context of both Ma'mar's *Jāmi'* and 'Abd al-Razzāq's *Muṣannaf*, elucidates the significance of the Prophet's anger considerably. The tradition of Ḥafṣah's reading the 'stories of Joseph' appears alongside a litany of others addressing the study and reading of *non*-qur'ānic scripture. The tradition trails a discussion of the famous and controversial *ḥaddithū 'an banī isrā'īl wa-lā ḥaraja* tradition, in which the Prophet enjoins his followers to transmit biblical traditions from Jews without fear of sinning.[44] Hence, Muḥammad's reaction expresses his displeasure at hearing Ḥafṣah read non-qur'ānic traditions about Joseph—her knowledge of the Qur'ān is neither contested here nor even the topic of the tradition.

Another tradition mirrors the Ḥafṣah exchange and clarifies this point further. In this tradition, the Prophet's interlocutor is not Ḥafṣah but rather her father, 'Umar. According to this tradition, 'Umar asks a Jew from Medina's Qurayẓah clan to copy for him sections of (*jawāmi' min*) the Torah, and when 'Umar then offers to present these writings to Muḥammad, "the Messenger of God's countenance changed (*fa-taghayyara wajh rasūl allāh*)." Muḥammad then likewise declares to 'Umar, "Were Moses to appear in your midst and

30 (2005): 104–107. Tradition also lists 'Umar among the seventeen men of Quraysh who knew how to read and write. See Balādhurī, *Liber expugnationis regionum (Futūḥ al-buldān)*, ed. M. J. de Goeje (Leiden: Brill, 1968), 470f. and Claude Gilliot, "Oralité et écriture dans la genèse, la transmission et la fixation du Coran," in Philippe Cassuto and Pierre Larcher (eds.), *Oralité et écriture dans la Bible et le Coran* (Aix-en-Provence: Presses Universitaires de Provence, 2014), 99–142,106–112. However, a common trope in the stories of 'Umar's conversion to Islam portrays him as hopelessly illiterate; e.g., see Ma'mar b. Rāshid, *Expeditions*, 20–21. On 'Umar's literacy, see also Maged A. Badahdah, *Ṣinā'at al-kitāb wa'l-kitābah fī'l-Ḥijāz: 'Aṣr al-nubuwwah wa'l-khilāfah al-rāshidah* (London: Furqan, 2006), 2.611–613.

44. 'Abd al-Razzāq, *Muṣannaf*, 6.109–110. Discussed in meticulous detail by M. J. Kister, "*Ḥaddithū 'an banī isrā'īla wa-lā ḥaraja*: A Study of an Early Tradition," *IOS* 2 (1972): 215–239. See also de Prémare, *Les fondations*, 452–454.

were you then to follow him and abandon me, you would go astray. Of all peoples, you are my lot; just as of all the prophets I am your lot."[45]

As seen above, the evidence that Khan offers readers for deducing that Ḥafṣah actively edited the codex is remarkably not only slim but virtually non-existent. However much Ḥafṣah and her persona in these early traditions may fascinate us, one cannot simply conjure evidence where none exists. In this case, the evidence for the editorial activities of Ḥafṣah as imagined by Khan is sorely wanting.

Marwān b. al-Ḥakam's (or ʿUthmān b. ʿAffān's?) Destruction of Ḥafṣah's Codex

The last central point in Khan's discussion of Ḥafṣah's codex focuses on Zuhrī's account of the destruction of Ḥafṣah's codex during the caliphate of Muʿāwiyah b. Abī Sufyān (r. 660–680). Khan highlights Ḥafṣah's resolve when facing the request of Medina's governor, Marwān b. al-Ḥakam, that she hand over her copy of the Qur'ān inherited from her father in order to have it destroyed. Khan writes:

> From a feminist perspective, Hafṣa's [sic] refusal here is a powerful example of female agency that stands out in these androcentric classical narratives. This act of refusal to comply with Marwān's demand was no small matter… What palpably comes across is the special and intense nature of the relationship between her and the *ṣuḥuf*. Western scholars of Qur'ānic studies need to ponder the not-so-obvious: of what significance, if any, is the vigilance and tenacity with which Hafṣa guarded the *ṣuḥuf*? What could Qur'ānic studies' [sic] scholars glean from the way in which Hafṣa "owned" or possessed the *ṣuḥuf* (especially since the intensity of this relation is evident in nearly all the classical narratives associated with the codification of the Qur'ān)? Is the special and intense nature of the relationship between Hafṣa and the *ṣuḥuf* simply due to them being ultimately *her* editorial product? Is this intensity a marker of her intellectual labor *vis-à-vis* the *ṣuḥuf*—that is, the Qur'ānic writings that she collected, recorded, and edited? There are other scenarios. Perhaps, the intensity is simply a function of the daughter–father bond because the *ṣuḥuf* were bequeathed to her by her father ʿUmar. Or perhaps the intensity of Hafṣa's relation to the *ṣuḥuf* is a function of the father–daughter joint effort as regards the collecting, copying, and editing the Qur'ān

45. ʿAbd al-Razzāq, *Muṣannaf*, 6.113, *wa-law aṣbaḥa fīkum mūsā thumma ittabaʿtumūhu la-ḍalaltum antum ḥaẓẓī min al-umam wa-anā ḥaẓẓukum min al-nabiyyīn*; Ibn Ḥanbal, *Musnad*, 25.198 and ibid., 30.280; Abū ʿUbayd al-Qāsim b. Sallām al-Harawī (d. *ca.* 224/834), *Gharīb al-ḥadīth*, ed. Ḥusayn M. M. Sharaf et al. (Cairo: al-Hay'ah al-ʿĀmmah li-Shu'ūn al-Maṭābiʿ al-Amīriyyah, 1984–1999), 2.322–325 and ibid., 5.55–60. Cf. Kister, "*Ḥaddithū*," 234.

> [sic]. It is plausible that if 'Umar possessed a copy, he would have his daughter Hafṣa help him make this copy, especially given the reports concerning her literacy. After all, according to the first Hadīth [sic] tradition (from Bukhārī's collection), it was 'Umar who was very invested in the project of assembling the Qur'ān (208–209).

Zuhrī—the earliest known scholar to emphasize the importance of Ḥafṣah's codex for the collection of the caliph 'Uthmān's recension—also serves as the authority for the accounts of the destruction of Ḥafṣah's scrolls (*ṣuḥuf*). Hence, we are likely dealing with two intimately intertwined narratives that originated with Zuhrī and his students. The extant iterations of Zuhrī's story of, on the one hand, the codification of the 'Uthmānic recension of the Qur'ān and, on the other, the destruction of the Ḥafṣah codex ought to be read as complimentary accounts, inasmuch as they posit Ḥafṣah's codex as simultaneously indispensable to the establishment of the 'Uthmānic recension carried out by Zayd b. Thābit and definitively surpassed by this recension.

Khan's reading of the Marwān-Ḥafṣah episode relies heavily on her previous readings of Ḥafṣah's alleged editorial activities, and suffers as a result. For Khan, Marwān's "obsession" with destroying Ḥafṣah's codex was not only because it was a pre-canonical *muṣḥaf*:

> Marwān's obsession with destroying these codical materials possibly was a function of not just what was in them, but also of who "owned" them—namely, a woman and a "once-divorced" widow of the prophet at that. (209)

Given that the evidence she adduces for Ḥafṣah's role as an editor of the Qur'ān and her lifelong stigmatization lacks any textual foundation or evidentiary support, it is unsurprising that Khan's reading of this episode collapses under scrutiny. Khan reads the episode as revealing Ḥafṣah's deeply personal attachment to the codex as indicative of her role in its redaction, but as framed by Zuhrī's account of the events, what Marwān destroys is not Ḥafṣah's *personally edited* codex but, rather, the codex compiled during Abū Bakr's caliphate at 'Umar's prompting—a codex she *inherited* (and perhaps curated) rather than edited.[46]

Khan cites Ḥafṣah's stipulation to the caliph 'Uthmān that her codex be returned to her after his recension is completed as further evidence for Ḥafṣah's investment in the codex as the product of *her* editorial work. But lacking an evidentiary basis in the source material, this interpretation is superfluous at best and even misleading. Ḥafṣah's demands that 'Uthmān return the codex

46. Balādhurī, *Ansāb*, 1/2.1063; Ibn Abī Dāwūd al-Sijistānī, *Kitāb al-maṣāḥif*, ed. Muḥibb al-Dīn 'Abd al-Sabḥān (Beirut: Dār al-Bashā'ir al-Islāmiyyah, 2002), 1.169, 202.

to her reflects rather her belief in the inviolability of her ownership rights over the codex—ownership that she fears will be annulled if she hands over the codex to the caliph. Indeed, one tradition portrays Ḥafṣah stating as much during her exchange with ʿUthmān. She explains her reluctance to hand over her codex as follows: "I fear that you will withhold [the *muṣḥaf*] from me (*innī akhāfu an taḥbisahu ʿannī*)!"[47] In other words, she fears that the codex will not be returned to her.[48] ʿUthmān cedes to her demands and agrees to return the codex to her. Since Ḥafṣah dies childless and without a husband—as do all the Prophet's wives—her property rights fall to her brother, ʿAbd Allāh b. ʿUmar, from whom Marwān demands the codex once again at a later date. Unlike his sister Ḥafṣah, Ibn ʿUmar consents to Marwān's demands, and Marwān has the codex either erased by washing the parchment (*ghasalahā ghaslan*),[49] torn to shreds (*shaqqaqahā wa-mazzaqahā*),[50] or burned to ashes (*fashāhā wa-ḥarraqahā*).[51]

47. Arthur Jeffery (ed. and trans.), *Two Muqaddimas to the Qur'anic Sciences: The Muqaddima to the 'Kitāb al-Mabānī' and the Muqaddima of Ibn ʿAṭiyya to His Tafsīr* (Cairo: al-Khaniji, 1943), 22. Once regarded as anonymous, Claude Gilliot has recently deduced the identity of the author of the *Kitāb al-mabānī* as being a scholar and belletrist of late tenth-century Khurasan, Abū Muḥammad Aḥmad b. Muḥammad al-ʿĀṣimī. See Gilliot, "La théologie musulmane en Asie Centrale et au Khorasan," *Arabica* 49 (2002): 135–203, 182f.

48. One may also speculate that she feared that the *ṣuḥuf* might be damaged. When the governor of Iraq, al-Ḥajjāj b. Yūsuf al-Thaqafī (d. 95/713), undertook the 'second canonization' of the Qur'ān between 703 and 705 on behalf of the Umayyad caliph ʿAbd al-Malik, Ḥajjāj sent the new vulgate to Medina, as well as other population centers, to serve as the official copy for public readings. ʿUthmān's kin in Medina soon protested the idea that ʿUthmān's copy would be surpassed. In response to their objections, Ḥajjāj demanded that they hand over ʿUthmān's codex for official use; however, much like Ḥafṣah, they refused to hand over the codex, claiming that it had been damaged during the caliph's assassination. Cf. ʿUmar b. Shabbah al-Numayrī (d. 264/877), *Tārīkh al-madīnah al-munawwarah*, ed. Fuhaym Shaltūt (Jeddah: Dār al-Iṣfahānī, 1979), 1.7f., "*uṣība al-muṣḥaf yawma qutila ʿuthmān*"; Samhūdī, *Wafāʾ*, 2.457.

49. Ibn Zabālah, *Muntakhab*, 37; Ibn Shabbah, *Tārīkh al-madīnah*, 3.1003; Balādhurī, *Ansāb*, 1/2.1064. Erasing the parchment of the *muṣḥafs* rather burning or shredding them is attested elsewhere, too. Cf. the account in *Ikhtilāf al-maṣāḥif* by the Zaydī scholar Abū Jaʿfar Muḥammad b. Manṣūr al-Murādī (d. *ca.* 290/903) cited in Raḍī al-Dīn Ibn Ṭāwūs (d. 664/1266), *Saʿd al-suʿūd* (Qum: n.p., 1944), 278, where ʿUthmān seizes the *muṣḥafs* of Ubayy b. Kaʿb, ʿAbd Allāh b. Masʿūd, and Sālim, Abū Ḥudhayfah's *mawlā*, and has them erased (*ghasalahā ghaslan*) rather than burning them. On the Zaydī scholar Murādī, see Etan Kohlberg, *A Medieval Muslim Scholar at Work: Ibn Ṭāwūs and his Library* (Leiden: Brill, 1992), 100, 188.

50. Ibn Shabbah, *Tārīkh al-madīnah*, 3.1004; Abū ʿUbayd al-Qāsim b. Sallām, *Kitāb Faḍāʾil al-Qurʾān*, ed. Marwān al-ʿAṭiyyah, Muḥsin Kharābah, and Wafāʾ Taqī al-Dīn (Damascus: Dār Ibn Kathīr, 1995), 284.

51. Ibn Abī Dāwūd, *Maṣāḥif*, 1.203.

But why this insistence on the destruction of Ḥafṣah's *ṣuḥuf*? Is this a plot, as Khan implicates, to conceal the spurned Ḥafṣah's role in editing the Qur'ān because she was a despised, stigmatized wife of the Prophet? Again, a close reading fundamentally contradicts this hypothesis. The Zuhrī-traditions about the destruction of the Ḥafṣah codex explicitly state the rationale behind Marwān's pursuit of Ḥafṣah's codex to have it destroyed. Marwān himself cites "the fear that there might be a cause to dispute that which ʿUthmān copied down because of something therein"—i.e., Ḥafṣah's codex must ultimately be subjected to the same fate all other codices of the Prophet's Companions faced.[52] If copies of ʿAbd Allāh b. Masʿūd's and Ubayy b. Kaʿb's codices must be destroyed, so must Ḥafṣah's, for otherwise the unassailable authority of ʿUthmān's recension would be open to question. Admittedly, this contention is in tension with a key premise of Zuhrī's account of the ʿUthmānic recension—namely, that the codex Ḥafṣah inherited served as the basis of, or merely confirmed the accuracy of, the project Zayd b. Thābit oversaw during ʿUthmān's caliphate.[53] Yet, it is also not entirely incompatible with fears that the mere existence of the codex Ḥafṣah inherited from ʿUmar, being both earlier and an important precursor, would mitigate and even undermine the authority of the ʿUthmānic recension.[54]

Also neglected in Khan's credulous treatment of the Marwān story are several important authorities who place Ḥafṣah's death not during Muʿāwiyah's caliphate but, rather, during ʿUthmān's.[55] The testimony of these authorities, which include such heavyweights as the Medinan scholar Mālik b. Anas (d. 179/795),[56] renders the entire Marwān story impossible. Indeed, at

52. Ibn Shabbah, *Tārīkh al-madīnah*, 3.1004, *makhāfata an yakūna fī shay'in min dhālika khilāfun li-mā nasakha ʿuthmān*; Abū ʿUbayd, *Faḍā'il*, 284.

53. Hence, according to at least one version of the Zuhrī account, it was only after ʿUthmān had himself seen the codex Ḥafṣah inherited and had confirmed that his copy matched it word for word that "[ʿUthmān's] soul was content, and he ordered the people to write down the codices" (*tābat nafsuhu wa-amara al-nās an yaktubū al-maṣāḥif*), Ibn Shabbah, *Tārīkh al-madīnah*, 3.1002.

54. Aziz al-Azmeh's recent monograph offers an important insight that further elaborates the need to destroy her codex from the perspective of the early Umayyads: "The rapidly centralizing state needed a 'master-copy,' the need for which was not purely technical... the state needed to additionally keep an Umayyad guarantee of the integrity of the Vulgate, and for the integrity to be in the custody of an emergent class of specialists," *The Emergence of Islam in Late Antiquity: Allāh and His People* (Cambridge: Cambridge University Press, 2014), 487.

55. Cf. Balādhurī, *Ansāb*, 1/2.1063, who lists two authorities who place her death during ʿUthmān's caliphate, albeit while rejecting the date himself.

56. Ibn Abī Zayd, *Jāmiʿ*, 321. The Egyptian scholar Ibn Wahb also asserted that his teacher Mālik b. Anas of Medina dated Ḥafṣah's death to the year of the conquest of North Africa—i.e., 27/647–648. See Abū Zurʿah al-Dimashqī (d. 281/894), *Al-*

least four versions of the Zuhrī account assert that the caliph ʿUthmān (and *not* Marwān) requested ʿAbd Allāh b. ʿUmar to hand over Ḥafṣah's *muṣḥaf* after his sister's death, whereupon the codex was either burned[57] or erased.[58] As is well known, ʿUthmān's destruction of all previous codices created a scandal, leading dissenters to excoriate him as "the codex-incinerator" (*ḥarrāq al-maṣāḥif*)[59]—indeed, some traditions even deny that ʿUthmān burned the codices at all, claiming rather that he buried them in a chest (*ṣundūq*) beneath the Prophet's pulpit (*minbar*), or that he merely ripped them to shreds because the idea of burning the codices grieved him.[60] Was the Marwān narrative invented, therefore, to exculpate ʿUthmān from the responsibility for the destruction of Ḥafṣah's codex?

Not likely. The incongruities between these accounts suggest that they are, to a large degree, literary constructions shaped by theological interests rather than simply straightforward records of the Qurʾān's compilation. For this reason, modern scholars must be wary of inferring that one can derive empirical data about the earliest copies of the Qurʾān from the minutiae of these accounts, which can exhibit a high degree of variance. In other words, the historicity of every detail of Zuhrī's account of the fate of Ḥafṣah's copy after her passing is elusive and, in all likelihood, ultimately unknowable.[61]

Tārīkh, ed. Luṭfī Maḥmūd Manṣūr (Beirut: Dār al-Fikr, 2007), 1.324–325. Abū Zurʿah attempts to harmonize Mālik's assertion with those accounts that place her death during the caliphate of Muʿāwiyah by positing that Mālik must have referred to a later campaign during the governorship of Marwān given the anachronism this creates for the story of Marwān's destruction of Ḥafṣah's codex (see ibid., 1.6); however, if ʿUthmān rather than Marwān destroyed the codex, the anachronism disappears.

57. Jeffery, *Two Muqaddimas, kitāb al-mabānī*, 22 (citing Zuhrī): *lammā halakat ḥafṣah arsala ʿuthmān ilā ʿabd allāh ibn ʿumar bi-ʿazīmatin lammā arsala ilayhi biʾl-ruqʿah fa-akhadhahā wa-aḥraqahā*; cf. Abu Nuʿaym al-Iṣfahānī, *Ḥilyat al-awliyāʾ wa-ṭabaqāt al-aṣfiyāʾ* (Beirut: Dār al-Fikr, 1996), 2.51.

58. Ṭabarī, *Jāmiʿ*, 1.56: *fa-lammā mātat ḥafṣah arsala [ʿuthmān] ilā ʿabd allāh ibn ʿumar fīʾl-ṣaḥīfah bi-ʿazīmatin fa-aʿṭāhum iyāhā fa-ghusilat ghaslan*. Cf. Ibn Shabbah, *Tārīkh al-madīnah*, 3.1003 and n. 3 thereto, where the editor has amended the text of the manuscript from "ʿUthmān' to 'Marwān,' erroneously assuming a copyist's error.

59. Ibn Shabbah, *Tārīkh al-madīnah*, 3.996; Muḥammad b. ʿAbd al-Karīm al-Shahrastānī, *Mafātīḥ al-asrār wa-maṣābīḥ al-abrār*, ed. Muḥammad ʿAlī Ādharshab (Tehran: Mīrāth-i Maktūb, 2008), 1.10, 12; cf. Sayf b. ʿUmar al-Tamīmī, *Kitāb al-Riddah waʾl-futūḥ*, ed. Qasim al-Samarrai (Leiden: Smtiskamp Oriental Antiquarium, 1995), 51f.

60. Ibn Shabbah, *Tārīkh al-madīnah*, 3.1003–1005.

61. Hence, while Motzki's conclusions regarding the transmission of Zuhrī's tradition are cogently argued and convincing (see n. 5 above), whether or not the accounts are in fact historical is another matter altogether. The distinction here, and one often missed by Motzki's readers, is between dating the origin of the reports and their historical authenticity. Cf. Nicolai Sinai, "When Did the Consonantal Skeleton

What modern scholars can deduce with greater certainty is that, whether historical or not, the diverse accounts of Ḥafṣah's codex serve as a literary means to add testimonies to the veracity and success of ʿUthmān's project.

As recently argued by Viviane Comerro, the theological function of the accounts of Ḥafṣah's codex can be seen more clearly when read against parallel accounts that reproduce a similar scenario, but swap out Ḥafṣah's codex for that of ʿĀ'ishah. According to a tradition recorded by Ibn Shabbah (d. 262/876), during his codification project, the caliph ʿUthmān sent Ibn al-Zubayr not to Ḥafṣah, to obtain the codex she inherited from ʿUmar, but rather to ʿĀ'ishah, asking her to bring "the sheets upon which the Messenger of God wrote the Qur'ān, which we compared with the sheets [in ʿUthmān's *muṣḥaf*] and rectified [ʿUthmān's *muṣḥaf*]. Later he ordered the rest of the sheets to be ripped to shreds."[62] According to another account, ʿUthmān asked ʿĀ'ishah to send him "the scraps of leather upon which the Qur'ān was written straight from the mouth of the Messenger of God, at the moment when God revealed it to Gabriel, and Gabriel revealed it to Muḥammad and brought it down to him—when the Qur'ān was still fresh (*wa-idh al-qur'ān ghaḍḍ*)."[63] The intent of the tradition, as Comerro notes, is to assert that

> ʿĀ'ishah possessed, in effect, a parchment that contained the original Qur'ān, exactly contemporary with the recitation of the Prophet, exactly contemporary with the moment of its revelation, and identical with that which God revealed to Gabriel—the exemplar most faithful to the heavenly original.[64]

That is, ʿĀ'ishah's copy ensures that the authenticity and accuracy of ʿUthmān's recension is vouchsafed and unimpeachable.

---

of the Quran Reach Closure? Part II," *BSOAS* 77 (2014): 509–521: "For all we know, the full narrative about the promulgation of the ʿUthmānic text could be teeming with later expansions, accretions, and embellishments. This possibility is augmented by the fact that al-Zuhrī… may legitimately be suspected of having been susceptible to the exigencies of Umayyad 'state expediency'" (512–513). Also, see now Viviane Comerro, "Pourquoi et comment le Coran a-t-il été mis par écrite?" in François Déroche, Christian J. Robin, and Michel Zink (eds.), *Les origines du Coran, le Coran des origines* (Paris: De Boccard, 2015), 191–206.

62. Ibn Shabbah, *Tārīkh al-madīnah*, 3.991, *baʿathanī ilā ʿāʾishah fa-jiʾtu bi'l-ṣuḥuf allatī kataba fīhā rasūl allāh al-qurʾān fa-ʿaraḍnāhā ʿalayhā ḥattā qawwamnāhā thumma amara bi-sāʾirihā fa-shuqqiqah.* Cf. *GdQ*, 2.53 (trans. Behn, 256).

63. Ibn Shabbah, *Tārīkh al-madīnah*, 3.997–998.

64. Comerro, *Les traditions*, 164, "ʿĀ'isha possède, en effet, un parchemin qui contient le Coran originel, exactement contemporain de la récitation du Prophète, exactement contemporain du moment de sa révélation, identique à celui que Dieu a révélé à Gabriel, l'exemplaire le plus fidèle à l'original céleste."

Comerro's cogent arguments are a far cry from Khan's speculation that Ḥafṣah's divorce stigmatized her and thus inspired the traditionists to suppress her decisive role in the establishment of the ʿUthmānic codex. What Comerro's reading demonstrates is precisely the opposite: the Prophet's wives, whether one reads the version featuring ʿĀ'ishah or the version featuring Ḥafṣah, confirm and vouchsafe the authority and accuracy of ʿUthmān's recension by virtue of the intimacy they enjoyed with the Prophet as members of his household.

In truth, readings of these traditions that deploy the historical-critical method bear rather bad news for any project burdened with the task of excavating feminine subjectivity in the scattered stories *about* (rather than *by*) women in the *ḥadīth* and *tafsīr* literature. The tradition only rarely presents us with independent female voices, and in the absence of substantial evidence unmediated by the androcentric frame of the early Islamic tradition, it is truly difficult to imagine how modern historians might create a reliable methodology for reconstructing a history of feminine subjectivity from these sources. These stories are men's stories about women, and what vestiges of women's independent voices did exist at some point in time are muffled by the anecdotal recollections of men. The women we encounter are often "anecdotal women"[65]—images of women and their lives devised to serve men's narratives. These difficulties should never dissuade us from writing the histories of women's lives, but as we do so, we must be wary of the perils of historical error awaiting us along the path to this goal. Worded in another way, the parameters of the tradition and its historicization of the Qur'ān are by default androcentric and, therefore, stifle feminist readings of the past and scripture. Feminist readings can only flourish when they can reveal, disrupt, and transcend said parameters: a process that the tools of the historical-critical method can facilitate considerably.

The Codices (*maṣāḥif*) of the Prophet's Wives and Their Scribes

Another line of inquiry worth pursuing is what these anecdotes about the Prophet's wives tell us about the codicological history of the Qur'ān and its preservation. The literature on the variant readings (*qirāʾāt*) of the Qur'ān also features the codices of the Prophet's wives—in particular the codices of Ḥafṣah, ʿĀ'ishah, and Umm Salamah—but in this literature, the codices play an altogether different role than the one seen above. In the *qirāʾāt*

65. An idea developed, albeit for a different literary context, by Fedwa Malti-Douglas in *Women's Body, Women's Word: Gender Discourse in Arabo-Islamic Writing* (Princeton: Princeton University Press, 1991), 29ff. It has fallen into disuse but perhaps the time is ripe for its revival.

literature, the role of the wives' codices is that of repositories for readings that depart from the ʿUthmānic recension. This contrasts with the role the wives' codices play in the narratives discussed above—i.e., to vouch for the accuracy and authenticity of the ʿUthmānic recension. Ostensibly, the codices of the Prophet's wives represent different collections undertaken by the Prophet's wives independently, but in actuality, the variant readings this literature attributes to the codices of the Prophet's wives are striking for their uniformity and homogeneity rather than their diversity.

Accounts of these codices' origins conspicuously follow the same narrative template, amounting to three iterations of the same story. Hence, ʿĀ'ishah's codex purportedly came to be when she commissioned her own copy of the Qur'ān from her slave-client (*mawlā*), Abū Yūnus. While Abū Yūnus copied the codex, ʿĀ'ishah intervened: she specified that he take care to write *āyat al-ṣalāt* (Q Baqarah 2:238) in the precise manner she heard the Prophet recite it to her, adding the words "and the afternoon prayer" (*wa-ṣalāt al-ʿaṣr*) to the ʿUthmānic text.[66] A nearly identical story about this same verse is told regarding Ḥafṣah's personal copy, too; however, in the Ḥafṣah story the scribe is named ʿAmr b. Rāfiʿ (*v. l.* Nāfiʿ), and he is the slave-client of her father ʿUmar.[67] Likewise is yet another, virtually identical story recounted about the codex of Umm Salamah where, again, *āyat al-ṣalāt* features foremost. In the Umm Salamah version, her personal scribe, the slave-client ʿAbd Allāh b. Rāfiʿ, undertakes the copy and receives instruction to copy *āyat al-ṣalāt* according to Umm Salamah's instructions.[68]

The codices of the Prophet's wives are all purported to have been copied down by scribes after the Prophet's death, presumably for each wife's personal use rather than public dissemination.[69] Owning a Qur'ān codex required a considerable expenditure of wealth during this time—a level of wealth that

66. Ibn Abī Dāwūd, *Maṣāḥif*, 366–369, where Abū Yūnus' daughter Ḥamīdah claimed ʿĀ'ishah bequeathed this *muṣḥaf* to her family.

67. Ibid., 374–376. The same story is repeated as well, in which the scribe is rather Ḥafṣah's *mawlā* Abū Rāfiʿ in ibid., 376–377.

68. Ibid., 377–379.

69. Jeffery claims that the wives' codices were completed *during* the lifetime of the Prophet, but this assertion is not supported by his sources (*Materials*, 212, citing Ibn al-Jazarī's [d. 833/1429] *Al-Nashr fī'l-qirā'āt al-ʿashar*). The cost of owning a personal copy of the Qur'ān would be too prohibitive prior to the influx of wealth that flooded Medina after the conquests. While reports of scribes recording parts of the Qur'ān during the Prophet's lifetime abound, such reports never mention Ḥafṣah among the so-called "scribes of the revelation" (*kuttāb al-waḥy*). See Balādhurī, *Ansāb*, 1/2. 1280–1281 and Claude Gilliot, "Collecte ou mémorisation du Coran: Essai d'analyse d'un vocabulaire ambigu," in Rüdiger Lohlker (ed.), *Ḥadīṯstudien – Die Überlieferungen des Propheten im Gespräch: Festschrift für Prof. Dr. Tilman Nagel* (Hamburg: Verlag Dr. Kovač, 2009), 77–132.

only the post-conquest affluence of Medinans rendered feasible.[70] All of this would lead one to infer that the codex Ḥafṣah commissioned from the scribe ʿAmr b. Rāfiʿ must be different, therefore, from the codex she inherited from her father. But in truth, the relationship between the two codices—one serving as the template for ʿUthmān's collection (according to Zuhrī) and the other as a source for variant readings—is unclear in historical terms. Inasmuch as these traditions are the best evidence we have for the Prophet's wives acting in anything resembling an editorial role in the commitment of the Qur'ān to writing, we have included a translation of Ibn Abī Dāwūd al-Sijistānī's (d. 316/929) compilation thereof in an appendix to this essay.

As was the case with roles attributed to the codices owned by Ḥafṣah and ʿĀ'ishah during the establishment of the ʿUthmānic recension, the replication of the same story about the same verse with different names in this second case does little to inspire confidence in the probative value of the accounts. The codices that ʿĀ'ishah, Ḥafṣah, and Umm Salamah commissioned from their scribes are theoretically different artifacts, but they are functionally identical in *qirā'āt* literature. All three codices serve as a repository for possible Qur'ān variants—and usually the same variants at that. Although it is certainly plausible that the wives of the Prophet owned their own copies of the Qur'ān, this *a priori* plausibility quickly becomes a rather trifling matter once the accounts are read horizontally as varying stories that hit upon either a single theme or a multitude of salient ones.[71] What such a reading reveals is that, regardless of the antiquity of these reports or how widely they circulated, they are impossible to read as simple, matter-of-fact accounts.

Yet, the cause of gleaning historical insight into the Qur'ān's codicological history from such literary accounts is not entirely hopeless, nor is the application of the modern methods of historical criticism entirely a destructive enterprise. With the aid of a little philological spadework and a dash of paleographic insight, one can discern that the aforementioned accounts do reflect, however obliquely, a modicum of historical reality, even if the details the accounts offer are merely factitious. One can see this in the striking verisimilitude found in the account of Ḥafṣah's commissioning ʿAmr b. Rāfiʿ to copy a *muṣḥaf* for her. As first noted by Alfred-Louis de Prémare, Ibn Saʿd identifies Ḥafṣah's scribe (*kātib*) as a member of the Banū Lakhm, a tribe famous for converting to Christianity prior to the advent of Islam.[72]

70. On the high cost of producing our earliest extant *muṣḥafs*, see François Déroche, *Qur'āns of the Umayyads* (Leiden: Brill, 2014), 112.

71. Jeffery already noted this, albeit somewhat reluctantly, in *Materials*, 213, n. 1.

72. Ibn Saʿd, *Ṭabaqāt*, 5.299; de Prémare, *Les fondations*, 455. On the Christianization of the Lakhmids, especially in Ḥīrah, see now Adam Talib, "Topoi and Topography in the Histories of al-Ḥīra," in Philip Wood (ed.), *History and Identity in the Late Antique*

The origins of Ḥafṣah's scribe accords very much with the recent findings of Alain George that, "The manuscript evidence... shows that some of the earliest scribes [of the Qur'ān] had become acquainted with Christian scribal techniques... either by personal contact, or because some of them were (or had been) Christian."[73] Indeed, the importance of Christianized Arabs and their role as scribes is a trope present in Arabic historiography and even Syriac historical accounts of early Islamic society.[74]

In other words, while theses accounts may be laced with *topoi* and theological tropes, the verisimilitude in which they are clothed is, in many cases, 'historical,' broadly speaking. Historians would be well advised not to dismiss these stories as mere concoctions even if the historical truth of the event in all its details may not find vindication in the methods of modern historical and literary criticism. The picture such stories paint is not merely plausible in a general sense; these stories are historically informed by, and deeply ensconced in, the world the accounts depict.

The caveat is, of course, that these sorts of observations can only take modern historians so far, *pace* Khan's inadvisable speculations that Ḥafṣah might be the former editor of one of our earliest extant Qur'ān manuscripts (let alone its editor). Khan cites Behnam Sadeghi and Uwe Bergmann's radiocarbon dating of a single folio from the Ṣanʿāʾ 1 palimpsest to before

---

Near East (Oxford: Oxford University Press, 2013), 123–148 and Isabel Toral-Niehoff, *Al-Ḥīra: Eine arabische Kulturmetropole im spätantiken Kontext* (Leiden: Brill, 2014), 151–211.

73. Alain George, *The Rise of Islamic Calligraphy* (London: Saqi, 2010), 52–53, where he also cites traditions from *ḥadīth* literature in which several early Muslims—both *ṣaḥābīs* (Companions) and *tābiʿīs* (Followers)—commission copies of the Qur'ān to be transcribed by Christian scribes from Ḥīrah (cf. Ibn Abī Dāwūd, *Maṣāḥif*, 2.501–502). Strikingly, some of the earliest extant qur'ānic palimpsests were repurposed by Christians rather than Muslims. See idem, "Le palimpseste Lewis-Mingana de Cambridge, témoin ancien de l'histoire du Coran," *Comptes Rendus des Séances de l'Année* 1 (2011): 377–429. Early jurists like Muḥammad b. Ḥasan al-Shaybānī (d. 189/805), to cite one example, regarded the purchase and sale of a Qur'ān codex by Christians as permissible but problematic. See Shaybānī, *Al-Aṣl*, ed. Mehmet Boynukalın (Beirut: Dār Ibn Ḥazm, 2012), 2.514: "Were a Christian to purchase a *muṣḥaf*, I'd force him to sell it, for his purchase was valid; likewise, were he to sell it, his sale of the *muṣḥaf* would be valid (*idhā ishtarā al-naṣrānī muṣḥafan ajbartuhu ʿalā bayʿihi wa-kāna shirāʾuhu jāʾizan ʿalayhi wa-kadhālika law bāʿahu kāna bayʿuhu jāʾizan*).

74. Jones, "The Word Made Visible"; Barbara Roggema, "The Debate between Patriarch John and an Emir of the Mhaggrāyē: A Reconsideration of the Earliest Christian-Muslim Debate," in Martin Tamcke (ed.), *Christen und Muslime im Dialog: Christlich-muslimische Gespräche im muslimischen Orient des Mittelalters* (BTS 117; Beirut: Ergon, 2007), 21–39, 23–26; Michael P. Penn, "John and the Emir: A New Introduction, Edition and Translation," *Le Muséon* 121 (2008): 65–91, 78–80; Luke Yarbrough, "Upholding God's Rule: Early Muslim Juristic Opposition to the State Employment of Non-Muslims," *ILS* 19 (2012): 11–85.

669 CE with a 95% probability, and then she upbraids them for failing to hypothesize that Ḥafṣah's copy of the Qur'ān could be behind the text (210–211).[75] However, it is Sadeghi and Bergmann's circumspection against equating the lower text of the palimpsest with a specific Companion codex that is warranted, not Khan's groundless speculation about the survival of Ḥafṣah's codex.[76] Moreover, while indubitably an extraordinary and exciting find, Sadeghi and Bergmann's dating of this parchment does not settle the historiographical problems associated with resolving the tensions between *literary* traditions about the Qur'ān's compilation and transmission and the current analysis of its material remains. Even the discovery of a complete Qur'ān manuscript from ʿUthmān's caliphate—regardless of the revolutionary importance such a find would be in other respects—would not instantly dispel the intrinsic historiographical problems embedded in the multifarious, and oftentimes contradictory, literary accounts of the rationale and methods underlying the Qur'ān's compilation during his caliphate.

Appendix: Ibn Abī Dāwūd al-Sijistānī's Account of the Codices of the Prophet's Wives

Among the many merits of the *Kitāb al-Maṣāḥif* (*Book of Qur'ānic Codices*) of Ibn Abī Dāwūd al-Sijistānī (230-316/844-929) is that he arranges his lists of variant qur'ānic readings (*qirāʾāt*) according the codices in which they appear. Ibn Abī Dāwūd's compilation serves our purposes particularly well in that it not only lists all the variant readings attributed to the codices of the Prophet's wives, but that it also assigns each wife's codex its own section. As noted above, Ibn Abī Dāwūd includes three codices in his treatise: the *muṣḥaf* of ʿĀ'ishah, the *muṣḥaf* of Ḥafṣah, and the *muṣḥaf* of Umm Salamah. However, the distinction between the codices is actually rather superficial. The variant readings attributed to the wives' codices are quite homogenous. The traditions Ibn Abī Dāwūd compiled almost entirely focus on the codices' expanded reading of Q Baqarah 2:238—each codex of the Prophet's wives inserts mention of the afternoon prayer (*ṣalāt al-ʿaṣr*) to the verse. The wives' expanded reading of this verse is, notably, also the Qur'ān reading favored by the Shi'ah.[77]

75. Behnam Sadeghi and Uwe Bergmann, "The Codex of a Companion of the Prophet and the Qur'ān of the Prophet," *Arabica* 57 (2010): 348–353 *et passim*.

76. Ibid., 360.

77. See Etan Kohlberg and Mohammad Ali Amir-Moezzi, *Revelation and Falsification: The* Kitāb al-qirā'āt *of Aḥmad b. Muḥammad al-Sayyārī* (Leiden: Brill, 2009), 81–82.

Scholars working in the Western academy predominately know the *Kitāb al-Maṣāḥif* via the edition included in Arthur Jeffery's *Materials for the History of the Text of the Qur'ān* published by Brill in 1937. However, we have based our translation below not just on Jeffery's edition (marked AJ) but also the second printing of Muḥibb al-Dīn ʿAbd al-Sabḥān's edition of the *Maṣāḥif* published in two volumes by Dār al-Bashā'ir al-Islāmiyyah in 2002 (marked AS), as the Arabic text of this edition surpasses Jeffery's edition in his *Materials* in many respects.

[AJ 83/AS 1.365]

The Codex of ʿĀ'ishah, the Wife of the Prophet

ʿAbd Allāh related to us from ʿAbd Allāh b. Isḥāq al-Nāqid[78] and Abū ʿAbd al-Raḥmān al-Adhramī,[79] who said: Zayd[80] related to us: Ḥammād[81] reported to us on the authority of Hishām[82] on the authority of his father [ʿUrwah],[83] who said:

> Written in ʿĀ'ishah's copy of the Qur'ān (*muṣḥaf*) was: "Take care to observe the prayers, especially the middle prayer and the afternoon prayer" (*ḥāfiẓū ʿalā al-ṣalāt wa-ṣalāt al-wusṭā wa-ṣalāt al-ʿaṣr*).[84]

[AS 1.366]

ʿAbd Allāh related to us from Muḥammad b. Ismāʿīl al-Aḥmasī, from Jaʿfar b. ʿAwn [AJ 84], who said: Hishām[85] reported to us on the authority of Yazīd,[86] on the authority of Abū Yūnus, ʿĀ'ishah's slave-client (*mawlā*), who said:

> I wrote down (*katabtu*) a copy of the Qur'ān for ʿĀ'ishah, and she said, "When you come to *āyat al-ṣalāt* (Q Baqarah 2:238), do not write it down until I dictate it to you" (*ḥattā umliyahā ʿalayka*). She later dictated it to me as: "Take care to

78. ʿAbd Allāh b. Isḥāq al-Nāqid al-Wāsiṭī al-Baghdādī (d. after 200/815).

79. ʿAbd Allāh b. Muḥammad b. Isḥāq al-Jazarī al-Adhramī, a scholar of Mosul who flourished during the reign of al-Wāthiq (r. 227–232/842–847).

80. Yazīd b. Hārūn b. Zādhān al-Sulamī al-Wāsiṭī (d. 206/821).

81. Uncertain: either Ḥammād b. Zayd al-Baṣrī (d. 179/795) or Ḥammād b. Salamah al-Baṣrī (d. 167/783).

82. Hishām b. ʿUrwah b. al-Zubayr (d. 146/763).

83. ʿUrwah b. al-Zubayr (d. *ca.* 94/713), ʿĀ'ishah's nephew.

84. Cf. Q 2:283 where the standard reading omits "the afternoon prayer" (*ṣalāt al-ʿaṣr*).

85. Hishām b. Saʿd al-Madanī (d. 160/776–777).

86. Probably Yazīd b. Nuʿaym b. Hazzāl al-Ḥijāzī, but perhaps "Yazīd" is a corruption of "Zayd [b. Aslam]"; cf. Jamāl al-Dīn al-Mizzī, *Tahdhīb al-kamāl fī asmā' al-rijāl*, ed. Bashshār ʿAwwād Maʿrūf (Beirut: Mu'assasat al-Risālah, 1983–1992), 3.205.

observe the prayers, especially the middle prayer and the afternoon prayer" (*ḥāfiẓū ʿalā al-ṣalāt wa-ṣalāt al-wusṭā wa-ṣalāt al-ʿaṣr*).

ʿAbd Allāh related to us from Abū'l-Ṭāhir,[87] who said: Ibn Wahb[88] reported to us and said: Mālik[89] reported to us on the authority of Zayd b. Aslam,[90] on the authority of al-Qaʿqāʿ b. Ḥakīm, on the authority of Abū Yūnus, the slave-client of ʿĀ'ishah the Mother of the Faithful, who said:

> ʿĀ'ishah ordered me to write down a copy of the Qur'ān for her. Later she said, "When you reach this *āyah*—'Take care to observe the prayers, especially the middle prayer' (*ḥāfiẓū ʿalā al-ṣalāt wa-ṣalāt* [AS 367] *al-wusṭā*)—consult me (*fa-ādhinnī*)." So when I reached the *āyah*, I consulted her, and she dictated to me: "Take care to observe the prayers, especially the middle prayer and the afternoon prayer" (*ḥāfiẓū ʿalā al-ṣalāt wa-ṣalāt al-wusṭā wa-ṣalāt al-ʿaṣr*).
>
> Then she said, "I heard this from the Messenger of God."

[AS 1.368]

ʿAbd Allāh related to us from Muḥammad b. Maʿmar, from Abū ʿĀṣim,[91] on the authority of Ibn Jurayj,[92] who said: Ibn Abī Ḥamīd[93] reported to me and said: Ḥamīdah[94] reported to me and she said:

> ʿĀ'ishah bequeathed to us her possessions (*awṣat lanā... bi-matāʿihā*), and in her copy of the Qur'ān it read, "Take care to observe the prayers, especially the middle prayer and the afternoon prayer" (*ḥāfiẓū ʿalā al-ṣalāt wa-ṣalāt al-wusṭā wa-ṣalāt al-ʿaṣr*).

ʿAbd Allāh related to us, from Isḥāq b. Ibrāhīm b. Zayd, from Abū ʿĀṣim, who said: Ibn Jurayj reported to us and said: ʿAbd al-Malik b. ʿAbd al-Raḥmān reported to us from his mother, Umm Ḥamīd bt. ʿAbd al-Raḥmān, that she asked ʿĀ'ishah the Mother [AS 1.369] of the Faithful about the middle prayer (*al-ṣalāh al-wusṭā*), and she said:

> We used to read in the original (*fī'l-ḥarf al-awwal*): "Take care to observe the prayers, especially the middle prayer and the afternoon prayer and stand

87. Aḥmad b. ʿAmr b. ʿAbd Allāh b. ʿAmr b. al-Sarḥ al-Miṣrī (d. 255/869).
88. ʿAbd Allāh b. Wahb al-Miṣrī (d. 197/812).
89. Mālik b. Anas (d. 179/795).
90. Zayd b. Aslam al-ʿAdawī al-Madanī (d. 136/754).
91. Al-Ḍaḥḥāk b. Mukhlad b. al-Ḍaḥḥāk al-Shaybānī al-Baṣrī (d. *ca.* 112/731).
92. ʿAbd al-Malik b. ʿAbd al-ʿAzīz b. Jurayj al-Makkī (d. 150/767–768).
93. Muḥammad b. Abī Ḥamīd al-Anṣārī, a Medinan tradent of ill repute.
94. Ḥamīdah bt. Abī Yūnus, the daughter of ʿĀ'ishah's *mawlā* Abū Yūnus.

in devotion before God" (*ḥāfiẓū ʿalā al-ṣalāt wa-ṣalāt al-wusṭā wa-ṣalāt al-ʿaṣr wa-qūmū li'llāh qānitīn*).

ʿAbd Allāh related to us, from Ismāʿīl b. Asad: Ḥajjāj[95] told us that Ibn Jurayj said: ʿAbd al-Malik b. ʿAbd al-Raḥmān reported to me on the authority of his mother, Umm Ḥamīd bt. ʿAbd al-Raḥmān, that she asked ʿĀ'ishah what God Most High decreed concerning "the middle prayer" (*al-ṣalāh al-wusṭā*). She said:

> We used to read in the original during the era (*ʿahd*) of the Prophet: "Take care to observe the prayers, especially the middle prayer and the afternoon prayer and stand in devotion before God" (*ḥāfiẓū ʿalā al-ṣalāt wa-ṣalāt al-wusṭā wa-ṣalāt al-ʿaṣr wa-qūmū li'llāh qānitīn*).

[AS 1.370]

ʿAbd Allāh related to us from Aḥmad b. al-Ḥabbāb, from Makkī,[96] from ʿAbd Allāh b. Lahīʿah,[97] on the authority of Ibn Hubayrah,[98] on the authority of Qabīsah [AJ 85] b. Dhu'ayb,[99] who said:

> In ʿĀ'ishah's copy of the Qur'ān was: "Take care to observe the prayers, especially the middle prayer and the afternoon prayer" (*ḥāfiẓū ʿalā al-ṣalāt wa-ṣalāt al-wusṭā wa-ṣalāt al-ʿaṣr*).

So said Ibn Abī Dāwūd.

ʿAbd Allāh related to us: Muḥammad b. Maʿmar told us: Abū ʿĀṣim related to us on the authority of Ibn Jurayj, who said: Ibn Abī Ḥamīd reported to me and said: Ḥamīdah reported to me and she said:

> ʿĀ'ishah bequeathed to us her possessions, and in her copy of the Qur'ān read "God and his angels continually bless the Prophet and those attain the highest ranks" (*inna'llāha wa-malā'ikatahu yuṣallūna ʿalā al-nabiyyi wa'lladhīna yaṣilūna al-ṣufūf al-uwal*).[100]

95. Ḥajjāj b. Muḥammad al-Maṣīṣī al-Aʿwar (d. 206/821).
96. Makkī b. Ibrāhīm b. Bashīr al-Tamīmī al-Balkhī (d. 215/830).
97. ʿAbd Allāh b. Lahīʿah al-Miṣrī (d. 174/790–791).
98. ʿAbd Allāh b. Hubayrah b. Asʿad al-Sabaʾī al-Miṣrī (d. 126/743–744).
99. Qabīsah b. Dhu'ayb b. Ḥalḥalah al-Khuzāʿī al-Madanī (d. *ca.* 86–87/705–706).
100. Q Aḥzāb 33:56 in the *textus receptus* has only *inna allāha wa-malā'ikatahu yuṣallūna ʿalā al-nabī*.

[AS 1.371]

The Codex of Ḥafṣah, the Wife of the Prophet

ʿAbd Allāh related to us from Muḥammad b. Bashshār,[101] from Muḥammad,[102] from Shuʿbah,[103] from Abū Bishr,[104] from ʿAbd Allāh b. Yazīd al-Azdī (one of them said 'al-Awdī' according to Ibn Abī Dāwūd), from Sālim b. ʿAbd Allāh:

> Ḥafṣah ordered someone to write down a copy of the Qurʾān for her (*amarat insānan an yaktuba lahā muṣḥafan*), and she said, "When you read this *āyah*—'Take care to observe the prayers, especially the middle prayer' (*ḥāfiẓū ʿalā al-ṣalāt wa-ṣalāt al-wusṭā*)—consult me (*fa-ādhinnī*)." When he reached it, he consulted her, and she said, "Write: 'Take care to observe the prayers, especially the middle prayer and the afternoon prayer (*ḥāfiẓū ʿalā al-ṣalāt wa-ṣalāt al-wusṭā wa-ṣalāt al-ʿaṣr*).'"

ʿAbd Allāh related to us, from Muḥammad b. Bashshār—and we wrote it down from no one else—from Ḥajjāj b. Minhāl, from Ḥammād b. Salamah, from ʿUbayd Allāh,[105] from Nāfiʿ,[106] from Ibn ʿUmar, from Ḥafṣah that:

> Ḥafṣah told the scribe for her copy of the Qurʾān, "If you reach the appointed times (*mawāqīt*) for the prayer, let me know so that I can let you know what I heard the Messenger of God say." When he told her, she said, [AS 1.372] "Write: 'Take care to observe the prayers, especially the middle prayer and the afternoon prayer' (*ḥāfiẓū ʿalā al-ṣalāt wa-ṣalāt al-wusṭā wa-ṣalāt al-ʿaṣr*)."

ʿAbd Allāh related to us: My uncle[107] and Isḥāq b. Ibrāhīm said: Ḥajjāj related to us: ʿUbayd Allāh b. ʿUmar reported to us on the authority of Nāfiʿ, from Ḥafṣah a similar report, but he did not mention Ibn ʿUmar in it.

ʿAbd Allāh related to us from Muḥammad b. Bashshār, from ʿAbd al-Wahhāb,[108] from ʿUbayd Allāh, from Nāfiʿ:

> Ḥafṣah ordered a slave-client of hers to write down a copy of the Qurʾān for her. She said, "When you reach 'Take care to observe the prayers, especially the middle prayer, and stand in devotion before God' (*ḥāfiẓū ʿalā al-ṣalāt wa-ṣalāt*

101. Muḥammad b. Bashshār al-Baṣrī (d. 252/866).

102. Muḥammad b. Jaʿfar al-Hudhalī al-Baṣrī (d. 193/809).

103. Shuʿbah b. al-Ḥajjāj al-Baṣrī (d. 160/776).

104. Jaʿfar b. Iyās al-Wāsiṭī (d. *ca.* 123–126/740–744).

105. ʿUbayd Allāh b. ʿUmar b. Ḥafṣ b. ʿĀṣim b. ʿUmar b. al-Khaṭṭāb al-Madanī (d. *ca.* 144–145/761–763).

106. Nāfiʿ, the slave-client of ʿAbd Allāh b. ʿUmar (d. 117/735).

107. Muḥammad b. al-Ashʿath al-Kindī al-Kūfī (d. *ca.* 66–67/685–687).

108. ʿAbd al-Wahhāb b. ʿAbd al-Majīd b. al-Ṣalt al-Thaqafī al-Baṣrī (d. 194/809–810).

> *al-wusṭā wa-qūmū li'llāh qānitīn*), do not write it down until I dictate it to you the way I heard the Messenger of God read it (*yaqra'uhā*)." When he reached it, she commanded him, and he wrote the verse as, "Take care to observe the prayers, especially the middle prayer and the afternoon prayer and stand in devotion before God" (*ḥāfiẓū 'alā al-ṣalāt wa-ṣalāt al-wusṭā wa-ṣalāt al-'aṣr wa-qūmū li'llāh qānitīn*).

Nāfi' added, "I read this myself in the codex and found the two *wāws*."

'Abd Allāh related to us from Ismā'īl b. Isḥāq, from Ismā'īl,[109] who said: [AS 1.373] My brother[110] related to me on the authority of Sulaymān,[111] from 'Abd al-Raḥmān b. 'Abd Allāh, from Nāfi':

> 'Amr b. Rāfi' (or Ibn Nāfi'), the slave-client of 'Umar b. al-Khaṭṭāb, informed him that he wrote down a copy of the Qur'ān for Ḥafṣah bt. 'Umar and she said, "When you reach *āyat al-ṣalāt*, consult me and I'll dictate to you the way I heard from the Messenger of God." When I reached "Take care to observe the prayers" (*ḥāfiẓū 'alā al-ṣalāt*), she said: "especially the middle prayer and the afternoon prayer" (*wa-ṣalāt al-wusṭā wa-ṣalāt al-'aṣr*).

'Abd Allāh related to us from Muḥammad b. Yaḥyā al-Naysabūrī, from Khālid, from Muḥammad b. Isḥāq on the authority of Abū Ja'far and Nāfi' the slave-client of Ibn 'Umar, from 'Amr b. Nāfi' [sic], the slave-client of 'Umar b. al-Khaṭṭāb, who said:

> While the wives of the Prophet were alive I used to write down copies of the Qur'ān (*kuntu aktubu al-maṣāḥif fī 'ahd azwāj al-nabī*), and Ḥafṣah bt. 'Umar sought me out to write down a copy of the Qur'ān for her (*fa-istaktabatnī ḥafṣah bint 'umar muṣḥafan lahā*). She told me, "Listen boy, when you reach this *āyah*—'Take care to observe the prayers' (*ḥāfiẓū 'alā al-ṣalāt*)—do not write it down until you come to me so I can dictate it to you the way I memorized it from God's Messenger."
>
> When I reached the verse, I carried my sheet and writing utensils (*al-waraqah wa'l-dawāh*) to go see her, and she said: "Take care to observe the prayers, especially the middle prayer and the afternoon prayer and stand in devotion before God" (*ḥāfiẓū 'alā al-ṣalāt wa-ṣalāt al-wusṭā wa-ṣalāt al-'aṣr wa-qūmū li'llāh qānitīn*).

'Abd Allāh related to us from Abū'l-Ṭāhir who said: Ibn Wahb reported to us and said: Mālik reported to me on the authority of Zayd b. [AJ 87] Aslam, from 'Amr b. Nāfi' [sic], that he said:

---

109. Ismā'īl b. 'Abd Allāh b. 'Abd Allāh b. Abī Uways al-Madanī (d. 227/842).

110. 'Abd al-Ḥamīd b. 'Abd Allāh b. 'Abd Allāh b. Abī Uways al-Madanī (d. 202/817–818).

111. Sulaymān b. Bilāl al-Taymī al-Madanī (d. 172/788–789 or 177/793–794).

> I used to write down a copy of the Qur'ān (*kuntu aktubu muṣḥafan*) [AS 374] for Ḥafṣah, the Mother of the Faithful, and she said, "When you reach this *āyah*, consult me: 'Take care to observe the prayers, especially the middle prayer' (*ḥāfiẓū ʿalā al-ṣalāt wa-ṣalāt al-wusṭā*)." When I reached the *āyah*, I consulted her, and she dictated: "Take care to observe the prayers, especially the middle prayer and the afternoon prayer and stand in devotion before God" (*ḥāfiẓū ʿalā al-ṣalāt wa-ṣalāt al-wusṭā wa-ṣalāt al-ʿaṣr wa-qūmū li'llāh qānitīn*).

[AS 1.376]

ʿAbd Allāh related to us from Muḥammad b. ʿAbd al-Malik,[112] from Yazīd,[113] from Muḥammad b. ʿAmr,[114] on the authority of Abū Salamah[115] who said: ʿAmr b. Nāfiʿ [sic] the slave-client of ʿUmar b. al-Khaṭṭāb said:

> Written in the codex of Ḥafṣah, the Prophet's wife, is "Take care to observe the prayers, especially the middle prayer and the afternoon prayer" (*ḥāfiẓū ʿalā al-ṣalāt wa-ṣalāt al-wusṭā wa-ṣalāt al-ʿaṣr*).

ʿAbd Allāh related to us from Hārūn b. Sulaymān, from ʿUthmān b. ʿUmar, from Abū ʿĀmir al-Khazzāz,[116] from Ibn Abī Rāfiʿ, on the authority of his father, Ḥafṣah's slave-client, who said:

> Ḥafṣah sought me out to write down a copy of the Qur'ān, and she said, "When [AS 1.377] you come to this *āyah*, come here so I can dictate to you the way it was recited to me (*ka-mā uqrītūhā*)." So when I came to the *āyah*—"Take care to observe the prayers" (*ḥāfiẓū ʿalā al-ṣalāh*)—she said, "Write: 'Take care to observe the prayers, especially the middle prayer and the afternoon prayer' (*ḥāfiẓū ʿalā al-ṣalāt wa-ṣalāt al-wusṭā wa-ṣalāt al-ʿaṣr*)."
>
> Then I met Ubayy b. Kaʿb, or perhaps Zayd b. Thābit, and I said, "O Abū'l-Mundhir![117] Ḥafṣah said the *āyah* went such-and-such way (*qālat kadhā wa-kadhā*). Ubayy replied, "It's just as she said. For is it not the case that at the time of the noon prayer (*ṣalāt al-ẓuhr*) we are most busy with our work and our camels (*fī ʿamalinā wa-nawāḍiḥinā*)?"

The Codex of Umm Salamah

---

112. Muḥammad b. ʿAbd al-Malik b. Marwān al-Wāsiṭī (d. 266/879–880).

113. Yazīd b. Hārūn b. Zādhān al-Sulamī al-Wāsiṭī (d. 198/813 or later).

114. Muḥammad b. ʿAmr b. ʿAlqamah al-Laythī al-Madanī (d. *ca.* 144–145/761–763).

115. Abū Salamah b. ʿAbd al-Raḥmān b. ʿAwf al-Zuhrī al-Madanī (d. 94/712–713 or 104/722–723).

116. Ṣāliḥ b. Rustam al-Mazanī al-Baṣrī al-Khazzāz.

117. Abū'l-Mundhir Ubayy b. Kaʿb (d. 19/640 or later).

ʿAbd Allāh related to us from Abū'l-Ṭāhir,[118] from Ibn Nāfiʿ,[119] from Dāwūd b. Qays on the authority of ʿAbd Allāh b. Rāfiʿ, the slave-client of Umm Salamah, that she said to him:

> Write down for me [AS 1.378] a copy of the Qur'ān. When you reach this *āyah*, let me know: "Take care to observe the prayers, especially the middle prayer" (*ḥāfiẓū ʿalā al-ṣalāt wa-ṣalāt al-wusṭā*." When I reached "Take care to observe the prayers, especially the middle prayer" (*ḥāfiẓū ʿalā al-ṣalāt wa-ṣalāt al-wusṭā*), she said, "Write down: 'Take care to observe the prayers, especially the middle prayer and the afternoon prayer' (*ḥāfiẓū ʿalā al-ṣalāt wa-ṣalāt al-wusṭā wa-ṣalāt al-ʿaṣr*)."

ʿAbd Allāh related to us from Hārūn b. Isḥāq and ʿAlī b. Muḥammad b. Abī al-Khaṣīb, who said: Wakīʿ related to us on the authority of Dāwūd b. Qays, from ʿAbd Allāh b. Rāfiʿ, from Umm Salamah:

> She [?] wrote a copy of the Qur'ān (*annahā k-t-b-t muṣḥafan*), and when she [?] reached (*fa-lammā b-l-gh-t*)[120] "Take care to observe the prayers, especially the middle prayer" (*ḥāfiẓū ʿalā al-ṣalāt wa-ṣalāt al-wusṭā*), she said, "Write down: 'Take care to observe the prayers, especially the middle prayer and the afternoon prayer' (*ḥāfiẓū ʿalā al-ṣalāt wa-ṣalāt al-wusṭā wa-ṣalāt al-ʿaṣr*)."

ʿAbd Allāh related to us [AJ 89] from Muḥammad b. Ismāʿīl al-Aḥmasī, from ʿUbayd Allāh,[121] from Sufyān,[122] on the authority of Dāwūd b. Qays, from ʿAbd Allāh b. Rāfiʿ, who said:

> I wrote down a copy of the Qur'ān for Umm Salamah, and she dictated to me "Take care to observe the prayers, especially the middle prayer and the afternoon prayer" (*ḥāfiẓū ʿalā al-ṣalāt wa-ṣalāt al-wusṭā wa-ṣalāt al-ʿaṣr*).

[AS 1.379]

ʿAbd Allāh related to us from Isḥāq b. Ibrāhīm, from Saʿd b. al-Ṣalt, from ʿAmr b. Maymūn b. Mihrān al-Jazarī on the authority of his father, who said:

> Umm Salamah told a scribe writing down a copy of the Qur'ān for her, "When you write 'Take care to observe the prayers, especially the middle prayer'(*ḥāfiẓū ʿalā al-ṣalāt wa-ṣalāt al-wusṭā*), write down: 'the afternoon prayer' (*al-ʿaṣr*)."

---

118. Aḥmad b. ʿAmr b. al-Sarḥ al-Umawī al-Miṣrī (d. 250/864).

119. ʿAbd Allāh b. Nāfiʿ al-Ṣā'igh al-Madanī (d. 206/822).

120. *Sic.* The text seems to be corrupt here, as the second half of the report has the scribe, rather than Umm Salamah, writing the *muṣḥaf* as in the above report.

121. ʿUbayd Allāh b. Mūsā b. Bādhām al-ʿAbsī al-Kūfī (d. 213/828–829).

122. Either Sufyān al-Thawrī or Sufyān b. ʿUyaynah.

JIQSA 1 (2016): 127–147

"NOTHING BUT TIME DESTROYS US": THE DENIERS OF RESURRECTION IN THE QUR'ĀN

PATRICIA CRONE†

Edited by Michael E. Pregill

Abstract

In this posthumously published paper, Patricia Crone (d. 2015) examines a corpus of verses in the Qur'ān in which the *mushrikūn*, the supposedly pagan opponents of the qur'ānic prophet, are portrayed as objecting to the doctrine of the resurrection, one of the central tenets of the Qur'ān. In contrast to the traditional understanding of the *mushrikūn* as idolaters ignorant of monotheism, the evidence of the Qur'ān itself suggests that the *mushrikūn* were familiar with the concepts of judgment and resurrection but were either skeptical about them or denied them outright. The Qur'ān attributes statements to them that indicate that the resurrection was an ancestral doctrine they had come to reject, not a new teaching. Not only do the *mushrikūn* appear to have been directly familiar with monotheistic concepts, but the Qur'ān attributes statements to them that seem to reflect biblical phraseology. The author concludes that the most radical deniers may have represented a strain of eternalism or rationalism current in the late antique world in which the Qur'ān was revealed.

Editor's Introduction: Patricia Crone (1945–2015)

In the preface to the first volume of her *Collected Studies in Three Volumes* (published not long after her passing in July 2015), Patricia Crone makes a poignant remark about legacy and remembrance:

> Would you not like to be understood for what you were in your own time rather than what some will make of you? We live short lives, try to make our

doi: http://dx.doi.org/10.5913/jiqsa.1.2017.a007

> mark, hoping for some kind of afterlife in memories about us. We owe it to past people to try to understand them, just as we hope future people will respect us.[1]

There are few scholars today whose legacy is as assured as that of Patricia Crone. Her influence on the contemporary study of the Qur'ān and Islamic origins is practically unmatched among scholars of her generation, and she is guaranteed a place among the titans in the field. Her contribution to the study of early and classical Islamic tradition has likewise been monumental.

Although Professor Crone is talking about Muḥammad in the quotation above, it is difficult not to detect a subtext to her observation that we would all prefer to be remembered for what we actually were and did rather than for what others said we were and did, for she was extremely conscious of the degree and frequency with which her work had been misrepresented. Like her mentor John Wansbrough, she is still often subject to attacks by people who have not read her carefully—sometimes one wonders if they have read her at all—but who claim to be able to refute or correct her, or seek to persuade others that her ideas have no merit.

It has seemed quite appropriate to introduce this piece in such a fashion because the subject at hand is, of course, immortality. When initial planning for this journal began some years ago, I approached Professor Crone about contributing to the inaugural issue. During one of the sessions of the Qur'ān Seminar organized by Gabriel Said Reynolds and Mehdi Azaiez at Notre Dame during 2012–2013, we discussed a recurring theme in her work over the years, namely that of a third site of importance to the proto-Islamic community alluded to in the Qur'ān besides Mecca and Medina—that is, another city, presumably in northern Arabia, that might have been an arena for the unfolding of the critical events that shaped the early *ummah* alongside the two Hijazi locations celebrated and sanctified by later tradition. We talked about the possibility of her revisiting this subject, perhaps in the light of new developments in the study of political consolidation and the spread of Christianity in northern Arabia.[2] After Professor Crone's passing, I contacted her literary executor, Michael Cook, in the hopes that she had commenced working on this piece. Investigation yielded the discovery that she had not been able to undertake the project of which we had spoken, but that she had

1. Patricia Crone, *The Qur'ānic Pagans and Related Matters. Collected Studies in Three Volumes, Volume 1*, ed. Hanna Siurua (IHC 129; Leiden: Brill, 2016) (hereafter *CS1*), xii.

2. Greg Fisher, *Between Empires: Arabs, Romans, and Sasanians in Late Antiquity* (Oxford: Oxford University Press, 2011); Therese Hainthaler, *Christliche Araber vor dem Islam: Verbreitung und konfessionelle Zugehörigkeit. Eine Hinführung* (Leuven: Peeters, 2007); see also now Greg Fisher (ed.), *Arabs and Empires before Islam* (Oxford: Oxford University Press, 2015) and Isabel Toral-Niehoff, *Al-Ḥīra: Eine arabische Kulturmetropole im spätantiken Kontext* (Leiden: Brill, 2014).

earmarked a talk on a different subject she had given at Notre Dame in 2011 as a potential contribution instead.[3]

The present piece is the result. It treats a group of statements by the opponents of the qur'ānic prophet in which they express skepticism about the resurrection. It should be located in the context of a larger collection of studies by Professor Crone concerning the worldview of these supposedly pagan adversaries, a worldview that—contrary to the assertions of the mature Islamic tradition—can hardly be reduced to "paganism" at all. As she herself acknowledged, Professor Crone's research in this area was spurred by the groundbreaking study of G. R. Hawting, *The Idea of Idolatry and the Emergence of Islam*, in which Hawting argues that based on the evidence of the Qur'ān itself, one would not naturally conclude that the qur'ānic *mushrikūn* were polytheists, but rather, it seems, subscribed to some form of monotheism that the qur'ānic prophet deemed insufficient or incomplete.[4] Professor Crone subsequently devoted a number of articles to the systematic attempt to discern the actual contours of the religious outlook of these "pagans."

Professor Crone discusses the subject of the denial of the resurrection by the *mushrikūn* at greater length in a two-part article published in the *Bulletin of the School of Oriental and African Studies* in 2012–2013.[5] There is significant overlap between the present piece and that article, but the material is approached from a somewhat different direction here. In particular, Professor Crone's focus in the present piece is on the interpretation of the qur'ānic statements about time, death, and future punishment attributed to the Prophet's opponents. Thus, despite the overlap with the *BSOAS* article, the treatment of the subject in its present form has particular value for those interested in the Qur'ān, and so has seemed entirely suitable for inclusion here in the inaugural issue of *JIQSA*.

In the aforementioned preface to volume 1 of her *Collected Studies*, Professor Crone is disarmingly candid about her scholarly engagement with the Qur'ān. She notes that after the publication of *Hagarism*, coauthored with Michael Cook—a work that earned both of them a seemingly unshakeable reputation as radical revisionists—she did not address the subject of the

3. The original talk, entitled "Who Were the Deniers of the Resurrection in the Qur'an?," was delivered on October 6, 2011 at the Medieval Institute at the University of Notre Dame. Professor Crone's contributions to the Qur'ān Seminar project are included in Mehdi Azaiez et al. (eds.), *The Qur'an Seminar Commentary: A Collaborative Study of 50 Qur'anic Passages* (Berlin: De Gruyter, 2016).

4. G. R. Hawting, *The Idea of Idolatry and the Emergence of Islam* (Cambridge: Cambridge University Press, 1999).

5. Patricia Crone, "The Quranic *Mushrikūn* and the Resurrection (Part I)," *BSOAS* 75 (2012): 445–472 (= *CS1*, 125–158); eadem, "The Quranic *Mushrikūn* and the Resurrection (Part II)," *BSOAS* 76 (2013): 1–20 (= *CS1*, 159–182).

Qur'ān or Islamic origins again for almost twenty years, being primarily interested in the intervening period in researching and writing about the history of Islam *per se* rather than the foundations of the tradition.[6] A handful of articles about the Qur'ān and related matters in the 1990s led to a much more prolonged engagement with the subject during the final two decades of Professor Crone's life; the majority of her relevant articles on the topic date to 2004–2016, a period during which she also continued a robust publication program on other topics, including two massively important monographs, *God's Rule* (2004) and *The Nativist Prophets of Early Islamic Iran* (2012).[7]

Professor Crone's pattern of publication during these years is important to note because the articles pertaining to the Qur'ān that she published in this period have now been brought together into the first volume of her *Collected Studies*. Taken as a whole, these groundbreaking articles constitute the equivalent of an indisputably important and deeply challenging monograph in Qur'ānic Studies, focusing on the Qur'ān's place in its late antique milieu and rigorously pursuing the method of allowing the Qur'ān to speak for itself, at least to the extent to which this is possible. The "chapters" of this potential monograph, as significant as any other publication in the field over the last ten years (and surely more significant than most of them), treat issues that have now become central again in the study of the Qur'ān after a prolonged period of neglect: the society and culture in which the Qur'ān was revealed, at least insofar as they may be discerned through their impact on the statements of the scripture itself; the development of the qur'ānic prophet's message to his opponents and the community he sought to reform or overthrow; and Arabian society's relationship to the larger late antique world, particularly the appropriation and adaptation of earlier textual traditions in the Qur'ān's message.

Taken collectively, the message of this collection of articles is loud and clear: not just the Qur'ān itself, but the culture of those who opposed its prophet was deeply imbricated in the larger late antique world, particularly the Jewish, Christian, and biblical traditions, and to see this properly, we must rely on the evidence of the Qur'ān itself and not on later Islamic representations of where the Qur'ān and its prophet came from. Thus, in the piece at hand—a concise rehearsal of Professor Crone's most important insights on the subject—we see that the religiosity implied by the statements the Qur'ān attributes to the *mushrikūn* indicates that these people came from a culture in which monotheistic ideas had significant traction. Not only were

---

6. Crone, *CS1,* xiii–xiv.

7. Patricia Crone, *God's Rule: Government and Islam* (New York: Columbia University Press, 2004); eadem, *The Nativist Prophets of Early Islamic Iran: Rural Revolt and Local Zoroastrianism* (Cambridge: Cambridge University Press, 2012).

the *mushrikūn* familiar with 'Judeo-Christian' ideas, but they appear to have lapsed and *rejected* them, so that we may align their perspective with a larger phenomenon of radical skepticism that was characteristic of the late antique age.

As recovered from her files, the original draft of the paper presented here was supplied with only the barest footnotes. I have added others to supply citations that have seemed indispensable, generally drawn from the longer piece Professor Crone published in *BSOAS* (or, in one instance, from another published article); these have been clearly marked to distinguish them from those she actually provided in the original text. A few of those citations have been altered slightly for the benefit of the reader, and two of her quotations of primary sources expanded slightly for the sake of clarity.

The editors of *JIQSA* must extend special thanks to Michael Cook, Sabine Schmidtke, and especially Hanna Siurua, editor of Professor Crone's *Collected Studies*, for their invaluable assistance. Those of us who were lucky enough to study with her or otherwise receive her advice and tutelage know well that her critiques of students, like her critiques of sources, were blunt and unsentimental, sometimes difficult to hear, but judicious, fair, and indisputably beneficial. We offer our condolences to those students, as well as to Professor Crone's family and friends; they surely need no reminder of her gracious personality and inimitable style of teaching, but we hope nevertheless that this presentation of a small, final part of her work serves as fitting testimony to her scholarly legacy, granting her an immortality that no one could ever deny.

***

Introduction

One of the main problems in studying the rise of Islam is that we know so little about the context. Our key source is the Qur'ān, but we have no literature from northern Arabia to relate it to, except for poetry that was collected later, and which rarely helps. Most scholars react by going to the exegetical works; there you get lots of information about both the Messenger, Muḥammad, and his opponents, but it does not always inspire trust. The early exegetes commented on each verse as an independent unit regardless of its qur'ānic context, which allowed them to fit each verse into a historical context that they themselves supplied. A generation ago you more or less had to follow the exegetical tradition, but then Muslims themselves began to reject this approach because they wanted to reinterpret the Qur'ān; now Islamicists are also interpreting the Qur'ān in the light of the Qur'ān itself, using the exegetical literature as secondary literature rather than as an authoritative source.

Yet we still need a context to which to relate the Qur'ān, and it is clear that we have to look for it outside Arabia, in the religious debates of the Near East. It would of course have been better if we had evidence for those debates in Arabia itself, but we do not, and there is enough overlap between what is going on in the world outside and in the Qur'ān for the external material to help.

The question that interests me is this: what kind of religious milieu was it that the Prophet broke away from? Who are the people he calls *mushrikūn*, 'polytheists' or 'pagans,' in the Qur'ān? Formerly, people thought they knew the answer, for the historical tradition, including the exegetes, tells us that the *mushrikūn* were idolaters who worshipped stones and images. However, in 1999 Gerald Hawting showed that this is not actually the picture you get from the Qur'ān.[8] Time and again it is clear that the so-called 'pagans' believed in God, and what is more, the *same* God as the Messenger himself, that is, the God of the biblical tradition. The Messenger calls them polytheists because they *also* believed in lesser beings, who are sometimes called angels and sometimes gods, who functioned more or less like saints in later Islam and Christianity: that is, you hoped they would intercede for you and help you. They were intermediaries.

Some of these intermediaries were, like some saints, female. Those named in the Qur'ān were pagan deities known from Arabian archaeology and epigraphy, such as the goddesses al-Lāt, Manāt, and al-ʿUzzā. Pagan deities were often reduced to angels in Late Antiquity. In a famous Greek inscription of the third century, Apollo speaks of himself and other Greek gods as "angels," and as small parts of God.[9] The old Near Eastern deities Nirig, Sin, Shamash, Bel, and Nanai appear as "holy angels" on an Aramaic magic bowl in Sasanian Iraq; the old deity Baalshamin turned into the angel Balsamos in Manichaeism.[10] Apparently, something similar was taking place in Arabia.

8. [Hawting, *The Idea of Idolatry and the Emergence of Islam*; see my comments above concerning Professor Crone's remarks about this work elsewhere. –MP]

9. A third-century inscription from Oenoanda in Lycia proclaims: "Born of itself, untaught, without a mother, unshakable, not contained in a name, known by many names, dwelling in fire, this is God. We, his angels, are a small part of God" (Stephen Mitchell, "The Cult of Theos Hypsistos between Pagans, Jews, and Christians," in Polymnia Athanassiadi and Michael Frede (eds.), *Pagan Monotheism in Late Antiquity* (Oxford: Oxford University Press, 1999), 81–148, 86).

10. [James Alan Montgomery, *Aramaic Incantation Texts from Nippur* (Philadelphia: University Museum, 1913), no. 36; *Cologne Mani Codex*, line 49, in Iain Gardner and Samuel N. C. Lieu (eds.), *Manichaean Texts from the Roman Empire* (Cambridge: Cambridge University Press, 2004), 54. These citations have been supplied from Patricia Crone,

So the *mushrikūn* were monotheists who operated with mediator figures, which were at least sometimes pagan deities by origin, and this outraged the Messenger. But apart from this, there is hardly anything pagan in the Qur'ān, and not a lot of disagreement between the Messenger and the so-called 'pagans' either. There are only three big points of disagreement between them: (1) the mediators, or "partners" (*shurakā'*), as the Messenger calls them; (2) the Day of Judgment and the resurrection; and (3) the Messenger's own prophetic status. That is all; agreement is presumed on all the rest. The Messenger and his opponents came from the same people, and apparently they had all grown up as monotheists, but not as *true* monotheists, as the Messenger eventually decides. What I want to do here is to look at those who denied the resurrection.

Believers, Doubters, and Deniers

As everyone knows, the Messenger of the Qur'ān was a doomsday prophet. People had to repent, for it would not be long before the Day of Judgment would come, and all sinners would go to Hell. This is the message of the *sūrahs* classified as Meccan, on which the present paper focuses. In one passage in Sūrat al-Ma'ārij the Messenger says:

> Someone has asked about the punishment to come. The unbelievers (*kāfirūn*) cannot avert it. ...They see it as far away (*ba'īd*), and We see it as close (*qarīb*). (Q Ma'ārij 70:1–2, 6–7)

So some unbelievers in Mecca *believed* in the Day of Judgment, they just did not think it would come anytime soon. But there were also unbelievers who had their doubts. For example, we hear about a rich man who

> went into his garden... and said, "I do not think that this will ever perish, nor do I think that the Hour is coming. But *if* I am brought back to my Lord, I shall surely find [there] something better in exchange." (Q Kahf 18:35–36)

This man sounds like an eternalist: he thought the world would last forever. Yet he was also willing to consider the alternative, and assumed that he would do fine under those circumstances too. He was not worried about the Day of Judgment, even as someone who believed in it. That was the trouble with a lot of the unbelievers in Mecca.

"The Religion of the Qur'ānic Pagans: God and the Lesser Deities," *Arabica* 57 (2010): 151–200, 186 (= *CS1*, 86), n. 73–74. –MP]

However, we often hear of people who express doubt about the Day of Judgment:

> When we are dust, shall we [return] in a new creation (*khalq jadīd*)? (Q Ra'd 13:5; similarly Isrā' 17:49, 98; Sabā' 34:7)
>
> When we die and become dust and bones, shall we be raised up again, and also our forefathers (*ābā'unā al-awwalūn*)? (Q Ṣāffāt 37:16–17)
>
> When we die and become dust and bones, shall be we judged? (Q 37:53)

And so on; there are many more examples. God retorts:

> Does man think that We cannot assemble his bones? (Q Qiyāmah 75:3)
>
> If you have doubts about the resurrection (*al-ba'th*), [remember that] We created you from dust... (Q Ḥajj 22:5)

You cannot always be sure whether the opponents doubt or actually deny the resurrection, but some are certainly described as categorically denying it:

> They deny the Hour... (Q Furqān 25:11)
>
> The unbelievers say, 'The hour will never come to us.' (Q Sabā' 34:3)

Sometimes they deny not only the resurrection but the afterlife altogether:

> There is nothing but our life down here; we will not be resurrected. (Q An'ām 6:29)

The leading people of a past nation, "who did not believe and who denied the meeting in the hereafter," said the same:

> There is nothing but our life down here. We die and we live, but we will not be resurrected. (Q Mu'minūn 23:37)

In the same vein, the Messenger's contemporaries said:

> There is nothing apart from our present life. We die and we live, and nothing but time destroys us (*mā yuhlikunā illā al-dahr*). (Q Jāthiyah 45:24)

So three positions are described in the Qur'ān: belief in the resurrection, skepticism about it, and outright denial of it. Those who denied the resurrection seem always to have denied the afterlife altogether—at least we never hear from them of any other form of the afterlife.

I want to zoom in on these hardline deniers. Who were they? They were certainly what the Qur'ān calls polytheists (*mushrikūn*), for in Sūrat al-Najm we find that

> those who do not believe in the hereafter (*lā yu'minūna bi'l-ākhirati*) name the angels by female names... (Q Najm 53:27)

—the angels in this *sūrah* being al-Lāt, al-'Uzzā, and Manāt.[11] Yet it is as believers in God that the polytheists deny the resurrection:

> They swear their strongest oath by God that God will never resurrect those who die. (Q Naḥl 16:38)

They sound rather like the fifteenth-century Diego de Barrionuevo:

> I swear to God that Hell and Paradise are nothing more than a way of frightening us, like people saying to children, "the bogeyman will get you."[12]

Ancient Fables

If the Messenger's opponents were biblical monotheists, then one would expect them to have grown up believing in the resurrection, like this Diego. In fact, some of them still believed in the resurrection and others merely doubted it. But even those who denied it outright speak of it as a stupid old doctrine, not as a new claim introduced by the Messenger:

> What, when we have become dust, we and our fathers, shall we be raised from the dead? We and our fathers were promised/threatened (*wu'idnā*) this before; it is nothing but fables of the ancients (*asāṭīr al-awwalīn*). (Q Naml 27:67–68)[13]

The unbelievers could, of course, be saying that their forefathers knew the doctrine of the resurrection as something that *others* believed in, but to which they had never subscribed themselves; however, in a review of the reasons that they might have for rejecting the Messenger, God Himself asks:

11. [As specified previously in vss.19–20 of Sūrat al-Najm. –MP]

12. John Edwards, "Religious Faith and Doubt in Late Medieval Spain: Soria *circa* 1450–1500," *Past and Present* 120 (1988): 3–25, 25.

13. [In "Quranic *Mushrikūn*," Professor Crone notes the attempts by both classical exegetes and modern scholars to discern what these "fables" could have been; see "Quranic *Mushrikūn* (I)," 455 (= *CS1*, 136), n. 21. –MP]

> Have they not pondered the words (*al-qawl*), or has anything come to them which did *not* come to their ancient fathers? (Q 23:68)

God's point is clearly that nothing the Messenger is saying departs from their own ancestral doctrines. Further evidence for this view appears in the following vignette:

> The one who says to his parents, "Ugh, are you promising (or threatening, *taʿidāninī*) me that I will be resurrected (lit. got out, *ukhraja*) even though generations have passed away before me?" And they [the parents] ask for God's help [saying to the son], "Woe to you, believe! God's promise/threat (*waʿd*) is true!" But he says, "It is nothing but fables of the ancients." (Q Aḥqāf 46:17)

What is so striking about this passage is that it is the parents who play the role of believers and the son who is cast as an arrogant denier of the resurrection. If the Messenger had introduced the doctrine of the resurrection to pagans who had been holding out against it, it should obviously have been the older generation that typified denial of this doctrine, while the son should have stood for the younger generation who were willing to break with their parents for the sake of the truth. Instead, the parents are believers while the son dismisses the doctrine as old nonsense. Thus the denial of the resurrection is here described as a new doctrine that was leading the young astray.

There is another passage that starts by telling us that the unbelievers dismiss the resurrection as ancient fables (Q 23:82–83) and continues by asking a series of questions designed to bring out the absurdity of the unbelievers' position:

> Say, "To whom belongs the earth and all in it, if you know?" They will say, "To God!" Say, "Why won't you let yourselves be admonished?" (Q 23:84–85)

And again:

> Say: "Who is lord of the seven heavens, and the lord of the mighty throne?" They will say, "[They are] God's!" ...Say: "In whose hand is the dominion (*malakūt*) over all things... ?" They will say, "God's!" Say: "How can you then be so deluded?" (Q 23:86–89)

The Messenger cannot understand how the unbelievers can think of God as the lord of the universe and yet deny the resurrection. However, here you have a passage showing that the opponents came from the same biblical tradition as he did: they think in terms of seven heavens and of God's having a throne, and they know the term *malakūt*.

The "First Death"

Now I want to adduce some more specific evidence. On one occasion the hardliners say,

> There is nothing apart from our first death—we will not be resurrected. (Q Dukhān 44:35)

Why not say there is nothing apart from our first *life*? Later in the same *sūrah*, the Messenger says of the people in Paradise:

> They will not taste death there, except the first death. (Q 44:56)

The first death here is the death they have already experienced.[14] So what is the *second* death? This expression is not actually used in the Qur'ān, and for this reason the exegetes had trouble with it. However, it does appear in the Jewish targums, the Talmud, the Apocalypse of John, Syriac texts, a Greek work preserved only in Ethiopic, and Manichaean literature. In this literature, the "second death" stands for eternal damnation.[15] What the unbelievers are saying when they insist that there is only one death is that they will not go to Hell, because there is no such thing: they will not be resurrected.

This is confirmed by another qur'ānic passage in which the unbelievers condemned to Hell tell God that they now realize that

> twice you have made us die (*amattanā*) and twice you have made us live (*aḥyaytanā*). (Q Ghāfir 40:11)

Again, the second death here is clearly the eternal damnation that the unbelievers are now suffering. In line with this, a story set in the future depicts people in Paradise chatting and passing the cup around. One man tells of how he had a friend who did not believe in the resurrection. He now saw the friend suffering in Hell for his denial and praises God for having himself escaped this fate. The Messenger then asks,

---

14. Zamakhsharī has an abstruse explanation involving the idea that we were dead before we were born, so that when we die it is for the second time. But this is disproved by the passage in which the Messenger himself says that people of Paradise will not taste death, except the first death. The reference must be to the death that they have already died, as Zamakhsharī himself accepts. In other words, our death down here is the first death, not the second. [Cf. "Quranic *Mushrikūn* (I)," 457–458 (= *CS1,* 139–140), citing Zamakhsharī, *Kashshāf ad* Q 44:35. –MP.]

15. [For detailed discussion and citation of these varied sources, see "Quranic *Mushrikūn* (I)," 458–461 (= *CS1,* 140–143). –MP]

> So will we [really] not die more than our first death and will we [really] not be punished? (Q 37:58–59)

The hapless friend is suffering the second death in Hell that the unbelievers denied.

It is almost always the unbelievers who speak of the first death, or have their own words turned against them. The Messenger uses the expression only once, in Q 44:56 (cited above); in other passages, he says of the one who enters the Fire *not* that he is dying a second death but, on the contrary, that he will never die there (Q Fāṭir 35:36) or that "he will neither die there nor live" (Q Aʿlā 87:13). So the idea of eternal damnation as the second death seems to have come more naturally to the unbelievers than it did to the Messenger. One may infer that they had all learned the expression as part of the religious vocabulary of the community in which they grew up. The *mushrikūn* are denying the resurrection and eternal damnation in the language in which these doctrines had been taught to them. It is the Messenger who is breaking away from this community and developing new imagery to express his own view of them.

"We Die and We Live"

In two of the qurʾānic passages we have already seen, the unbelievers say,

> *We die and we live*, but we will not be resurrected. (Q 23:37)
>
> *We die and we live*. Nothing but time destroys us. (Q 45:24)

Why do they use that word order? The exegetes explain that the unbelievers meant that "we die but our children live on" or "some of us die but others live." However, the Messenger uses the same word order himself:

> [The unbelievers] have adopted gods who do not create, who can do nothing and who have no power over *death, life, or the resurrection*. (Q 25:3)[16]

We have seen it also in the verse in which the unbelievers in Hell say,

> Twice You have made us die (*amattanā*) and twice You have made us live (*aḥyaytanā*). (Q 40:11)

We seem to be dealing with a fixed expression. This is what it seems to reflect:

16. The exegetes do not say anything about the word order here.

> I, even I, am He; there is no god besides me. I kill/make dead (*āmît*) and I make alive (*ăḥayeh*)... (Deut 32:39)

Another passage echoes God's speech in Deuteronomy:

> The Lord kills (*mēmît*) and brings to life (*məḥayeh*)... (1 Samuel 2:6)

In 2 Kings 5:7, an Israelite king asks:

> Am I God to kill and to make alive (*ləhāmît ûlhaḥăyôt*)?

I don't know why God used this word order in His first book, but it came in handy when Jewish exegetes began to look for proof of the resurrection in their scripture. It now seemed self-evident to them that when God said, "I kill and I make alive," He was talking about death and resurrection. Jews who denied the resurrection said no—that it meant that God killed one person and gave life to another. The rabbis responded by adducing the next part of Deuteronomy 32:39, "I wound and I heal," which proved to them that God was talking about one and the same person: just as God healed whomever He had wounded, so He would resurrect those whom He had killed. At least, that is what Raba, a Babylonian rabbi who died in 322, argued.[17]

The commentators on the Qur'ān may well be right when they take the *mushrikūn* to be saying that "some of us die and some of us live," or "we die and our children live on," but you need the Hebrew Bible passage to see why they expressed themselves like that. The Qur'ān uses the same word order in refutation of the polytheists on two occasions, as we have seen, but elsewhere God says of Himself:

> Say: it is God who gives life and kills/makes dead (*yuḥyī wa-yumītu*). (Q 44:8)
>
> It is We who give life and We who bring death. (Q Ḥijr 15:23)
>
> It is He who gives life and death. (Q Ḥadīd 57:2)

He is correcting the inversion. Like the expression "the first death," the inverted word order shows the polytheists to be closer to the biblical or parabiblical literature than the Messenger was. It is the *mushrikūn* who deny the inverted word order derived from the community, because that was the

---

17. Yifat Monnickendam, "'I Bring Death and Give Life, I Wound and Heal' (Deut. 32:39): Two Versions of the Polemic on the Resurrection of the Dead," *Hen* 35 (2013): 90–118 (Hebrew original published in *Tarbiz* 76 (2007): 329–352). My thanks to Menahem Kister for drawing my attention to this study and to Dr. Monnickendam for allowing to me read the English version before publication.

formulation in which the doctrine was defended in communities in which the Pentateuch, or books derived from it, were authoritative. For his part, the Messenger is correcting the word order because he no longer feels bound by their scripture.

The concept of damnation as the second death was common among Jews and Christians, as well as Mandaeans and Manichaeans, but the allusion to Deuteronomy 32:39 points in a Jewish direction. It was the Jews who had to find their prooftexts for the resurrection in the Pentateuch. Still, there were some Christians who used it as well. The Pseudo-Clementine *Homilies*, probably composed in Antioch or Edessa around 300–320, used it.[18] More strikingly, so does Aphrahat, a Christian from the Sasanian side of the border who died around 345. He tells us that it is right for us to fear the second death, and that terrible suffering awaits the wicked who do not believe in the resurrection, concluding (after diverse other points) that the living mouth testifies, "I kill and I make alive." He also adduces other pentateuchal passages used by the rabbis concerning the second death.[19] The Pseudo-Clementines are Jewish Christian, and Aphrahat represents a Christianity that is both close to the traditions of the rabbis and deeply hostile to Judaism, probably because the local Jewish and Christian communities were not fully distinct in his time. In short, the religious environment in which the *mushrikūn* and the Messenger had grown up seems to belong somewhere on the spectrum between Judaism and a Christianity close to its Jewish roots.

I have to remind you that you should not envisage the qur'ānic environment as some place in the desert full of bedouin. The Qur'ān indicates that we are in an agricultural community within the olive-growing zone, with a fair degree of literacy. You also hear a lot about religious disputation, and the disputations seem to have been of the formal kind popular all over the Near East. So it was quite a developed environment.

In line with this, the so-called 'pagans' come across as a varied lot. There were at least three different kinds of them. The first were what you might call traditional believers, who saw God as the creator and ruler of everything, venerated the lesser beings as intercessors, and believed in the resurrection as

18. *The Clementine Homilies* 20.3 (*ANF* 8.82).

19. [In "Quranic *Mushrikūn* (I)" Professor Crone cites Aphrahat in the Latin edition of Parisot and the English translation of Valavanolickal; here I substitute references to the more recent and widely available translation of Adam Lehto instead: *The Demonstrations of Aphrahat, the Persian Sage* (Gorgias Eastern Christian Studies 27; Piscataway, NJ: Gorgias, 2010). For Aphrahat's discussion of the second death, see *Demonstrations* 8.19–25 (trans. Lehto, 232–236), and cf. 7.25 (trans. Lehto, 215–216). For his citation of Deut 32:39, see 8.10, 25; 22.3 (trans. Lehto, 226, 236, 461); for Deut 33:6, see 22.1–3 (trans. Lehto, 460–462). Professor Crone acknowledges Joseph Witztum for drawing her attention to Aphrahat's use of Deut 32:39. –MP]

well as in messengers. Their error, from the Messenger's point of view, lay in their veneration of the lesser beings, their lack of anxiety about the Day of Judgment, and their rejection of him. The second lot are really a subgroup of the first. They also believed in God as the creator and governor of all things (see Q 23:82–89), and they too venerated lesser beings, but they had lost faith in the resurrection: some doubted it, others denied it outright. You can call them the traditional deniers.

The third lot are the radicals, and there are only a few passages on them, so they are unlikely to have been numerous. The only certain passage about them is the one in which the unbelievers say, "We die and we live, and nothing but time destroys us." In other words, God does not bring death or life, as He claims in Deuteronomy and as the unbelievers deny by using the Deuteronomic word order. They cannot have seen Him as the creator, ruler, or judge of the universe either. Then there is the rich man who went into his garden saying, "I do not think that this will ever perish." Maybe he was just speaking hyperbolically, but, as I said, he sounds like an eternalist, someone who believes that the universe has no beginning or end, and so no creator, ruler, or judge either. This third lot use a strikingly reductionist formulation, and you have that elsewhere too: "nothing but time destroys us"; "there is nothing but our life down here"; the resurrection is "nothing but fables of the ancients." Reductionism is characteristic of positivists, who hold reason to rule out claims based on revelation. Did they believe in God or the lesser beings? I would assume not, but there is no way of proving it.

I do wish to mention, though, that you also meet people who sound like positivists in Medinan *sūrahs* as well. They pretend to believe in God and the Last Day, but they don't, and when they are told to, they say, "Shall we believe as the fools believe?" (Q Baqarah 2:13). The Messenger angrily responds that *they* are the fools, perhaps with reference to Psalms 14:1, "The fool says in his heart: there is no God." We also hear of People of the Book, and specifically Jews, who do not believe in God and the Last Day in the Medinan *sūrahs*, but this material is extremely complicated, so I leave it aside to go outside Arabia.[20]

Deniers of Resurrection outside Arabia

There is plenty of evidence outside Arabia of people who denied the resurrection and/or the afterlife altogether, usually in a rationalist vein. You find them among Zoroastrians, Christians, and Jews alike.[21]

20. [Professor Crone discusses the Medinan material briefly in "Quranic *Mushrikūn* (I)," 471–472 (= *CS1*, 157–158). –MP]

21. [This section represents only a brief rehearsal of the main points of the

On the Zoroastrian side, the attestations start to appear in the third century, when the priest Kerdīr put up three big inscriptions proclaiming that he had been on a heavenly journey and seen Paradise and Hell with his own eyes:

> He who sees this text
> May he not be incredulous of the things beyond
> for he should hold it to be certain that there is a Paradise,
> there is a Hell, and the one who does good will go to Paradise,
> the one who sins will be cast into hell.[22]

There were clearly people who had doubted or denied this. In fact, there are surprisingly many references to disbelief in the afterlife and in God or the gods in Zoroastrian literature, several of them dating to the sixth century.[23]

On the Jewish side, there is nothing unusual about denial of the afterlife, at least not if you go sufficiently far back in time.[24] There is a fair amount of evidence relating to the period from around 200 to 400, but let me go straight to 553. In that year, Justinian (r. 527–565) issued a famous novella in which he took it upon himself to legislate about the language to be used in the synagogue service and in which he added the following warning on a completely different subject:

> And if there are some people among them who shall attempt to introduce ungodly nonsense, denying either the resurrection or the last judgement or that the angels exist as God's work and creation, we want these people expelled from all places, and that no word of blasphemy of this kind and absolutely no erring from that knowledge of God shall be spoken. We impose the harshest punishments on those attempting to utter such nonsense, completely purifying in this way the nation of the Hebrews from the error introduced into it.[25]

---

second part of Professor Crone's *BSOAS* article on this topic, "Quranic *Mushrikūn* (II)," 1–20 (= *CS1,* 159–182). –MP]

22. [Cited in "Quranic *Mushrikūn* (II)," 4 (= *CS1,* 162), n. 11: trans. D. N. Mackenzie in Georgina Herrmann, *The Sasanian Rock Reliefs at Naqsh-i Rustam: Naqsh-i Rustam 6, The Triumph of Shapur I* (Iranische Denkmäler 13, Reihe 2, Iranische Felsrelief I; Berlin: D. Reimer, 1989), 61; Philippe Gignoux (ed. and trans.), *Les Quatres inscriptions du mage Kirdīr* (Cahiers de Studia Iranica 9; Leuven: Peeters, 1991), 99. –MP]

23. [Professor Crone relates these in more detail in "Quranic *Mushrikūn* (II)," 4–5 (= *CS1,* 162–164). –MP]

24. [The most famous example is that of the Sadducees, whom Professor Crone discusses briefly in "Quranic *Mushrikūn* (II)," 7 (= *CS1,* 166). –MP.]

25. [Originally cited in abbreviated form, and here given in full as cited in "Quranic *Mushrikūn* (II)," 7–8 (= *CS1,* 166–167): Novella 146 (*Peri Hebraiōn*), cap. 2, in Amnon Linder (ed. and trans.), *The Jews in Roman Imperial Legislation* (Detroit: Wayne

Here there are two heresies addressed: denial of the resurrection and the Last Judgment, and denial that the angels exist as God's creation. Whether the first heresy amounts to a denial of the afterlife altogether one cannot tell. The second heresy was not to the effect that the angels did not exist at all, but rather that they were uncreated. Apparently, they were regarded as divine. This is nothing if not intriguing: it is exactly the same concatenation of heresies that we meet in the Qur'ān. It is hard to believe that there is no connection.

On the Greco-Roman side, there was also nothing unusual about denial of life after death back in the days when the empire was pagan, but you hear much about such denial after the victory of Christianity as well. Gregory of Nyssa (d. after 394) composed a dialogue in which he takes the role of the doubter who suspects that the soul dies with the body. He explains to his sister that scripture orders one to believe in the immortality of the soul, so one does so "by a kind of interior slavery, rather than assenting to the argument by a voluntary impulse."[26] The problem is this:

> [T]he body, being composite, must be dissolved into those elements from which it is composed. When the combination of the elements in the body is broken up, each element is likely to be drawn to its own kind. The very nature of the elements returns each to its own kind by some inevitable attraction... So where will the soul be after this? Anyone who says that it is in the elements will have to admit that it is identical with them. ...It cannot be in the elements if its nature is different, and there is no other place in the universe where the soul could be...[27]

That everything was composed of four elements (earth, air, fire, water) or four elementary qualities (hot, cold, wet, dry) was the axiom on which all late antique science was based. But if that was true of the soul, it could not survive as an independent entity, and how could the soul be an exception? Gregory's sister groans that he is arguing like the Stoics and Epicureans. She does not deny that the universe is made of four elements; she just thinks there are also things that you can only see with the mind. People who deny that even go so far as to eliminate the very divinity that maintains the universe, she says. But whoever says that "there is no God" is a fool: she explicitly quotes Psalms 14:1. Gregory agrees, and so she manages to convince him.

State University Press and Jerusalem: Israel Academy of Sciences and Humanities, 1987), 409. –MP.]

26. St Gregory of Nyssa, *On the Soul and the Resurrection*, trans. Catharine P. Roth (Crestwood, NY: St Vladimir's Seminary Press, 1993), 29.

27. Ibid., 30–31. [The passage from Gregory of Nyssa is cited in a slightly different way in "Quranic *Mushrikūn* (II)," 11–12 (= *CS1*, 171–172). –MP]

The doubter here is envisaged as an educated Christian who continues to think in the empirical terms associated with non-Platonic philosophy: all beliefs must ultimately be grounded in sense perception. If you take that view, there are only two arguments in favor of God: one is the fact that all humans seem to have the idea, and the other is that the universe is so well ordered that there must be a mind behind it. You could also respond, however, that God is not a separate being up there; rather, He permeates the world and is in everything—this was the Stoic position. You could also argue that chance can account for the order—this was the Epicurean position. But the idea of the world as the outcome of chance struck most people as implausible until the discovery of natural evolution, so the standard argument for God's existence was that from design: just look around you and see how ingeniously everything is organized. It is a very old argument, and it is constantly used in the Qur'ān in proof of God's power and the resurrection.

We meet deniers of providence again in Nemesius of Emesa, who wrote around the year 390, and then once more in the work of Theodoret of Cyrrhus, who died around 460 and who wrote a book against such people. They too denied the afterlife. Theodoret tells them,

> Now the [pagan] Greeks... were directed by nature alone and were convinced of the truth of these things. ...Their poets and philosophers alike believed and taught that the wicked would be punished and the just rewarded in a future life. ...Perhaps you, too, persuaded by nature, instructed by these truths... will join your voice to theirs and agree that these things are so.[28]

They seem to have been Christians, nominally at least, but you had to base your arguments on nature and the ancient Greeks to persuade them.

Around the year 500, we have the famous story of the Seven Sleepers of Ephesus, written to convince people of the reality of the resurrection. It became enormously popular, and the Qur'ān also has it.[29] The attestations of the narrative continue after the Arab conquests: around 700 there were Syrians who wished to know,

> How is it clear that the soul does not die when one does? Some people think so.

The author, Pseudo-Athanasios, himself retorts,

---

28. [Theodoret, *On Providence* 9.24: *Theodoret of Cyrus, On Divine Providence*, trans. Thomas P. Halton (Ancient Christian Writings 49; Mahwah, NJ: Paulist Press, 1988), 126–127. Professor Crone deviates slightly from the Halton translation in citing it here, as it preserves a textual error; see the parallel citation in "Quranic *Mushrikūn* (II)," 13 (= *CS1*, 173–174), n. 66 for clarification. –MP]

29. [This is the narrative of the *aṣḥāb al-kahf*; see Q Kahf 18:7–26. –MP]

> Some foolish people think that the human being does not differ from animals in anything. The death of a human being is just like that of an animal, since [humans] don't have an immortal soul. For, it is said, humans and animals have the same death once their blood has been spilt.[30]

In Iraq, on the former Sasanian side, John of Phenek tells us around 690 that the demons are responsible for a number of errors. Some of them have persuaded men

> that there is no God at all, and others that there is a God but that He is not providential. ... They have persuaded others to call the mute elements "God."[31]

We hear much more about such people from the Muslims, who tell us about them under the label of "Dahris."[32]

The Dahris were nominal Muslims who came in endless varieties. Some just denied creation from nothing, while others denied the creation altogether. The most radical of them were eternalists who denied that the world had a creator, ruler, or judge, or that there were any angels, spirits, prophets, or revealed books. They were empiricists who accepted evidence only in the form of sense impressions, above all personal observation, and a limited amount of reasoning. They were also materialists who held everything to be composed of four elementary qualities (*tabāʾiʿ*), which were combined and recombined forever. Some held there to be a fifth principle, spirit, which permeates and regulates everything, in the Stoic style. Most of them were doctors, astrologers, and others studying natural phenomena, and they are often called "physicists" or "naturalists" (*aṣḥāb al-ṭabāʾiʿ*). All denied that

30. [Cited in "Quranic *Mushrikūn* (II)," 15 (= *CS1,* 176), n. 73: Ps.-Athanasios, "Quaestiones ad ducem Antiochum," *MPG* 28, 608, 681 (questions 17, 134); cf. Gilbert Dagron, "L'Ombre d'un doute: l'hagiographie en question, VIe–XIe siècle," *Dumbarton Oaks Papers* 46 (1992): 59–68, 62ff. Professor Crone here acknowledges Yannis Papadoyannakis as the source for these references. –MP]

31. [Cited in "Quranic *Mushrikūn* (II)," 15 (= *CS1,* 176), n. 75: John of Phenek, *Book of the Main Points of the History of the Temporal World*, MS Mingana Syr. 179, *memrā* 9. Professor Crone here acknowledges Richard Payne as the source for this reference. –MP]

32. [Or *dahriyyah*, discussed in greater detail in "Quranic *Mushrikūn* (II)," 15–19 (= *CS1,* 176–181). In the address presented as the author's preface to the third volume of her *Collected Studies,* Professor Crone poignantly notes that, but for lack of time, she would have devoted a book to the Dahris, "Godless people on whom I have written some articles" ("Remarks on Receipt of the 2014 Middle East Medievalists (MEM) Lifetime Achievement Award," *Al-ʿUṣūr al-Wusṭā* 23 (2015): iii–vi, vi; reprinted in *Islam, the Ancient Near East and Varieties of Godlessness. Collected Studies in Three Volumes, Volume 3,* ed. Hanna Siurua (IHC 131; Leiden: Brill, 2016), xi–xv, xv). –MP]

there was any form of afterlife. When the body died, the entire human being, including what others called the soul, reverted to the elementary qualities of which it was composed. Their views can be followed down to the sixth/twelfth century, and to some extent beyond.

The reason they were called Dahris is undoubtedly that the Muslims identified them with the qur'ānic unbelievers who said that nothing but time (*al-dahr*) would destroy them. From the tenth century onwards, this is made explicit. Al-Shahrastānī (d. 548/1153), for example, mentions that some Arab pagans said:

> There is nothing but our life down here, we die and we live.

Then he explains:

> They are referring to the elementary qualities (*al-ṭabāʾiʿ*) which are perceptible in this lower world: they are reducing life and death to the composition and dissolution of these qualities. That which brings them together is nature (*al-ṭabʿ*), and that which destroys them is time: "Nothing but time destroys us..."[33]

Fakhr al-Dīn al-Rāzī (d. 606/1209) says much the same, adding that they held the movement of the heavenly sphere to act on the elementary qualities, sometimes resulting in life and sometimes in death, so that there was no need to postulate a maker who makes the choice.[34]

Shahrastānī and his like did not have any independent evidence for such beliefs in pre-Islamic Arabia. They simply inferred from the Qur'ān that they must have existed there.[35] We do not have any independent evidence for the existence of such beliefs in Arabia either, but we do at least know that they existed outside of Arabia at the time of the revelation of the Qur'ān. On this basis I would say that their inference is right: the deniers of the resurrection in the Qur'ān belong to a wider trend in the Near East of trying to get away

33. [Cited in "Quranic *Mushrikūn* (II)," 17 (= *CS1,* 178), n. 79: Abū ʿĪsā al-Warrāq in Qāḍī ʿAbd al-Jabbār, *Al-Mughnī,* vol. 5 (ed. M. M. al-Khuḍayrī; Cairo: Wizārat al-Thaqāfah wa'l-Irshād al-Qawmī, 1965), 156. –MP]

34. [Cited in "Quranic *Mushrikūn* (II)," 19 (= *CS1,* 181), n. 92: Fakhr al-Dīn al-Rāzī, *Tafsīr ad* Q 45:24. –MP]

35. [In "Quranic *Mushrikūn* (II)" Professor Crone elaborates at greater length on the points raised here at the end of the conclusion to this paper. There, she notes that the clear implication is that some of the exegetes in fact read the qur'ānic passages discussed here in such a way that they were able to recognize that the *mushrikūn* were not pagans but rather monotheists. That is, the tradition does at times preserve an authentic, or at least non-doctrinaire, conception of the worldview of the *mushrikūn.* –MP]

from a cosmology and morality based on revelation. All have their intellectual roots in pagan systems of thought, and the deniers of the Qur'ān may still be 'pagans' in the sense that they have not formally converted to either Judaism or Christianity. But it is still some Jewish or Christian system that they are trying to get out of.

JIQSA 1 (2016): 149–172

BUKHĀRĪ'S *KITĀB TAFSĪR AL-QUR'ĀN*

CHRISTOPHER MELCHERT

Abstract

The celebrated *Ṣaḥīḥ* of al-Bukhārī (d. 256/870) includes a long book of qur'ānic commentary. It is unusual in the *Ṣaḥīḥ* as a whole in relying heavily on reports from Companions: 72 percent of all the unique reports given full *isnāds* in the book, as opposed to only about 9 percent of all reports in the whole *Ṣaḥīḥ*. It is also unusual in the density of comment from later authorities (without *isnāds*) and in the number of comments from Bukhārī himself. Bukhārī accepts without demur that the Qur'ān includes loan words. In comparison with other commentaries on the Qur'ān such as those of ʿAbd al-Razzāq before him and al-Ṭabarī and Ibn Abī Ḥātim after, Bukhārī's evidently plays down disagreement over the interpretation of words, legal applications, and textual variants. In comparison with the commentaries of al-Tirmidhī and al-Nasā'ī, Bukhārī's includes very many comments from philologists. Bukhārī's commentary is valuable for making out the larger history of Qur'ān commentary inasmuch as it testifies to the development of genre expectations in the mid-ninth century CE. It shows that the synthesis of *ḥadīth* and *adab* approaches was already under way, as well as other developments previously remarked in commentaries of the tenth and eleventh centuries.

The celebrated *Ṣaḥīḥ* (full title: *Al-Jāmiʿ al-musnad al-ṣaḥīḥ al-mukhtaṣar*, meaning roughly "the comprehensive, fully supported, sound epitome") of Abū ʿAbd Allāh Muḥammad b. Ismāʿīl al-Bukhārī (d. 256/870) is divided into ninety-seven chapters, of which the second largest is *kitāb tafsīr al-Qur'ān* ("the book of qur'ānic commentary"). It constitutes about 7 percent of the whole work. Marston Speight has a useful discussion of it in a 1988 article, recently revisited by Aisha Geissinger, but I should like to go further by way of measuring the extent of Bukhārī's reliance on Companions and other later authorities in comparison with his reliance on the Prophet; otherwise comparing this book with the rest of the *Ṣaḥīḥ*; and comparing this book with other notable collections of *ḥadīth*.[1] It confirms Bukhārī's unusual attention

1. R. Marston Speight, "The Function of *ḥadīth* as Commentary on the Qur'ān, as Seen in the Six Authoritative Collections," in Andrew Rippin (ed.), *Approaches to the*

doi: http://dx.doi.org/10.5913/jiqsa.1.2017.a008

to *adab* (belles-lettres), more pronounced than ever in this book. It seems a valuable witness to the state of qur'ānic commentary in the mid-ninth century CE, a time from which we have few others.

Verses and Comments

As for sizes, Ibn Ḥajar's (Shihāb al-Dīn Abū'l-Faḍl Aḥmad b. ʿAlī al-ʿAsqalānī, d. 852/1449) estimates in the introduction to his commentary on Bukhārī's *Ṣaḥīḥ* may be cited to indicate orders of magnitude: it comprises 7,275 *ḥadīth* reports with full *isnād*, 2,602 excluding repeats (i.e., multiple appearances of the same reports with variant *isnād*s and small changes of wording under different headings), with a further 1,341 mentioned with incomplete *isnād*s for the purpose of corroboration (*taʿālīq*).[2] By the standard numbering, *kitāb tafsīr al-Qurʾān* comprises 503 *ḥadīth* reports, which means that it constitutes about 7 percent of the whole collection and is longer than all but one other book (*kitāb al-maghāzī*) of the *Ṣaḥīḥ*. By contrast, Muslim's *Ṣaḥīḥ*, for example, includes 11,000 to 12,000 *ḥadīth* reports (about half of them repeats), but its *kitāb al-tafsīr* at the end is a much more modest collection of about forty *ḥadīth* reports.[3]

On the other hand, there is a substantially higher proportion of repeated *ḥadīth* reports in Bukhārī's *kitāb al-tafsīr* than in the *Ṣaḥīḥ* as a whole. Marston

---

History of the Interpretation of the Qurʾān (Oxford: Clarendon, 1988), 63–81, 73–75; Aisha Geissinger, *Gender and Muslim Constructions of Exegetical Authority* (IHC 117; Leiden: Brill, 2015), Chapter 4. Bukhārī's *kitāb al-tafsīr* is also remarked by Walid Saleh, "Preliminary Remarks on the Historiography of *tafsīr* in Arabic," *JQS* 12 (2010): 6–40, 26–27.

2. Ibn Ḥajar al-ʿAsqalānī, *Hady al-sārī*, ed. ʿAbd al-ʿAzīz b. ʿAbd Allāh Bin Bāz (Beirut: Dār al-Fikr, 1428–1429 [2008]), 562. The *Hady* is Ibn Ḥajar's introduction to his commentary on the *Ṣaḥīḥ*, *Fatḥ al-bārī*, normally published as its first volume. To my knowledge, this particular edition is as textually adequate as others and easily available commercially. However, I do not propose it as a standard edition to be preferred, except that it numbers sections and *ḥadīth* reports after that of Muḥammad Fu'ād ʿAbd al-Bāqī for Muḥibb al-Dīn al-Khaṭīb's edition of Ibn Ḥajar's commentary, the numbering of which I do endorse as the standard: *Fatḥ al-bārī: Sharḥ Ṣaḥīḥ al-Bukhārī*, ed. Muḥibb al-Dīn al-Khaṭīb (14 vols.; Cairo: al-Maṭbaʿah al-Salafiyyah, 1380 [1960]). One example of repetition: Bukhārī, *Ṣaḥīḥ*, *al-tafsīr* 2, *ad* Q 2:198, no. 4519 appears earlier with an overlapping *isnād* and similar but not identical wording at *al-ḥajj* 150, *bāb al-tijārah ayyām al-mawsim*, no. 1770. The restriction of *ḥadīth* to what is traced back to the Prophet, *athar* to reports of later Muslims, was established well after Bukhārī's time and has not influenced my usage here.

3. Saleh's observation, "In the compilations of ḥadīth, the sections on prophetic qur'ānic interpretation are rather short," applies to some compilations but not others. Walid A. Saleh, *The Formation of the Classical* Tafsīr *Tradition: The Qurʾān Commentary of al-Thaʿlabī (d. 427/1035)* (TSQ 1; Leiden: Brill, 2004), 192.

Speight has counted sequential repetitions: "it contains 457 *ḥadīth*, not counting repetitions within the same chapter, having to do with different versions of the same report."[4] But the overwhelming majority of reports in *kitāb al-tafsīr* are repeated in other books. By my count, *kitāb al-tafsīr* includes just sixty-eight unique *ḥadīth* reports, excluding all repeats. This means that it constitutes somewhat less than 3 percent of unique *ḥadīth* reports in the whole collection. It seems to be a special concern of Bukhārī's to show that Qur'ān and *ḥadīth* are complementary, the latter normally explaining the former. He quotes the Qur'ān in about a quarter of all his topic headings, far more than any other major *ḥadīth* collector.[5] Repeating *ḥadīth* reports that mention the Qur'ān in a long book of *tafsīr* is then another way to stress that complementarity.

Bukhārī's style is to go systematically through the Qur'ān in the canonical order from start to finish. Unlike other ninth-century *ḥadīth* collectors, and much more often than in other books of the *Ṣaḥīḥ*, Bukhārī usually begins sections of *kitāb al-tafsīr* with comments. These are most often glosses of obscure words and phrases, taken from various commentators, normally without any *isnād*, and occasionally with an incomplete one. For example, he begins the section on Q Maryam 19 with four comments from the Companion ('Abd Allāh) Ibn 'Abbās (d. 68/687–688), starting with an expansion of verse 38 ("*abṣir bihim wa-asmi'*, God says, whereas today they do not hear or see"); one from (Sufyān) Ibn 'Uyaynah (d. Mecca, 198/814) glossing an obscure expression in verse 83 (*ta'uzzuhum azzan*); one from Mujāhid (b. Jabr; d. Mecca, 104/722–723?) glossing an obscure word in verse 89 (*iddan*); then eight more apparently attributed to Ibn 'Abbās again (although Ibn Ḥajar's commentary identifies one of them rather as coming from the Basran grammarian Abū 'Ubaydah [d. 208/823–824?]); then one last gloss from Mujāhid.[6] For twenty-

4. Speight, "Function," 73. For example, Bukhārī, *Ṣaḥīḥ*, *al-tafsīr* 2, *ad* Q 2:223, nos. 4526–4527 are reports < Ibn 'Umar with overlapping *isnāds*, on which see more below.

5. Christopher Melchert, "Bukhārī and His *Ṣaḥīḥ*," *Le Muséon* 123 (2010): 425–454, 448. Cf. Scott C. Lucas, "The Legal Principles of Muḥammad ibn Ismā'īl al-Bukhārī and Their Relationship to Classical Salafi Islam," *ILS* 13 (2006): 289–324, esp. 299.

6. Ibn Ḥajar, *Fatḥ*, 9.272. Q 19:38 actually begins *asmi' bihim wa-abṣir*. Ibn 'Abbās' reversal, presumably the result of quoting by memory, was evidently remarked by Bukhārī, who mentions the correct order before going on to the next gloss. As an example of the textual weakness of the Bin Bāz edition, I observe that the final gloss from Mujāhid is mentioned only in the commentary, not in the text of Bukhārī's *Ṣaḥīḥ* given on the previous page. In the Sulṭāni edition of 1311–1313/1893–1895, the closest we have to a standard text of the *Ṣaḥīḥ*, Mujāhid's gloss appears in a marginal note (repr. Liechtenstein: Thesaurus Islamicus Foundation, 2001, 6.93). Bukhārī's involvement with philologists of the generation before him is treated at length in M. Fuat Sezgin, *Buhârî'nin kaynakları* (Ankara Üniversitesi İlâhiyat Fakültesi yayınlarından

nine chapters, he offers only comments without *isnād* (23, 29, 35, 51, 57, 58, 64, 67, 73, 76, 81, 82, 85–90, 94, 97, 100–107, and 109).

For most chapters, Bukhārī goes on to relate *ḥadīth* with *isnād* from the Prophet or Companions relevant to the chapter in question, usually to some particular verse. Sometimes, comments follow *ḥadīth*. (Occasionally, the order depends on which recension of the *Ṣaḥīḥ* is being followed, e.g., for Sūrat Hūd, where only the recension of Abū Dharr has comments all at the beginning.[7]) Although he usually offers Companion comments without *isnād*, he also includes notably many Companion comments with *isnād* in *kitāb al-tafsīr*—about 72 percent of all the unique reports in this book (and over a third of all reports in it with *isnād*), as opposed to about 9 percent of all the reports in the whole *Ṣaḥīḥ*. On Q Tawbah 9:40, "When the two of them were in the cave and he said to his companion, 'Do not grieve. God is with us,'" he hangs explanations from Ibn ʿAbbās of why he did not actively support his relative Ibn al-Zubayr in the Second Civil War, namely that Ibn al-Zubayr never actively sought his support.[8] He occasionally quotes illustrative poetry, for example to explain *ḥāmīm* as an apparent battle cry at the beginning of Sūrat Ghāfir. The Kufan jurist Sufyān al-Thawrī (d. 161/777–778?) is quoted as saying that he found no verse of the Qurʾān harder on him than Q Māʾidah 5:68, "you have no base until you observe the Torah and the Gospel and what has been sent down to you."[9]

I have counted 299 comments expressly attributed (but excluding *ḥadīth* with full *isnād*). These are dominated by Mujāhid and Ibn ʿAbbās, each responsible for 103 (34 percent). The Basrans al-Ḥasan (d. 110/728) and Qatādah b. Diʿāmah (d. 117/735–736?) and the Kufans Sufyān b. ʿUyaynah and Saʿīd b. Jubayr (d. 95/713–714?) are the next most prominent, with ten, eight, nine, and six quotations, respectively. On the other hand, of Abū

13; Istanbul: Ibrahim Horoz Basimevi, 1956), 124–163. Anonymous comments (i.e., Bukhārī's own) are collected in appendices at 321–368 (in *kitāb al-tafsīr*) and 369–379 (in other books of the *Ṣaḥīḥ*). Chapter names will be given as in printed Qurʾāns today, but Bukhārī's usage is often very different; e.g., Q 19 is 'Sūrat *khyʿṣ*' (of uncertain pronunciation).

7. Ibn Ḥajar, *Fatḥ*, 9.195, *ad* Q 11. For recensions of the *Ṣaḥīḥ*, see Johann Fück, "Beiträge zur Überlieferungsgeschichte von Buḫārī's Traditionssammlung," *ZDMG* 92 (1938): 60–87, now also available as "On the Transmission of Bukhārī's Collection of Traditions," trans. Gwendolyn Goldbloom, in Claude Gilliot (ed.), *Education and Learning in the Early Islamic World* (FCIW 43; Farnham: Ashgate, 2012), 245–270.

8. Cf. Claude Gilliot, "ʿAbdallāh ibn ʿAbbās," *EI*[3], s.v. on reports of the quarrels of Ibn ʿAbbās and Ibn al-Zubayr. All translations of the Qurʾān here are from Alan Jones (trans.), *The Qurʾān* (Exeter: Gibb Memorial Trust, 2007).

9. Bukhārī, *Ṣaḥīḥ*, *kitāb al-tafsīr*, introductory glosses *ad* Q 5; also at *al-riqāq* 19, *bāb al-rajāʾ maʿa al-khawf*, before no. 6469.

Ẓabyān (d. 90/708–709), al-Ḍaḥḥāk (d. 106/724–725?), and Muḥammad b. Abī Muḥammad (recently enumerated by Harald Motzki as "the earliest authorities of qur'ānic exegesis which seem to be historically tangible" besides Mujāhid), only al-Ḍaḥḥāk appears.[10] Two recensions identify a comment on Sūrat al-Ṣaff as coming from "Yaḥyā." Ibn Ḥajar's commentary indicates that the source is Yaḥyā b. Ziyād al-Farrā', the famous Kufan grammarian (Baghdad, d. 207/823–824), in particular his book *Ma'ānī al-Qur'ān*.[11] Ibn Ḥajar indicates that a substantial number of purely anonymous comments are also from him, even more from Abū 'Ubaydah.[12] I am not sure why Bukhārī was reluctant to name them. Certainly, they were fairly recent authorities—older contemporaries of Bukhārī himself.

It was usual to rely more heavily on later authorities when it came to the Qur'ān (as opposed to the law), less heavily on the Prophet and his Companions. Bukhārī himself relies more heavily on Companions and Followers in his chapter on the Qur'ān than in the *Ṣaḥīḥ* as a whole. At the same time, it cannot be said that Bukhārī consistently avoids citing more recent authorities. His section on Sūrat al-Ḥajj begins with a gloss from Ibn 'Uyaynah: *mukhbitīn* means *muṭma'innīn*. According to Ibn Ḥajar's commentary, a *tafsīr* attributed directly to Ibn 'Uyaynah and the *Tafsīr* of (Muḥammad) Ibn al-Mundhir (d. 318/930?) relate this gloss < Ibn 'Uyaynah < Ibn Abī Najīḥ < Mujāhid. At least we can generalize that Bukhārī's standard of accuracy in his *ta'līqāt* (comments and quotations without full *isnād*) is lower than for fully supported quotations, just as the tradition has recognized.

A prominent feature of the qur'ānic commentary tradition is multiple alternative interpretations of obscure words. An example is *ill* in Q Tawbah 9:8 ("They will not observe any *ill* or *dhimmah* with you"). 'Alī b. Muḥammad al-Māwardī (d. 450/1058) is typical:

10. Harald Motzki, *Analysing Muslim Traditions* (IHC 78; Leiden: Brill, 2010), 271. "Muḥammad b. Abī Muḥammad" is an obscure reference. Bukhārī mentions two such men in his *Al-Tārīkh al-kabīr*, but it seems doubtful whether either is the one Motzki has in mind. See Bukhārī, *Kitāb al-Tārīkh al-kabīr* (2nd ed.; 4 vols. in 8; Hyderabad: Maṭba'at Jam'iyyat Dā'irat al-Ma'ārif al-'Uthmāniyyah, 1377/1958; repr. 8 vols. with index; Beirut: Dār al-Kutub al-'Ilmiyyah, 1986), 1.225–256.

11. Ibn Ḥajar, *Fatḥ*, 9.485, confirmed by al-Farrā', *Ma'ānī al-Qur'ān*, ed. Muḥammad 'Alī al-Najjār et al. (3 vols.; Cairo: Maṭba'at Dār al-Kutub al-Miṣriyyah, 1955–1972), 3.153. On Farrā', see Fuat Sezgin, *Geschichte des arabischen Schrifttums* [*GAS*] (9 vols.; Leiden: Brill, 1967–1984), 8.123–125, 9.131–134; also Muḥammad b. Aḥmad 'Abd Allāh Shams al-Dīn al-Dhahabī, *Tārīkh al-islām*, ed. 'Umar 'Abd al-Salām Tadmurī (52 vols.; Beirut: Dār al-Kitāb al-'Arabī, 1987–2000), 14.293–295, with further references.

12. On Abū 'Ubaydah, see Sezgin, *GAS*, 8.67–71, 9.65–66, also Dhahabī, *Tārīkh*, 14.397–400, with further references.

Concerning *ill* there are seven interpretations.
One is that it means a pact (*ʿahd*), this being the position of Ibn Zayd.
The second is that it is a name of God, as Mujāhid said…
The third is that it is an alliance (*ḥilf*), this being the position of Qatādah.
The fourth is that *ill* is an oath while *dhimmah* is a guarantee. Abū ʿUbaydah said this…
The fifth is that it means permission (*jawāz*), as al-Ḥasan said.
The sixth is that it is relatedness (*qarābah*), as said by Ibn ʿAbbās and al-Suddī…
The seventh is that it means a pact, a contract, a covenant, and an oath, whereas *dhimmah* is where one is considered blameworthy who has no pact, as a certain Basran said.[13]

By contrast, Bukhārī says only, "*Ill* means relatedness."[14]

Bukhārī seems unafraid of foreign words in the Qurʾān. Concerning Q Hūd 11:75 ("Abraham was prudent, tender-hearted and penitent"), he quotes the Kufan Follower Abū Maysarah (d. 63/682–683?), "*Awwāh* means merciful in Ethiopic." Concerning Q Yūsuf 12:31 ("She invited them and prepared for them a couch"), he quotes Mujāhid, "*Muttakaʾ* means a citrus fruit (*utrujj*) in Ethiopic," taking it that Potiphar's wife prepared for them fruit (which they were peeling when they cut themselves) rather than places to lean. Concerning the mysterious letters at the beginning of Sūrat Ṭāhā 20, he quotes Saʿīd b. Jubayr, "In Nabataean, *ṭāhā* is 'O man.'" Concerning Q Nūr 24:35 ("His light is like a niche in which there is a lamp"), he quotes another Kufan Follower, Saʿd b. ʿIyāḍ al-Thumālī, "*Mishkāh* is an aperture (*kuwwah*) in Ethiopic." He quotes Mujāhid apropos of Q Najm 52, "*Ṭūr* means mountain in Syriac." But there is obviously no special preference for identifying foreign origins. For example, *sijill* (from Latin by way of Byzantine Greek *sigíllon*) is simply glossed as *ṣaḥīfah* ("scroll") at Q Anbiyāʾ 21:104 ("The day We roll up the heavens as a recorder rolls up records").[15] Presumably, Bukhārī accepted that Arabic included loan words.

13. Abūʾl-Ḥasan ʿAlī b. Muḥammad b. Ḥabīb al-Māwardī, *Al-Nukat waʾl-ʿuyūn: Tafsīr al-Māwardī*, *ad* Q 9:8; ed. Sayyid b. ʿAbd al-Maqṣūd b. ʿAbd al-Raḥīm (6 vols.; Beirut: Dār al-Kutub al-ʿIlmiyyah and Muʾassasat al-Kutub al-Thaqāfiyyah, 1992), 2.343.

14. Bukhārī, *Ṣaḥīḥ*, *kitāb al-tafsīr*, introductory glosses *ad* Q 9.

15. See Arthur Jeffery, *The Foreign Vocabulary of the Quran* (Gaekwad's Oriental Series 79; Baroda: Oriental Institute, 1938; repr. Lahore: Al-Biruni, 1977), 163–164.

Variant Readings

Bukhārī occasionally reports variant readings (*qirā'āt*), sometimes fairly obscure ones without significant followings in later times. Giving full *isnāds*, he reports that Ibn ʿAbbās read *yuṭawwaqawnah* at Q Baqarah 2:184, whereas the Ten Readers all read *yuṭīqūnah* ("for those who are able to do it").[16] He mentions that one of those who became the Seven Readers, ʿĀṣim, read *adbār* in Q Qāf 50:40 ("and glorify Him at the *ends* of prostrations") but *idbār* in Q Najm 52:49 ("and glorify Him at the *setting* of the stars"). The first was controversial: three of the Seven Readers (Nāfiʿ, Ibn Kathīr, and Ḥamzah) and five of the Ten (additionally Abū Jaʿfar and Khalaf) favored *idbār* there. But only one of the Ten (Yaʿqūb) favored *adbār* in Q 52:49.[17] The Prophet himself is said to have recited *fa-hal min muddakir* at Q Qamar 54:15, a fairly uncontroversial reading—only Qatādah is reported to have interpreted it otherwise.[18] Al-Aʿmash and ʿĀṣim read *fa-ʿadalaka* at Q Infiṭār 82:7, Bukhārī says, whereas the people of the Hijaz read *fa-ʿaddalaka*. This is to name two Kufans of the earlier second/eighth century, one of the Fourteen and one of the Seven, respectively. It is to overlook others of the Seven and Ten who read *fa-ʿadalaka* (the other Kufans Ḥamzah, al-Kisā'ī, and Khalaf) and *fa-ʿaddalaka* (the Basran Abū ʿAmr and the Damascene Ibn ʿĀmir, unless Bukhārī counted Abū ʿAmr among the people of the Hijaz).[19] Bukhārī says that Jarīr, ʿĪsā b. Yūnus, and Abū Muʿāwiyah read *tarā'l-nāsa sakrā wa-mā hum sakrā* instead of *sukārā* (Q 22:2). This refers to Jarīr b. ʿAbd al-Ḥamīd al-Rāzī (d. 187/802–803), ʿĪsā b. Yūnus al-Sabīʿī (d. 187/802–803?), and Abū Muʿāwiyah Muḥammad b. Khāzim (d. 195/810–811?), all transmitters from the Kufan traditionist and Qur'ān reader al-Aʿmash (Sulaymān b. Mihrān, d. 148/765?), one of the Fourteen. Bukhārī apparently ignores the preference of others for *sakrā*—Ḥamzah and al-Kisā'ī among the Seven, as well as Khalaf among the Ten.[20] Bukhārī observes that the Meccan preacher (*qāṣṣ*) ʿUbayd b. ʿUmayr (d. 68/687–688?) read *tatalaẓẓā* at Q Layl 92:14 ("I have warned you of a fire

---

16. Aḥmad Mukhtār ʿUmar and ʿAbd al-ʿĀl Sālim Mukram, *Muʿjam al-qirā'āt al-Qur'āniyah: maʿa muqaddimah fī'l-qirā'āt wa-ashhar al-qurrā'* (8 vols.; Kuwait: Dhāt al-Salāsil, 1982–1985; repr. n.p.: Intishārāt-i Uswah, 1991–1992), 1.143; Muḥammad b. al-Ḥusayn al-Qalānisī, *Al-Kifāyah al-kubrā fī'l-qirā'āt al-ʿashr*, ed. ʿUthmān Maḥmūd Ghazāl (Beirut: Dār al-Kutub al-ʿIlmiyyah, 2007), 142.

17. ʿUmar and Mukram, *Muʿjam*, 6.237–238, 263; Qalānisī, *Kifāyah*, 382, 384.

18. *Mudhdhakir* or *mudhakkir* (reports vary), according to ʿUmar and Mukram, *Muʿjam*, 7.34.

19. ʿUmar and Mukram, *Muʿjam*, 8.89; Aḥmad b. al-Ḥusayn b. Mihrān, *Al-Mabsūṭ fī'l-qirā'āt al-ʿashr*, ed. Subayʿ Ḥamzah Ḥākimī (Damascus: Majmaʿ al-Lughah al-ʿArabiyyah, n.d.), 465.

20. ʿUmar and Mukram, *Muʿjam*, 4.161–163.

that blazes") instead of the shortened form *talaẓẓā* (what one finds in printed Qur'āns today) or (a variant form of Ibn Kathīr's reading) *ttalaẓẓā*.[21]

Plainly, then, Bukhārī had no idea of restricting the acceptable readings to so small a range as seven or ten. He offers (evidently) his own opinion concerning Q Ḍuḥā 93:3, *mā wadda'aka rabbuka wa-mā qalā* ("Your Lord has not said farewell to you nor does He hate you"), "This may be read with either a double or single *dāl* ('d'), with the same meaning," when all of the Fourteen agreed on *wadda'aka* and only a few others are remembered as reading *wada'aka*.[22] Likewise, it seems to be his own saying of Q Sabā' 34:19 ("They said, 'Our Lord, make the stages of our journey longer'"), "*bā'id* and *ba''id* are the same." The Ten Readers are divided on this two and a half for *ba''id*, one for *bā'ada*, six and a half for *bā'id*.[23] Again, Bukhārī seems to advocate indifference, although in this case there was more disagreement among the most famous experts. (It has been remarked that he avoids reports of divergent Syrian and Iraqi readings of the Qur'ān before 'Uthmān's authoritative collection, perhaps because, conversely, this is a point over which disagreement was disturbingly consequential.[24]) It apparently fits the style of Basran scholarship that Bukhārī should quote grammarians more often than qur'ānic readers.[25]

On the other hand, Bukhārī apparently disapproves of trying to come up with one's own interpretation of the consonantal outline on the basis of sense, quoting 'Abd Allāh b. Mas'ūd (d. 32/652–653?) as saying, "We recite it only as we have been taught it."[26] The Qur'ān reciter Muḥammad b. al-Ḥasan b. Miqsam (d. 354/965) was famously put on trial in 322/934 and forced to renounce his defense of inventing new readings consistent with the consonantal outline. We do not know that it was ever considered a crime

21. Ibn Mujāhid, *Kitāb al-Sab'ah fī'l-qirā'āt*, ed. Shawqī Ḍayf (Cairo: Dār al-Ma'ārif, 1972; repr. 1988), 690.

22. 'Umar and Mukram, *Mu'jam*, 9.179–180, mentioning the Companion Ibn 'Abbās, the Medinan Followers 'Urwah b. Zubayr and Hishām b. 'Urwah, the Syrian Follower Abū Baḥriyyah, and the later Syrians Ibn Abī 'Ablah and Abū Ḥaywah.

23. In favor of *ba''id* are remembered Ibn Kathīr, Abū 'Amr, and Ibn 'Āmir according to Hishām; in favor of *bā'ada*, Ya'qūb; in favor of *ba''id*, all the rest (Qalānisī, *Kifāyah*, 352).

24. Viviane Comerro, *Les traditions sur la constitution du muṣḥaf de 'Uthmān* (Beiruter Texte und Studien 134; Würzburg: Ergon, 2012), 63.

25. C. H. M. Versteegh, *Arabic Grammar and Qur'ānic Exegesis in Early Islam* (Studies in Semitic Languages and Linguistics 19; Leiden: Brill, 1993), 182.

26. Another, longer version *apud* 'Abd al-Razzāq b. Hammām al-Ṣan'ānī, *Tafsīr al-Qur'ān*, *ad* Q 12:23; ed. Muṣṭafā Muslim Muḥammad (3 vols. in 4; Riyadh: Maktabat al-Rushd, 1410 [1989]), 1/2.320 or ed. 'Abd al-Mu'ṭī Amīn Qal'ajī (2 vols.; Beirut: Dār al-Ma'rifah, 1991), 1.279. Its *isnād* intersects with Bukhārī's only at the transmitter from Ibn Mas'ūd, Abū Wā'il Shaqīq b. Salamah (Kufan, d. ca. 100/718–719).

before him, but Bukhārī's quotation indicates that opinion was hardening against it in the mid-ninth century.[27]

Bukhārī quotes Ibn Mas'ūd to explain his reading of Q 12:23, the command *hayta lak* in particular. Ibn Mujāhid's Seven Readings include this, *hīta lak*, and *haytu lak*.[28] Ibn 'Abbās, the authority Bukhārī most often quotes, goes unmentioned at this point. The reason may be uncertainty over what his reading was. The commentary of al-Ṭabarī (d. 310/923) quotes Ibn 'Abbās as considering the word Ḥawrāni, an opinion for which Bukhārī quotes 'Ikrimah. Al-Suddī, on the other hand, thought it was Coptic (which agrees with the presumed Egyptian setting), al-Ḥasan that it was Syriac, Mujāhid that it was Arabic. Then Ṭabarī quotes Ibn 'Abbās for the readings *hi'tu* and *hītu*.[29] From other sources, 'Umar and Mukram's comprehensive encyclopedia of variant readings also quotes Ibn 'Abbās as favoring *huya'tu*, *huyaytu*, *haya'tu*, and *hayti*.[30] Bukhārī was not indifferent to the pronunciation of this odd word, else he would not have quoted Ibn Mas'ūd. Bukhārī's refusal to quote Ibn 'Abbās may have come of uncertainty as to which reading he most likely preferred but probably also of reluctance to call attention to disagreement over the meaning of the Qur'ān.

It is instructive to compare a short book of the *Sunan* of Abū Dāwūd Sulaymān b. al-Ash'ath al-Sijistānī (d. 275/889), *kitāb al-ḥurūf wa'l-qirā'āt*. This includes two versions of the *ḥadīth* report by which Ibn Mas'ūd preferred *hayta lak* and defended it by saying, "I prefer to recite it as I have learnt it."[31] However, Abū Dāwūd is also more willing than Bukhārī to report disagreement over the readings. One prominent disagreement concerns Q 1:4, whether *malik yawm al-dīn* (a majority of the Seven) or *mālik* (two Kufans: 'Āṣim and al-Kisā'ī). Abū Dāwūd quotes one *ḥadīth* report (with Medinan *isnād*) by which al-Zuhrī says that the Prophet, Abū Bakr, 'Umar, and 'Uthmān all recited *malik*. "The first to read it as *mālik yawm al-dīn* was Marwān."[32] He follows this by a report (with Meccan *isnād*) attributing this reading to the Prophet (no.

27. See Christopher Melchert, "Ibn Mujāhid and the Establishment of Seven Qur'anic Readings," *SIs* 91 (2000): 5–22, 20.

28. Ibn Mujāhid, *Sab'ah*, 347.

29. Abū Ja'far Muḥammad b. Jarīr al-Ṭabarī, *Jāmi' al-bayān 'an ta'wīl āy al-Qur'ān*, *ad* Q 12:23; *Tafsīr al-Ṭabarī: Jāmi' al-bayān 'an ta'wīl āy al-Qur'ān*, ed. Maḥmūd Muḥammad Shākir and Aḥmad Muḥammad Shākir (16 vols. [incomplete]; Cairo: Muṣṭafā al-Bābī al-Ḥalabī, 1954–1969), 16.25–31.

30. 'Umar and Mukram, *Mu'jam*, 3.158–161.

31. Abū Dāwūd Sulaymān b. al-Ash'ath al-Sijistānī, *Sunan*, *kitāb al-ḥurūf wa'l-qirā'āt*, nos. 4004–4005. These both intersect with 'Abd al-Razzāq's version at the Kufan al-A'mash.

32. Abū Dāwūd, *Sunan*, no. 4000. This is quoted < Aḥmad Ibn Ḥanbal < 'Abd al-Razzāq, but I have not found it in 'Abd al-Razzāq's *Tafsīr*.

4001). Finally, he quotes Ibn Ḥanbal as saying, "The ancient reading is *mālik yawm al-dīn*." Bukhārī offers no advice as to the wording of Sūrat al-Fātiḥah, apparently another example of reluctance to call attention to disagreement.

Of Q ʿAlaq 96:15, *la-nasfaʿan biʾl-nāṣiyah*, Bukhārī comments that this means "we will surely take it," the verb to be written with a *nūn*, not doubled (representing, other commentators tell us, a lightened form of the energetic mood). In printed Qurʾāns, this normally appears with *tanwīn fatḥah* rather than the letter *nūn*, although in Ibn Ḥajar's commentary it is written exactly as Bukhārī describes it, with *nūn*.[33] Bukhārī does not comment on the other place in the Qurʾān where a lightened energetic verb is written with *tanwīn fatḥah*, Q 12:32. Neither was the spelling of major concern to other medieval exegetes. For example, as Bukhārī remarks the example at Q 96:15 but not 12:32, the later commentator Abū ʿAbd Allāh Muḥammad b. Aḥmad al-Qurṭubī (d. 671/1273?) remarks the example at Q 12:32 but not 96:15.[34] Bukhārī's comment is a reminder that the exact written presentation of the Qurʾān was subordinate to the sound of the letters as it was recited. (When I began to teach selected passages of the Qurʾān at Oxford, I used a library copy printed in Damascus in the late nineteenth century. It often diverged from student copies in spelling but not pronunciation, e.g., as to writing the feminine ending as *tāʾ marbūṭah* or *tāʾ*.)

Comparisons

Bukhārī's *kitāb al-tafsīr* may be compared with the *tafsīr* of Abū Bakr ʿAbd al-Razzāq b. Hammām al-Ṣanʿānī (d. 211/827), likewise from a major *ḥadīth* collector, although not part of his major *ḥadīth* collection, *Al-Muṣannaf*. What has come down to us is evidently the recension of ʿAbd al-Razzāq's *Tafsīr* by Salamah b. Shabīb (d. 247/861–862?), while Ṭabarī is said to have drawn on another recension by Abū ʿAlī b. Abīʾl-Rabīʿ al-Jurjānī (d. 263/877).[35] It comprises 3,759 numbered items. Not every verse of the Qurʾān is covered, but only one chapter (63) goes without any comment. Over three-quarters of the items in our version come from Maʿmar b. Rāshid (d. 153/770?), a Basran client who transferred to Yemen. Its ultimate authorities are the Prophet at about 14 percent of all items, Companions at 10 percent, and later figures,

33. Ibn Ḥajar, *Fatḥ*, 9.560.

34. Abū ʿAbd Allāh Muḥammad b. Aḥmad al-Qurṭubī, *Al-Jāmiʿ li-aḥkām al-Qurʾān*, ed. Muḥammad Ibrāhīm al-Ḥifnāwī and Maḥmūd Ḥāmid ʿUthmān (22 vols.; Cairo: Dār al-Ḥadīth, 1994), 9.190, 20.125, or ed. ʿAbd al-Razzāq al-Mahdī (20 vols. in 10; Beirut: Dār al-Kitāb al-ʿArabī, 1997), 9.157–158, 20.115–116.

35. ʿAbd al-Muʿṭī Amīn Qalʿajī, introduction to ʿAbd al-Razzāq, *Tafsīr*, 1.31–33; Sezgin, *GAS*, 1.99.

nearly all Followers, at 76 percent. Leaving aside items from the Prophet and Companions, it is about two-thirds Basran, one-seventh Kufan, and one-tenth Meccan. About two-fifths of all items come from the Basran Qatādah alone (figures based on a random sample of 200). It comprises only reports with *isnāds*.

ʿAbd al-Razzāq's commentary is unlike Bukhārī's, then, in that Bukhārī offers almost no Follower *ḥadīth* reports with full *isnād*, whereas Follower reports with full *isnāds* dominate ʿAbd al-Razzāq's collection. It is also unlike Bukhārī's collection in offering comments only from the Prophet, Companions, and later traditionists—no grammarians or philologists. Like Bukhārī, ʿAbd al-Razzāq occasionally but unsystematically mentions variant readings, e.g., ʿUmar read *lā yuḍārar kātib* at Q 2:282 ("let not a scribe... be harmed"), whereas nine of the Ten read *yuḍārra* and one *yuḍāra*; al-Aʿmash read *tassāqaṭ* at Q 19:25 ("you will cause... to fall down"), in agreement (as it happens) with eight of the Ten Readers.[36] ʿAbd al-Razzāq tends not to mention non-Arabic languages, though. Of *awwāh*, for example (Q 11:75), he reports not that it has an Ethiopic meaning but that ʿUbayd b. ʿUmayr used to allude to it by saying *awh awh* at the mention of the Fire.[37] Of *muttaka'* (Q 12:31), he quotes Qatādah as saying it means food (*ṭaʿām*).[38] Of the mysterious letters at the beginning of Q 20, *ṭā-hā*, he quotes Qatādah and al-Ḥasan as saying that they mean "O man," but not that this is Nabataean.[39] ʿAbd al-Razzāq is more likely than Bukhārī to report disagreement. For example, he addresses a now-famous controversy, namely whether Abraham took up Isaac or Ishmael to sacrifice. He mentions three Companions, three Followers, and Maʿmar himself as identifying the son in question as Isḥāq, one Companion and two Followers as identifying him as Ismāʿīl, one of them (Saʿīd b. al-Musayyab) expressly in the face of someone's assertion that it was Isḥāq.[40] Bukhārī says nothing in his short chapter on Sūrat al-Ṣaffāt.

Among the Six Books, just one other has a large book of *tafsīr*, *Al-Jāmiʿ al-ṣaḥīḥ* of Abū ʿĪsā Muḥammad b. ʿĪsā al-Tirmidhī (d. 279/892), which comprises some 420 *ḥadīth* reports, over 98 percent of them from the Prophet. (Ibn Mājah, like ʿAbd al-Razzāq, assembled a separate Qur'ān commentary, but it is not extant.[41]) It covers all but twenty-one chapters of the Qur'ān

---

36. ʿUmar and Mukram, *Muʿjam*, 1.225–227, 4.39–41; Qalānisī, *Kifāyah*, 209, 307; Ibn Mihrān, *Mabsūṭ*, 288–289; ʿAbd al-Razzāq, *Tafsīr*, ed. Muḥammad, 1.111, 2.7.

37. ʿAbd al-Razzāq, *Tafsīr*, ed. Muḥammad, 1/2.309 = ed. Qalʿajī, 1.269.

38. ʿAbd al-Razzāq, *Tafsīr*, ed. Muḥammad, 1/2.322 = ed. Qalʿajī, 1.281.

39. ʿAbd al-Razzāq, *Tafsīr*, ed. Muḥammad, 2.15.

40. ʿAbd al-Razzāq, *Tafsīr*, ed. Muḥammad, 2.152 = ed. Qalʿajī, 2.124–125.

41. ʿAbd al-Karīm b. Muḥammad al-Rāfiʿī, *Al-Tadwīn fī tārīkh Qazwīn*, ed. ʿAzīz Allāh al-ʿUṭāridī (4 vols.; Hyderabad: al-Maṭbaʿah al-ʿAzīziyyah, 1404 [1984]), 2.49; Kātib Çelebī, *Kitāb al-Kashf al-ẓunūn*, ed. Şerefettin Yaltkaya and Rifat Bilge (2 vols.;

(46, 65, 67, 71, 73, 76–79, 82, 86–87, 90, 100–101, 103–107, and 111), of which fourteen coincide with chapters for which Bukhārī offers no *ḥadīth* with *isnād*. The few comments that Tirmidhī quotes that are not from the Prophet come from Companions. He offers no comments from Followers, let alone ninth-century philologists. He glosses words only as he has glosses from the Prophet, as when the Prophet explains that *al-ṣūr* in Q Zumar 39:68 is a horn that will be blown.[42] The comparison confirms Bukhārī's closeness to the classical style of Qur'ān commentary, copiously quoting Followers, and especially in the realm of *adab*. Tirmidhī does twice quote anonymous glosses from "the people of knowledge." A long *ḥadīth* report in which the Prophet describes a series of heavens and earths above and below ours concludes with his saying, apparently, that if one could let down a rope to the lowest earth, it would land on God, then quoting Q Ḥadīd 57:2 ("His is the sovereignty of the heavens and the earth. He brings life and He brings death. He has power over everything"), the reason for placing it in the book of *tafsīr*. After commenting on the *isnād*, Tirmidhī says, "Some of the people of knowledge have commented on this *ḥadīth* report, saying [pl.] that it would land on God's knowledge, power, and authority, God's knowledge, power, and authority being in every place, whereas He is on the Throne as described in His Book."[43] Thus he defends traditionalist theology. Bukhārī's selection of *ḥadīth* in the *Ṣaḥīḥ* more consistently supports semi-rationalist Sunni theology against the more thoroughgoing traditionalists. (Tirmidhī calls this one *gharīb*, meaning uncorroborated, as he does with a quarter of all reports in his book of *tafsīr*.)

Bukhārī's *kitāb al-tafsīr* may also be compared with that of Abū ʿAbd al-Raḥmān Aḥmad b. Shuʿayb al-Nasāʾī (d. 303/915?) at the end of his *ḥadīth* collection *Al-Sunan al-kubrā*, usually counted outside the Six Books (in Speight's time thought lost).[44] It comprises 735 *ḥadīth* reports, or about 6 percent of the

Istanbul: Maarif Matbaası, 1941, 1943), 1.439. Outside the Six Books, there are likewise occasional reports of a *tafsīr* by Mālik (b. Anas, d. 179/795), also apparently not extant: Ibn al-Nadīm, *Kitâb al-Fihrist*, ed. Gustav Flügel, with Johannes Roedigger and August Mueller (Leipzig: F. C. W. Vogel, 1872), 33 (*fann* 3, *maqālah* 1); al-Qāḍī ʿIyāḍ b. Mūsā b. ʿIyāḍ al-Yaḥṣubī, *Tartīb al-madārik wa-taqrīb al-masālik li-maʿrifat aʿlām madhhab Mālik*, ed. Muḥammad b. Tāwīt al-Ṭanjī et al. (8 vols.; Rabat: n.p., 1966–1983), 1.81.

42. Abū ʿĪsā Muḥammad b. ʿĪsā al-Tirmidhī, *Al-Jāmiʿ al-ṣaḥīḥ, kitāb tafsīr al-Qurʾān*, *ad* Q 39, no. 3244.

43. Tirmidhī, *Jāmiʿ*, *tafsīr al-Qurʾān ad* Q 57, no. 3298. The other such gloss appears shortly before at *tafsīr al-Qurʾān, ad* Q 56, no. 3294.

44. In modern times, it is Nasāʾī's smaller collection, *Al-Mujtabā*, that has usually been included among the Six Books. It has often been referred to simply as *Al-Sunan*. See Christopher Melchert, "The Life and Works of Al-Nasāʾī," *JSS* 59 (2014): 377–407.

whole book—a slightly smaller proportion than the 504 in Bukhārī's *kitāb al-tafsīr*. Whereas 95 percent of *Al-Sunan al-kubrā* as a whole goes back to the Prophet, in *kitāb al-tafsīr* within it, about 70 percent of all *ḥadīth* reports go back to the Prophet, 30 percent to the Companions, very similarly to *ḥadīth* in Bukhārī's *kitāb al-tafsīr*. Like ʿAbd al-Razzāq and Bukhārī, Nasāʾī goes through the Qur'ān in canonical order, offering glosses on various verses, although far from all verses. Whereas Bukhārī offers only comments without *isnād* for thirty chapters, Nasāʾī offers no comments without *isnād* and skips only nine chapters altogether (71, 90, 94, 100–101, 103, 105, and 113–114). Like Bukhārī, Nasāʾī provides accounts of the occasions of revelation, the legal application of verses, glosses of words, and occasionally clarifications from transmitters. For example, Nasāʾī quotes Ibn ʿAbbās as explaining that Q Ibrāhīm 14:28 ("Have you not looked at those who changed the blessing of God for ingratitude?") refers to the people of Mecca, then Sufyān b. ʿUyaynah (who is in the *isnād* going back to Ibn ʿAbbās) as saying "that is, the unbelievers among them."[45] Concerning a prophetic gloss on Q Furqān 25:68, a further clarification is interpolated from Ḥamzah, the transmitter of *Al-Sunan al-kubrā*, from Nasāʾī.[46] But there seem to be no comments drawn from famous commentators such as Qatādah and Saʿīd b. Jubayr, nor philologists such as Farrā' and Abū ʿUbaydah. Likewise, I have found not one alternative reading.

A controversial juridical question in the ninth century was *ityān al-nisā' fī adbārihinn*, "going into women in their rears." In the *Muṣannaf*, ʿAbd al-Razzāq mentions Companions Ibn ʿAbbās, the Caliph ʿUmar, ʿAbd Allāh b. ʿAmr, Abū'l-Dardā', and Abū Hurayrah in opposition, as well as two Followers, although he apparently quotes the Prophet on both sides.[47] Non-prohibition is associated especially with the early Maliki school.[48] Both sides cite Q 2:223,

45. Abū ʿAbd al-Raḥmān Aḥmad b. Shuʿayb al-Nasāʾī, *Al-Sunan al-kubrā*, ed. ʿAbd al-Ghaffār Sulaymān al-Bundārī and Sayyid Kisrawī Ḥasan (Beirut: Dār al-Kutub al-ʿIlmiyyah, 1991), *kitāb al-tafsīr*, no. 11268 (*ad* Q 14). But Bukhārī quotes Ibn ʿAbbās by two other *isnād*s, both through Sufyān b. ʿUyaynah, in both of which it is Ibn ʿAbbās himself who specifies that the verse refers to the unbelievers in particular, not all the Meccans or all the Quraysh: Bukhārī, *Ṣaḥīḥ*, *al-maghāzī* 8, *bāb qatl Abī Jahl*, no. 3977, and ibid., *al-tafsīr* 14/3, *bāb a-lam tara*, no. 4700.

46. Nasāʾī, *Al-Sunan al-kubrā*, *al-tafsīr*, no. 11373 (*ad* Q 25). Ḥamzah's was the only extant recension of Nasāʾī's *kitāb al-tafsīr* according to Ibn Ḥajar, *Kitāb Tahdhīb al-Tahdhīb* (12 vols.; Hyderabad: Majlis Dā'irat al-Maʿārif al-Niẓāmiyyah, 1325–1327 [1907–1909]; repr. Beirut: Dār Ṣādir, n.d.), 1.6.

47. ʿAbd al-Razzāq, *Al-Muṣannaf*, ed. Ḥabīb al-Raḥmān al-Aʿẓamī (11 vols.; Johannesburg: Majlis al-ʿIlmī, 1970–1972), 11.442–443. There are just two relevant items (both implicitly opposed) in ʿAbd al-Razzāq, *Tafsīr*, *ad* Q 2:223; ed. Muḥammad, 1.89–90 = ed. Qalʿajī, 1.103.

48. E.g., Nasāʾī, *Al-Sunan al-kubrā*, 5.315–316. It is held against the Malikis in

"Your women are a tillage. Go to your tillage as you wish."[49] Bukhārī's *kitāb al-tafsīr* includes four Companion *ḥadīth* reports in explanation of it, the three from Ibn ʿUmar incomplete:

> No. 4526 < Isḥāq < al-Naḍr b. Shumayl < Ibn ʿAwn < Nāfiʿ: "Ibn ʿUmar..., when he recited the Qur'ān, would not speak until he had finished. I was with him one day. He recited Sūrat al-Baqarah until he reached a place. He said, 'Do you know about what this was sent down?' I said, 'No.' He said, 'It was sent down concerning such-and-such.' Then he went on."
>
> No. 4527 (< Isḥāq < al-Naḍr b. Shumayl) < ʿAbd al-Ṣamad < his father[50] < Ayyūb < Nāfiʿ < Ibn ʿUmar (concerning) "Go to your tillage as you wish." He said, "He goes into her in..." This was related by Muḥammad b. Yaḥyā b. Saʿīd < his father < ʿUbayd Allāh < Nāfiʿ < Ibn ʿUmar.
>
> No. 4528 < Abū Nuʿaym < Sufyān < Ibn al-Munkadir < Jābir: "The Jews used to say, 'If he has sex with her (*jāmaʿahā*) from behind, the child will turn out cross-eyed.' Then there came down 'Your women are a tillage. Go to your tillage as you wish.'"[51]

Apparently, no known recension of Bukhārī's *Ṣaḥīḥ* includes what Ibn ʿUmar said, so it must have been Bukhārī himself who could not bring himself to repeat it. However, Isḥāq b. Rāhawayh's *Musnad* and *Tafsīr* included the first version, which quotes Ibn ʿUmar as saying, "It came down concerning going into women's rears."[52] Ṭabarī quotes three overlapping versions < Ibn ʿAwn on up in his commentary at Q 2:223 to exactly the same effect. Ṭabarī also

---

polemics from other schools; e.g., Ibn Abī Yaʿlā, *Ṭabaqāt al-Ḥanābilah*, ed. Muḥammad Ḥāmid al-Fiqī (2 vols.; Cairo: Maṭbaʿat al-Sunnah al-Muḥammadiyyah, 1371 [1952]), 1.316, and al-Qāri' al-Harawī, *Manāqib al-imām al-aʿẓam, apud* Abī'l-Wafā', *Al-Jawāhir al-muḍiyyah* (2 vols.; Hyderabad: Dā'irat al-Maʿārif al-Niẓāmiyyah, 1332 [1913–1914]), 2.465–466. Denied by some early Malikis: e.g., Saḥnūn, according to Abū Bakr al-Mālikī, *Riyāḍ al-nufūs*, ed. Bashīr al-Bakkūsh, supp. Muḥammad al-ʿArūsī al-Muṭṭawwī (3 vols.; Beirut: Dār al-Gharb al-Islāmī, 1401–1403 [1981–1983]), 1.355.

49. So Abū ʿAbd Allāh Muḥammad b. Idrīs al-Shāfiʿī, *Kitāb al-Umm* (7 vols. in 4; Bulaq: al-Maṭbaʿah al-Kubrā al-Amīriyyah, 1321–1325 [1903–1908]; repr. Cairo: Kitāb al-Shaʿb, 1968), 5.84, 156.

50. "From his father" is omitted in the edition of Bin Bāz but supplied here from Aḥmad b. Muḥammad al-Qasṭallānī, *Irshād al-sārī li-sharḥ Ṣaḥīḥ al-Bukhārī* (10 vols.; Bulaq: al-Maṭbaʿah al-Kubrā al-Amīriyyah, 1304–1305 [1886–1888]), 7.34.

51. Muslim's *Ṣaḥīḥ* includes a close parallel to the last, < Qutaybah b. Saʿīd, Abū Bakr b. Abī Shaybah, and ʿAmr al-Nāqid < Sufyān on up. Muslim, *Ṣaḥīḥ*, *nikāḥ* 19, *bāb jawāz jimāʿihi imra'atahu fī qubulihā*, no. 1435.

52. Ibn Ḥajar, *Fatḥ*, 9.36, *ad* nos. 4526–5428. This section of the *Musnad* appears to be no longer extant. Cf. Isḥāq b. Rāhawayh, *Al-Musnad*, ed. ʿAbd al-Ghafūr ʿAbd

has an overlapping version of Bukhārī's second, no. 4527, < Abū Qilābah < 'Abd al-Ṣamad < his father < Ayyūb on up in which Ibn 'Umar's gloss is simply "in the rear." The unnumbered *ḥadīth* report through Muḥammad b. Yaḥyā b. Sa'īd on up was found in al-Ṭabarānī (d. 360/971), *Al-Mu'jam al-awsaṭ*, in which Ibn 'Umar says, "There came down on the Messenger of God 'Your women are a tillage for you' just to give permission (*rukhṣatan*) to go into the rear."[53]

Bukhārī treats a related Prophet *ḥadīth* report in his great biographical dictionary *Al-Tārīkh al-kabīr*: Khuzaymah b. Thābit < the Prophet, "God is not embarrassed by the truth. Do not go into women's backsides (*a'jāzihinn*)." He recounts nine different *isnāds* for it and rejects them all.[54] Since he has nothing else on the problem in the *Ṣaḥīḥ*, it seems likely that his opinion was similar to that reported of Nasā'ī: that there was no sound *ḥadīth* report on either side (at least from the Prophet), so that the safest course was not to prohibit something that early jurists had thought licit (Ibn 'Umar evidently foremost among them, although Ṭabarī also quotes the Hijazi Ibn Abī Mulaykah).[55] Nasā'ī himself relates a long series of relevant *ḥadīth* reports in *Al-Sunan al-kubrā*.[56] It includes one report that Ibn 'Umar, on being asked about going into the rear ends of concubines, responded, "Does a Muslim do this?" But it also includes two reports by which Ibn 'Umar said there was no harm in it, one of them related by Mālik b. Anas, who is independently quoted as himself seeing no harm in it.[57] (All three reports from Ibn 'Umar are also related by Ṭabarī. A different sort of counter-report comes from Abū Dāwūd, by which Ibn Mas'ūd [!] laments, "Ibn 'Umar—God forgive him—was imagining things."[58] Ṭabarī includes a counter-report that accuses Nāfi' of misquoting Ibn 'Umar.) On this point, then, Bukhārī implicitly sides with Mālik rather than Shāfi'ī (Muḥammad b. Idrīs al-Shāfi'ī, d. 204/820).[59] Nasā'ī expressly comes down

al-Ḥaqq Ḥusayn al-Balūshī (5 vols. in 4; Medina: Maktabat al-Īmān, 1990–1995); or ed. Muḥammad Mukhtār Ḍirār al-Muftī (Beirut: Dār al-Kitāb al-'Arabī, 2002).

53. Ibn Ḥajar, *Fatḥ*, 9:36, *ad* nos. 4526–4528.

54. Bukhārī, *Al-Tārīkh al-kabīr*, 8.256–257. Another report against going into a woman's rear is rejected at *Al-Tārīkh al-kabīr*, 3.16–17; yet another is not expressly rejected, but the possibility of its being from a Companion only and not the Prophet is raised at 8.303.

55. Nasā'ī quoted in Ibn al-Manẓūr, *Mukhtaṣar Tārīkh Dimashq*, ed. Rūḥiyyah al-Naḥḥās et al. (29 vols.; Damascus: Dār al-Fikr, 1984–1989), 3.101; al-Maqrīzī, *Kitāb al-Muqaffā al-kabīr*, ed. Muḥammad al-Ya'lawī (8 vols.; Beirut: Dār al-Gharb al-Islāmī, 1991), 1.401.

56. Nasā'ī, *Al-Sunan al-kubrā*, 5.314–325, *kitāb 'ishrat al-nisā'*, §§ 24–32.

57. Nasā'ī, *Al-Sunan al-kubrā*, 5.315.

58. Abū Dāwūd, *Sunan*, *kitāb al-nikāḥ* 44, *bāb fī jāmi' al-nikāḥ*, no. 2164.

59. Shāfi'ī, *Umm*, Bulaq ed., 5.84, 156 = ed. Rif'at Fawzī 'Abd al-Muṭṭalib (11 vols.; al-Manṣūrah: Dār al-Wafā', 2001; 2nd printing, 2004), 6.244–246, 443–444.

on the same side in the end but, characteristically, after presenting reports both for and against. By contrast, and equally characteristically, Bukhārī implicitly expresses his opinion by presenting reports on one side only. Perhaps this is a reason why *al-mukhtaṣar* is part of the full title of Bukhārī's *Ṣaḥīḥ*: it is not only a small selection of all known *ḥadīth*, even the sound; it is restricted to the rules of just one school (Bukhārī's own, in this case) rather than all the rules entertained by respectable Sunnis.[60]

Another useful comparison is the Qur'ān commentary of Abū Muḥammad ʿAbd al-Raḥmān b. Abī Ḥātim Muḥammad al-Rāzī (d. 327/938), from a major *ḥadīth* critic but independent of any larger collection.[61] Even more than Bukhārī's or Ṭabarī's commentaries, this apparently deserves to exemplify *al-tafsīr bi'l-maʾthūr*, for it normally includes an *isnād* with every comment and almost no comments on the Qur'ān from the compiler himself.[62] Mehmet Akif Koç reports that, over the course of a dozen volumes, Ibn Abī Ḥātim's own comments would cover no more than two pages.[63] Koç also reports that the extant portions comprise 16,283 reports in all, of which nearly 4 percent are from the Prophet, 22 percent from Companions (of which 80 percent are from Ibn ʿAbbās), 74 percent from Followers and later figures (my own rougher estimates indicate altogether half from Followers, a quarter from later figures).[64] This means a similar percentage of Prophet *ḥadīth* to that in the book of *tafsīr* in Muslim's *Ṣaḥīḥ* but hugely more post-Companion *ḥadīth*—almost exactly the same percentage as in ʿAbd al-Razzāq. Therefore, it is evidently not possible to identify preference for Prophet or Companion *ḥadīth* with traditionalist preference for *ḥadīth* (i.e., transmitted knowledge) over recent opinion.

Koç finds that twenty-two transmitters of opinions in Ibn Abī Ḥātim's *Tafsīr* are aspersed in his massive encyclopedia of *rijāl* criticism, *Kitāb al-Jarḥ wa'l-taʿdīl*; twenty-three are identified there but not characterized at all, and

---

60. On the juristic *mukhtaṣar* as not just an "abridgement," see Jonathan E. Brockopp, "Early Islamic Jurisprudence in Egypt: Two Scholars and Their *Mukhtaṣars*," *IJMES* 30 (1998): 167–182, esp. 174.

61. For the manuscripts, see *GAS*, 1.179, no. 3. Two editions are *Tafsīr al-Qurʾān al-ʿaẓīm*, ed. Asʿad Muḥammad al-Ṭayyib (14 vols.; Mecca: Maktabat Nizār Muṣṭafā al-Bāz, 1419 [1999]), and *Tafsīr Ibn Abī Ḥātim al-Rāzī*, ed. Aḥmad Fatḥī ʿAbd al-Raḥmān Ḥijāzī (7 vols.; Beirut: Dār al-Kutub al-ʿIlmiyyah, 2006).

62. The distinction between *al-tafsīr bi'l-maʾthūr* (explication by transmitted material) and *al-tafsīr bi'l-raʾy* (explication by opinion) has seemed polemically useful to Salafis but quickly fails on testing against actual Qur'ān commentaries across the centuries. See Saleh, "Preliminary Remarks," 21–37, and Saleh, *Formation*, 16.

63. Mehmet Akif Koç, "*Isnāds* and *rijāl* Expertise in the Exegesis of Ibn Abī Ḥātim (327/939 [sic])," *Der Islam* 82 (2005): 146–168, 163.

64. Koç, "*Isnāds*," 167n.

three are often cited in the *Tafsīr* but not mentioned at all in *Al-Jarḥ*. He explains the evident discrepancy by a conscious lowering of standards when theology and law are not at stake. A weaker standard of proof does less harm when the subject is encouraging piety, not identifying forbidden acts or acceptable dogmatic views. Elsewhere than the *Tafsīr*, Ibn Abī Ḥātim expressly quotes the prominent traditionist ʿAbd Allāh b. al-Mubārak (d. 181/797) as allowing transmission of *ḥadīth* from a weak transmitter concerning etiquette, exhortation, and renunciation (*adab, mawʿiẓah, zuhd*).[65] But Koç's distinction is weakened by our lack of a body of legal *ḥadīth* from Ibn Abī Ḥātim. That is, we cannot be sure that, had he collected 16,000 legal *ḥadīth* reports, they would have included fewer or no transmitters aspersed in *Al-Jarḥ wa'l-taʿdīl*. Bukhārī's *kitāb al-tafsīr* includes more comments from Companions than the rest of the *Ṣaḥīḥ*, but he does not give nearly so much space as Ibn Abī Ḥātim to Followers. He also includes hugely more philological clarifications and comments far more often himself.

One outstanding feature of the classical *tafsīr* tradition is alternative interpretations. A certain reluctance on Bukhārī's part to call attention to disagreement has been remarked already. Here it is conspicuous that Bukhārī seldom offers one interpretation after another of the same locution. One place where he does so is Q Yūnus 10:2, *anna lahum qadama ṣidq* ("that they will have a sure footing"); he quotes the Medinan Zayd b. Aslam (d. 136/754) as explaining that this refers to Muḥammad, then cites Mujāhid that it refers to goodness (*khayr*). By comparison, however, Ṭabarī names Mujāhid among five who said it refers to a reward of some sort, and Zayd b. Aslam among three who said it refers to Muḥammad. Māwardī offers four interpretations, but instead of quoting Zayd b. Aslam as saying it refers to Muḥammad, he quotes this interpretation of Muqātil b. Ḥayyān, a Khurasani client (d. bef. 150/767–768) cited just once by Bukhārī. To Mujāhid he attributes the

65. ʿAbd al-Raḥmān b. Abī Ḥātim Muḥammad al-Rāzī, *Kitāb al-Jarḥ wa'l-taʿdīl* (9 vols.; Hyderabad: Jamʿiyyat Dā'irat al-Maʿārif al-ʿUthmāniyyah, 1360–1371 [1941–1952]; repr. Beirut: Dār Iḥyā' al-Turāth al-ʿArabī, n.d.), 2.30–31. Koç interprets Ibn Abī Ḥātim as strongly endorsing the double standard, citing pages 27–32. However, this quotation from Ibn al-Mubārak is the only one that addresses it expressly. For an argument that the double standard has been overstressed on the basis of theoretical literature from the tenth century and later, citing the equal proportion of strong and weak among legal and non-legal *ḥadīth* included in Aḥmad's *Musnad*, see Christopher Melchert, "The *Musnad* of Aḥmad ibn Ḥanbal: How It Was Composed and What Distinguishes It from the Six Books" *Der Islam* 82 (2005): 32–51, 45–47. To the contrary, Brown has observed that Tirmidhī identifies as *gharīb* considerably more *ḥadīth* reports in his chapter on proper behavior (*al-birr wa'l-ṣilah*) than in his chapter on inheritance law (*al-farāʾiḍ*): Jonathan A. C. Brown, *Hadith: Muhammad's Legacy in the Medieval and Modern World* (Oxford: Oneworld, 2009), 235.

opinion that it refers to a previous truth-telling such as had earlier brought them to faith.[66] The most careful of the three, on this point, appears to be Ṭabarī with his complete *isnād* for every quotation.

Shortly afterwards, Bukhārī apparently quotes Mujāhid again as glossing Q 10:26, *wa-ziyādah* ("Those who do good will have the fairest [reward] and more"), as "forgiveness and satisfaction (*maghfirah wa-riḍwān*)," whereas someone else said it means looking at the face of God. Ṭabarī cites ten persons (including the Prophet and three Companions) said to have explained *wa-ziyādah* as looking at God's face, and just one, Mujāhid, as saying it means forgiveness and satisfaction. The *ḥadīth* report by which the Prophet himself connected Q 10:26 with looking at God's face is included by Muslim and other leading collectors with a Basran *isnād*, although not Bukhārī himself.[67] Bukhārī does testify elsewhere (in *kitāb al-tafsīr* apropos of Q 50:39, "and glorify your Lord by praising Him before the rising and the setting of the sun") that the Prophet promised the saved that they would see God in the afterlife, as clearly as they see the full moon on a cloudless night.[68] Māwardī cites the same three Companions as Ṭabarī as saying that *wa-ziyādah* means to look at His face, Mujāhid alone as saying it means forgiveness and satisfaction.[69] On this point, as at some others, Bukhārī's selection may reflect wariness of anthropomorphism.[70]

Bukhārī's *Tafsīr* and the Rest of the *Ṣaḥīḥ*

Bukhārī's immediate sources for *ḥadīth* in the *tafsīr* are geographically fairly similar to his immediate sources for *ḥadīth* in the rest of the *Ṣaḥīḥ*. Where identifiable, his immediate authorities are as follows: Basran 26 (27%); Kufan 16 (17%); Baghdadi 8 (8%); all Iraq 50 (53%); Egyptian 8 (8%); Syrian 10 (11%); Meccan 5 (5%); Medinan 3 (3%); Jibali 4 (4%); Khurasani and

66. Māwardī, *Nukat*, 2.421, *ad* Q 10:2.

67. Muslim, *Ṣaḥīḥ*, *kitāb al-īmān* 80, *ithbāt ruʾyat al-muʾminīn*, no. 181; Tirmidhī, *Jāmiʿ*, *ṣifat al-jannah* 16, *ruʾyat al-rabb*, no. 2552, and *tafsīr al-Qurʾān*, *ad* Q 10, no. 3105; Ibn Mājah Abū ʿAbd Allāh Muḥammad b. Yazīd, *Sunan*, *al-muqaddimah* 13, *fīmā ankarat al-jahmiyyah*, no. 187.

68. Bukhārī, *Ṣaḥīḥ*, *mawāqīt al-ṣalāh* 16, *bāb faḍl ṣalāt al-ʿaṣr*, no. 554; *mawāqīt al-ṣalāh* 26, *bāb faḍl ṣalāt al-fajr*, no. 573; *al-adhān* 129, *bāb faḍl al-sujūd*, no. 806; *al-tafsīr* 50, *ad* Q 50:39, no. 4851; *al-riqāq* 52, *bāb al-ṣirāt jisr Jahannam*, no. 6573; *al-tawḥīd* 24, *bāb* Q 7:52–53, nos. 7434–7437.

69. Māwardī, *Nukat*, 2.433, *ad* Q 10:26.

70. Cf. Melchert, "Bukhārī," 453–454, on the creation of Adam in God's image.

Transoxanian 15 (16%). Here for comparison is a chart showing percentages from the same regions in the whole *Ṣaḥīḥ*[71]:

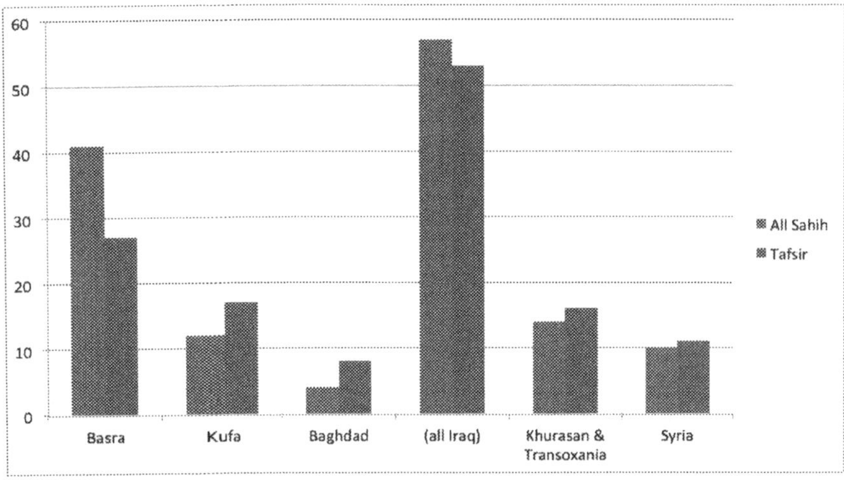

Bukhārī's ultimate authorities are rather more different. In his *kitāb al-tafsīr*, about 68 percent of all *ḥadīth* reports with *isnād*s (including repeats) go back to the Prophet, 31 percent to Companions, and less than 1 percent to a Follower. In the *Ṣaḥīḥ* as a whole, by contrast, over 90 percent of all *ḥadīth* reports go back to the Prophet. Bukhārī was much more concerned to report sayings from the Prophet than (for example) Muslim, in whose small *kitāb al-tafsīr* only about 5 percent go back to the Prophet, but the state of qur'ānic commentary still evidently constrained him to bring up the Companions more often than usual.

Bukhārī's *kitāb al-tafsīr* passes systematically through the whole Qur'ān only in the sense that it has something to say about each chapter. It is far from being a systematic treatment; for example, its choice of which variant readings to consider seems downright capricious. The *Ṣaḥīḥ* as a whole makes the Qur'ān unusually prominent, as by quoting it in over a quarter of all topic headings. The *kitāb al-tafsīr* shows that this is partly a matter of overlapping with the realm of *adab*. S. R. Burge has proposed that Bukhārī's arrangement of *ḥadīth* shows that he meant for readers to go through his *Ṣaḥīḥ* in order, not to use it as an encyclopedia in which one looks things up here and there.[72] The Qur'ān was of great interest to Muslim *littérateurs*, if nothing

71. Based on a sample of 230 *ḥadīth* reports in the *Ṣaḥīḥ*, from Melchert, "Bukhārī," 427.

72. S. R. Burge, "Reading between the Lines: The Compilation of *ḥadīṯ* and the Authorial Voice," *Arabica* 58 (2011): 168–197, 194–195.

else as the paragon of Arabic prose style. In Bukhārī's time, the specialized study of variant qur'ānic readings developed above all in Baghdadi belletrist circles.[73] *Adab* was also the field where out-of-the-way information, presented according to no obvious plan, was most prized. Bukhārī's literary talent has occasionally provoked comment.[74] The *kitāb al-tafsīr* confirms that he was part of that tradition. Tirmidhī, Nasā'ī, and Ibn Abī Ḥātim, by contrast, worked much more exclusively in the *ḥadīth* tradition.

Compared with the rest of the *Ṣaḥīḥ*, Bukhārī's *kitāb al-tafsīr* includes unusually much material without full *isnāds*. The tradition clearly distinguishes between the respect due to what Bukhārī presents with full *isnāds* and what he presents without, as *ta'ālīq*. The carelessness evident in *kitāb al-tafsīr*, as when he attributes something to Sufyān b. 'Uyaynah that Sufyān's *tafsīr* attributes rather to Mujāhid, or when he implicitly attributes something to Ibn 'Abbās that is actually from Farrā', confirms that Bukhārī maintained different standards for the different sections of his collection. In particular, it reflects the strong attraction between *tafsīr* and *adab*, the latter realm relatively indifferent to complete *isnāds* by comparison with works of *ḥadīth*. Bukhārī's attraction to *adab* is evident elsewhere in the *Ṣaḥīḥ*, as in frequent glosses on words. It seems to be strongest, however, in *kitāb al-tafsīr*. There is also a notable contrast between Bukhārī's *kitāb al-tafsīr* and the rest of the *Ṣaḥīḥ* in the frequency with which Bukhārī inserts his own comments: by Sezgin's count, 248 times in *kitāb al-tafsīr*, 45 times in all the rest of the *Ṣaḥīḥ*.[75] In *kitāb al-tafsīr*, Bukhārī seems to be working in a slightly different, less self-effacing tradition. It is conceivable, of course, that he came up on his own with the idea of treating qur'ānic commentary differently from the law and other concerns of the *Ṣaḥīḥ*. However, inasmuch as Bukhārī's *kitāb al-tafsīr* is anomalous both by comparison with *kitāb al-tafsīr* in other leading *ḥadīth* collections of its century and by comparison with other books of the *Ṣaḥīḥ* itself, it seems more likely that he took a different approach in *kitāb al-tafsīr* under the influence of earlier, *adab*-oriented approaches (as by the philologists whose glosses he quotes), possibly also because a developing genre of *tafsīr* in the mid-ninth century made that seem the normal approach.

Bukhārī's *Tafsīr* and the Genre of *Tafsīr*

In the end, one also wishes to know what Bukhārī's *kitāb al-tafsīr* tells us about the historical development of qur'ānic commentary. A weak reason for excluding Bukhārī from the history of qur'ānic commentary is that his

73. Melchert, "Ibn Mujāhid," 7–11.

74. See Melchert, "Bukhārī and His *Ṣaḥīḥ*," 448.

75. See note 6 above.

kitāb al-tafsīr is just a part of the *Ṣaḥīḥ*, not an independent work. In fact, it sometimes was referred to as a separate work.[76] As late as Ibn al-Nadīm in the tenth century, works we now consider unitary are often referred to by what we now think of as their constituent parts. A stronger reason is that Bukhārī only weakly influenced the later commentary tradition, partly because persecution at the end of his life limited the circulation of the *Ṣaḥīḥ* until the tenth century.[77] He is cited very often by the later Qur'ān commentator Qurṭubī, one possible measure of his influence, but Muslim is cited almost as often, so it cannot be argued that the attention paid Bukhārī is related to the importance of his *kitāb al-tafsīr*.

Influence is hard to measure, though. Walid Saleh asserts that it was al-Thaʿlabī (d. 427/1035), not Ṭabarī, who ushered in the classical style of qur'ānic exegesis.[78] A count of express citations suggests that the most important earlier commentaries for Qurṭubī were those of Ṭabarī, then Māwardī, then al-Qushayrī (Abū Naṣr, son of the famous Sufi, d. 465/1072), only then (and some distance behind) Thaʿlabī.[79] Does this show that Ṭabarī and Māwardī ought to be the most studied? Saleh is also puzzled by some of what Thaʿlabī identifies as the constituents of proper qur'ānic commentary: *ʿilal, iḥtijājāt*, and *al-akhbār al-mutaʿalliqāt*.[80] The first two are commonplaces of *ḥadīth*-based law: respectively, subtle defects in *isnād*s and arguments based on *ḥadīth* reports that suffice to establish points of law. Bukhārī's separate book of *ʿilal* mentioned by Ibn Ḥajar is not extant, but over three-quarters of all items in Tirmidhī's book *Al-ʿIlal al-kabīr* are comments from Bukhārī.[81] The term *mutaʿalliq* reminds one strongly of Bukhārī, since, as mentioned above, his *Ṣaḥīḥ* is distinguished by over a thousand reports with incomplete *isnād*s attached (hence the name) as commentary (especially to document parallel lines of transmission). Use of these terms by Thaʿlabī cannot demonstrate that Bukhārī was a direct influence, but they do tend to show that the culture of qur'ānic commentary overlapped with that of *ḥadīth* collection and criticism, even for an *adab*-oriented commentator as little obsessed with *isnād*s as Thaʿlabī. (Aisha Geissinger proposes that Bukhārī meant to influence the

---

76. E.g., Kātib Çelebī, *Kashf*, 1.443, mentioning both the one he included as a book of his *Ṣaḥīḥ* and another, larger commentary referred to by its transmitter from him, al-Firabrī. My guess is that there was only one commentary, the one included in the *Ṣaḥīḥ* (Melchert, "Bukhārī and His *Ṣaḥīḥ*," 433).

77. See Melchert, "Bukhārī and His *Ṣaḥīḥ*," 451–453.

78. Saleh, *Formation*, 5.

79. According to Qurṭubī, Ṭabarī is cited 179 times, Māwardī 154, Qushayrī 148, and Thaʿlabī 80.

80. Saleh, *Formation*, 86–87.

81. Al-Tirmidhī, *ʿIlal al-Tirmidhī al-kabīr, tartīb Abū* [sic] *Ṭālib al-Qāḍī*, ed. Ḥamzah Dīb Muṣṭafā (2 vols.; Amman: Maktabat al-Aqṣā, 1986).

development of qur'ānic commentary by discrediting what was not assembled by expert *ḥadīth* critics such as himself.[82] By this criterion, his *kitāb tafsīr al-Qur'ān* must be judged a failure, since not only did later commentators not confine themselves to well-attested *ḥadīth*, but those after Ṭabarī even tended to dispense with *isnāds*. However, the contrast between Bukhārī's plentiful quotation of philologists and Companions and Tirmidhī's stingier quotation of such sources suggests to me that Bukhārī's claims for *ḥadīth* specialists were more modest than Geissinger perceives.)

Norman Calder defined the genre of *tafsīr* by its reviewing the whole of the text in canonical order, citing named authorities, with polyvalent interpretations but mistrustful of mystical and allegorical readings.[83] Bukhārī has something to say about every chapter of the Qur'ān, so the whole text in canonical order is there. He does not yet have something on every verse—Ṭabarī seems to have been the first to pull this off. There is a heavy stress on named authorities. Bukhārī offers *isnāds* for all sayings of the Prophet, most but not all Companion sayings, and no sayings of Followers and later authorities. Here is some polyvalency but muted. It is hard to find mystical and allegorical readings. Bukhārī seems to be at least well on the way to producing a classical *tafsīr* text according to Calder's definition without fully meeting the proposed criteria.

Ahmed El Shamsy has contrasted the commentaries of two who studied with the disciples of Shāfiʿī, Ṭabarī and Ibn Abī Ḥātim, with commentaries of Shāfiʿī's time and before:

> The significant novelty in the Quran commentaries by al-Shāfiʿī's second-generation students is thus twofold. First, they exhibit a scientific distance between the author and the subject, which manifests itself in the open presentation of multivocal evidence. Earlier commentaries, such as those by ʿAbd al-Razzāq or Muqātil b. Sulaymān (d. 150/767), present authoritative opinions and coherent narratives, respectively, but do not display such a scientific distance; rather, they project the timeless and unchanging aura of a tradition. Second, this absence of a univocal tradition necessitates a new basis for authority, which is supplied by a hierarchy of sources…[84]

Bukhārī's *tafsīr* falls chronologically between. ʿAbd al-Razzāq's commentary already presents multiple contrary positions, as on the question of which son

82. Geissinger, *Gender*, 168–169.

83. Norman Calder, "*Tafsīr* from Ṭabarī to Ibn Kathīr: Problems in the Description of a Genre," in G. R. Hawting and Abdul-Kader A. Shareef (eds.), *Approaches to the Qur'ān* (London: Routledge, 1993), 101–140.

84. Ahmed El Shamsy, *The Canonization of Islamic Law* (Cambridge: Cambridge University Press, 2013), 216.

Abraham set out to sacrifice. Clearly (*contra* El Shamsy), the commentary tradition was moving in this direction independently of Shāfiʿī. Bukhārī's apparent reluctance to expose disagreement looks relatively conservative. But Bukhārī stands out by integrating the *ḥadīth* and *adab* approaches, ʿAbd al-Razzāq offering only the former. And Bukhārī clearly respects a hierarchy of sources, possibly under Shāfiʿī influence, but more likely, again, because of a general movement in this direction across the ninth century.

As noted, Walid Saleh has proposed that it is not Ṭabarī but Thaʿlabī who stands at the beginning of the classical commentary tradition. That he overstates his case has been sufficiently observed before now.[85] Some of what he expounds as innovations of Thaʿlabī's commentary have clear antecedents in Bukhārī's *kitāb al-tafsīr*. He disparages Ṭabarī for his fulsome provision of *isnāds* to support everything and praises Thaʿlabī for dispensing with them.[86] Bukhārī's *tafsīr* falls between Ṭabarī and Thaʿlabī, usually providing full *isnāds* for statements from the Prophet and his Companions but dispensing with them for more recent commentators, and often when quoting the Companion Ibn ʿAbbās. (Kātib Çelebī also thought commentaries bereft of *isnāds* constituted an important new stage, but he does not attribute it to Thaʿlabī. Rather, the commentators he names as introducing this style are the Baghdadi grammarians Abū Isḥāq al-Zajjāj [d. 310/922–923?] and his student Abū ʿAlī al-Fārisī [d. 377/987].[87])

Saleh thinks it significant that Thaʿlabī often quotes the Prophet not directly commenting on a verse, but exposing the meaning of something that comes up in a verse, such as the meaning of "patience."[88] Bukhārī, like Ṭabarī, most often quotes *ḥadīth* in which the Prophet quotes the Qur'ān or in which a revelation comes to cap something the Prophet has just said. But the connection between prophetic dictum and qur'ānic revelation may be fairly remote, inessential to the meaning of the prophetic dictum. For example, Bukhārī places reports of an incident at the Last Judgment, when death will be slaughtered in the form of a black and white ram, either in *kitāb al-tafsīr* or *kitāb al-riqāq* ("sayings to soften the heart") depending on whether the Prophet at the end quotes Q Maryam 19:39 ("Warn them of the day of anguish when the matter will have been decided while they are still in a state of heedlessness").[89] Such reports can hardly be called *exegetical*.

---

85. See review by Hans-Thomas Tillschneider, *WI* 48 (2008): 112–117.

86. Saleh, *Formation*, 224.

87. Kātib Çelebī, *Kashf*, 1.431. On these two, see respectively C. H. M. Versteegh, "al-Zadjdjādj," *EI*², s.v. and C. Rabin, "al-Fārisī," *EI*², s.v.

88. Saleh, *Formation*, 193–198.

89. Bukhārī, *Ṣaḥīḥ*, *tafsīr* 19, no. 4730; *al-riqāq* 5, *bāb yadkhulu al-jannah sabʿūna alfan*, no. 6544; *al-riqāq* 6, *bāb ṣifat al-jannah wa'l-nār*, no. 6548.

Perhaps there is an analogy in the rabbis' finding allusions to the rules of the Mishnah in the Pentateuch. Like them, Bukhārī is connecting two genetically independent textual corpora, in his case the Qur'ān and *ḥadīth*. If Bukhārī anticipates Thaʿlabī at points where he supposedly improved on Ṭabarī, it weakens Saleh's case for Thaʿlabī's originality and importance. However, it also shows how useful Saleh's description of Thaʿlabī can be for the history of qur'ānic commentary and, of more lasting consequence, demonstrates that qur'ānic commentary developed gradually (and unevenly), not by occasional great leaps.

To sum up, Bukhārī's example shows that there were multiple approaches to *tafsīr* in the mid-ninth century, just as there were later. His integration of the *ḥadīth* and *adab* approaches to the Qur'ān makes an important precedent for Ṭabarī's integration of them (although Ṭabarī need not have got the idea from Bukhārī, whose *Ṣaḥīḥ* he probably never saw). His combination of items with and without *isnād* furnishes a precedent for Thaʿlabī's doing without *isnād*s (although, again, there is no need to suppose direct influence, since he had other examples before him). Bukhārī's minimization of disagreement seems aberrant even for his own time, at least when it comes to *ḥadīth* and qur'ānic commentary; however, it agrees with the style of ninth-century legal *mukhtaṣar*s. Differences between his *kitāb al-tafsīr* and the rest of the *Ṣaḥīḥ* suggest that his special approach in the former reflects contemporary developments in the genre of *tafsīr*, although in the absence of extant examples from the mid-ninth century, it is impossible to say for sure.

JIQSA 1 (2016): 173–183

AFTERWORD: THE ACADEMIC STUDY OF THE QUR'ĀN—ACHIEVEMENTS, CHALLENGES, AND PROSPECTS

DEVIN STEWART AND GABRIEL SAID REYNOLDS

Qur'ānic Studies is a broad field that includes many categories and subtopics, including grammar, lexicon, rhetoric, theology, law, textual history, textual variants, the history of interpretation, and many others, any one of which is, or has the potential to be, large and complex. The investigation of these fields is not new but goes back to the early Islamic centuries. As the Islamic societies matured and spread, so did the scholarly genres that grew up around the Qur'ān, including *tafsīr, qiṣaṣ al-anbiyā'*, grammatical treatises, rhetorical manuals, and so on. Such works were penned in all corners of the Islamic world, primarily in Arabic, but also in other Islamic languages. Translations and primers were written in Persian, Turkish, Urdu, Malay, and other languages in order to facilitate comprehension of the Qur'ān on the part of Muslims who were not native speakers of Arabic. Study of the Qur'ān was also taken up by non-Muslims, including Jews and Christians in the Islamic world, and Jews and Christians in Western Europe. If the immediate motive for this interest was often polemical—the urge to counter Muslim claims to exclusive or superior access to the will of God—the result was an increase in general knowledge of Islamic doctrine and of Islam's sacred text. The Qur'ān was translated into Latin in the twelfth century, retranslated in the seventeenth century, and subsequently translated into many of the modern European languages. In a sense, then, Qur'ānic Studies has been a large, international project for centuries. It has involved Muslims, Christians, Jews, adherents of other religions, and adherents of no religion. And it will continue to do so.

It is indeed simplistic to imagine that critical investigation of the Qur'ān was the invention of the moderns, for the scholarship of medieval Islamic tradition already included such investigations. Muslim scholars such as Ibn Abī Dāwūd al-Sijistānī (d. 316/928), Abū Sa'īd al-Dānī (d. 444/1052), and others critically analyzed the orthography of the Qur'ān, and carefully investigated the form and rhyme schemes of the Qur'ān's *sūrah*s and verses in order to determine where to place verse divisions. In addition, *sūrah*s were

doi: http://dx.doi.org/10.5913/jiqsa.1.2017.a009

analyzed historically and divided into two classes, Meccan and Medinan, indicating the historical period in which they were revealed. In order to determine which verses could have abrogated—that is, canceled the legal effect of—other verses, medieval scholars endeavored to figure out the exact chronology of revelation of the *sūrahs*. Classical chronological lists of qur'ānic *sūrahs* were established in the works on "sciences of the Qur'ān" (*ʿulūm al-Qur'ān*) of al-Zarkashī (d. 794/1392), in his *Al-Burhān fī ʿulūm al-Qur'ān*, and al-Suyūṭī (d. 911/1505), in *al-Itqān fī ʿulūm al-Qur'ān*.

Meanwhile, an entire science of "readings" (*qirā'āt*) was devoted to the collection and examination of textual variants. The study of *qirā'āt* included speculation on reports of what was once found in the codices of Companions of the Prophet that were destroyed (according to the standard historical account) by the caliph ʿUthmān as part of his program to eliminate all competing texts to his authorized version. These "Companion variants" often involve significantly different material, including whole words and phrases not found in the standard text. A variant reading attributed to Ubayy b. Kaʿb (d. 29/649) adds to Q Ṣaff 61:6 (after "whose name will be Aḥmad") the phrase "the community of whom will be the last community and with whom God will place a seal on the prophets and messengers." The study of *qirā'āt* also involved the organization and codification of variant readings of the standard text. These "canonical variants" involve smaller changes than the "Companion variants" inasmuch as they do not affect the consonantal text attributed to ʿUthmān. Eventually such variants were organized into seven (or ten or fourteen) acceptable manners of reading the text of the Qur'ān, in part through the work of Ibn Mujāhid (d. 324/936). On such questions, we might note, indeed admire, the degree of freedom that the culture of medieval Islamic scholarship allowed to scholars to explore different readings and interpretations of the qur'ānic text.

Nevertheless, we should not allow our admiration to cross into naiveté or anachronistic assumptions about medieval Islamic scholarship. In this culture certain doctrinal boundaries were not crossed, large and important topics were nearly entirely ignored, and traditional views that had limited support in the text itself but had arisen for extraneous reasons were accepted almost without question. To illustrate this point, we might note that the term *al-kawthar*, a *hapax legomenon* that appears prominently in Sūrat al-Kawthar, is often interpreted in traditional commentaries as a pool or river in which the believers are cleansed before entering Paradise. The evidence for this interpretation in the text is non-existent—the context does not support it. Instead, it appears that *al-kawthar* is related to the common root *k-th-r* and means an abundance of some sort, probably the numerous spiritual "progeny" of the Prophet; in other words, the family of believers.

In addition, Muslim scholars eventually developed a largely skeptical perspective on the legitimacy of referring to Jewish and Christian tradition to explain the (considerable) biblical material of the Qur'ān. Only a small number of medieval Muslim scholars including Ismaili Shi'a such as Abū Ḥātim al-Rāzī (d. 322/934) and the Sunni exegete Ibrāhīm b. ʿUmar b. Ḥasan al-Biqāʿī (d. 885/1480) actively investigated the Hebrew Bible, the New Testament, and other Jewish and Christian texts as a means toward understanding the qur'ānic versions of biblical stories (but even then not as a source of new or different understandings of legal principles). Many actively discouraged the use of biblical tradition in this manner, preferring to arrive at interpretations that were entirely independent of "outside" traditions. In practice this was difficult because the traditional Islamic commentaries had early on assimilated much biblical material. Thus, for example, most traditional Muslim commentators—even those who refuse on principle to consult Jewish and Christian traditions—report (in line with the Bible) that the prophet Jonah was sent to the city of Nineveh.

As for exegesis proper, most Muslim commentaries are marked by an atomistic verse-by-verse approach to the Qur'ān, and also by an openness to a diversity of interpretations of any particular verse. Commentaries by al-Ṭabarī (d. 310/923) and Fakhr al-Dīn al-Rāzī (d. 606/1210) are encyclopedic inasmuch as they include considerable discussion of the views of earlier scholars, even those with whom they disagree pointedly. For example, on the meaning of the disconnected (or "mysterious") letters which open twenty-nine of the Qur'ān's *sūrahs*, they speculate widely. Indeed, at times their openness extends even to the possibility of admitting disagreement or uncertainty, to establishing only the "more correct" (*aṣaḥḥ*) meaning, or to concluding that the true meaning of a verse is known to God alone. Nevertheless, dogmatic ideas about the Qur'ān's revelation and proclamation also affected the history of Muslim scholarship. The idea that a passage of the Qur'ān could have been added into the Qur'ān or significantly modified after the time of the Prophet was not considered a real possibility, and indeed was considered blasphemous. Even the possibility that ʿUthmān's particular collection of the Qur'ān (which, according to the tradition itself was only one of many) was less than perfect was eventually considered unacceptable.

Scholarship on the Qur'ān in the West was of course free from the dogmatic concerns of Muslim scholars but it too had a particular history that shaped its development. The interest in the Qur'ān in the West was related to the history of biblical scholarship. Beginning in the sixteenth century, and spurred on, in some sense, by the challenge of Protestantism and the Wars of Religion, a new mode of studying the Bible developed in Christian Europe. It was not expressly aimed at undermining tradition, but the scholars who championed this mode of scholarship set out to investigate the biblical text in a scientific manner without adhering closely to traditional sources, methods, and modes of interpretation. They tried to find the oldest textual materials related to the Bible. They studied languages like Old Slavonic, Syriac, Georgian, and Armenian. They produced massive polyglot Bibles that made it possible to compare six versions of the biblical text in six different languages, quickly. They produced concordances and dictionaries. They examined apocryphal texts that had not made it into the canon. By the nineteenth century, scholars of the Bible had become adept at textual criticism, which they had learned from the Classicists, and they made significant breakthroughs in the analysis of the biblical text.

Julius Wellhausen (d. 1918), building on the work of previous scholars, proposed the Documentary Hypothesis, according to which the Pentateuch, the first five books of the Bible, was produced by combining four traditions. Scholars of the New Testament worked assiduously to characterize the relationship between the Synoptic Gospels—the Gospels of Matthew, Mark, and Luke—so called because they related parallel accounts of Jesus Christ (in contrast to the Gospel of John). After long debate, a "two-source hypothesis" emerged by which the Gospel of Mark was the earliest gospel, and Matthew and Luke both wrote their gospels using the Gospel of Mark as a source, along with another work that preserved a collection of Jesus' sayings, which New Testament scholars term Q (which comes from *Quelle*, the German word for "source"). Both of these hypotheses have been widely accepted and have informed the scholarly understanding of the Bible since the late nineteenth century. Scholars of the Bible have continued to produce a great deal of scholarship in the same vein, and now, in the twenty-first century, biblical scholarship is a massive enterprise, involving hundreds of academic journals and learned societies.

Scholars of biblical tradition turned their attention to the Qur'ān in a systematic way in the nineteenth century. The progression was natural. Just as scholars of the sixteenth century such as Joseph Scaliger and Thomas Erpenius had developed an interest in Arabic and the qur'ānic text, scholars in nineteenth-century Europe sought to expand the purview of their field to include a cognate tradition. The Qur'ān clearly shared a great deal with the texts from Jewish and Christian tradition with which they were familiar, not only in terms of individual stories but also in terms of concepts, forms, and textual history. Abraham Geiger, Gustav Weil, Gustav Wüstenfeld, Theodor Nöldeke, and others applied elements of biblical criticism to the Qur'ān and related texts. Of particular note in this regard is the 1833 work of Abraham Geiger, "Was hat Mohammed aus dem Judenthume aufgenommen?," in which Geiger discusses the relationship of the Qur'ān with Bible, Talmud, and midrash.

Another noteworthy moment in the history of nineteenth-century scholarship on the Qur'ān was a competition announced by the Académie des Inscriptions et Belles-lettres de Paris in 1857, which challenged scholars to study the history of the Qur'ān within the lifetime of the Prophet, or more specifically to

> research the primitive division [of the text] and the character of the different passages of which it is composed and to determine, as much as possible and with the aid of Arab historians and commentators, and in light of an examination of the passages themselves, the moments in the life of Muḥammad to which they are related.

The guidelines of this competition reflect the fundamental presuppositions of nineteenth-century scholarship on the Qur'ān, above all that the traditional method of explaining certain passages of the Qur'ān through accounts (*asbāb al-nuzūl*) found in medieval Islamic literature, which purport to explain when and why those passages were revealed, is reliable. These guidelines also reflect a certain confidence—represented famously by Ernest Renan (d. 1892), one of the judges of the Paris competition—that this literature, even if it included certain mythical elements, also contained reliable historical information on the circumstances of the Qur'ān's revelation. "Islam was born in the full light of history (*pleine histoire*)," quipped Renan. Among the three winners of the competition—along with the Italian Michele Amari (d. 1889) and the Austrian Aloys Sprenger (d. 1893)—was a young German named Theodor Nöldeke (d. 1930). Nöldeke would later translate his Latin entry to the competition into German as "Geschichte des Qorans" (1860, "History of the Qur'ān"), the first volume of which was dedicated to establishing a chronology of qur'ānic *sūrahs*. Subsequent volumes would be written by Friedrich Schwally (d. 1919) on the collection of the text, and then by Gotthelf Bergsträßer (d. 1933) and Otto Pretzl (d. 1941) on the subsequent history of the qur'ānic text, especially the Islamic literature on variant readings (*qirā'āt*) and variant codices. Together these three volumes would become a sort of canon for the study of the Qur'ān in the academy.

Building on the advances in Arabic philology made in France with the founding of the École des Langues Orientales, and working individually at first, such scholars succeeded in creating a tradition of qur'ānic scholarship centered in Germany and Austria. Thereafter, this academic specialization spread to Britain, France, and Sweden in the early twentieth century.

The European scholars of Qur'ānic Studies had an approach that differed significantly and was thus, to an extent, complementary to the customary modes of Islamic scholarship. Their strong point was their knowledge of biblical tradition and other Semitic languages, and so a major facet of their work was the identification of references to and adaptations of biblical material in the Qur'ān. Abraham Geiger had begun this in 1833, and it was pursued by a series of scholars such as Hartwig Hirschfeld, Alphonse Mingana, Josef Horovitz, Daniel Sidersky, and others, culminating in the work of Heinrich Speyer, *Die biblischen Erzählungen im Qoran* (1931). They were also less restrained in their investigation of the text, and they could suggest that this or that feature was due to the purposeful action of the Prophet Muḥammad or that it had been interpolated at a later date. They could likewise suggest that this or that aspect of the biblical tradition had been garbled, miscomprehended, or misconstrued.

The European tradition of Qur'ānic Studies, however, never gained a strong, international presence. It was interrupted by the rise of the Nazi regime in Germany, the consequent flight of Jewish scholars from Germany, and the interruption of normal academic life. What had been a continuous tradition for several generations was broken up, and it was not reconstituted in England, the United States, Israel, or other nations to which scholars fled. For the remainder of the twentieth century, qur'ānic scholarship was often undertaken by individuals working in relative isolation. Key works of qur'ānic scholarship from the late nineteenth and early twentieth centuries were out of print and inaccessible. What is more, most scholars who decided to write on the Qur'ān during this period were actually specialists in other areas of Arabic and Islamic Studies. They had undergone no rigorous training under accomplished specialists in the investigation of the Qur'ān. Recognized curricula, courses of study, and reference works were next to non-existent. Scholars were unaware of the works of their predecessors and made unfounded claims of originality. They also failed to build on the work of their colleagues in a regular fashion.

One area in which scholarship on the Qur'ān continued at a great pace was translation. In 1937, the Scottish scholar Richard Bell published a translation of the Qur'ān accompanied by detailed notes meant to illustrate additions and edits which took place during its composition. In his original 1949 annotated French translation of the Qur'ān, Régis Blachère rearranged the *sūrahs* according to their supposed chronological order. In 1962, Rudi Paret published his German translation of the Qur'ān, followed in 1971 by his *Kommentar und Konkordanz*, a reference work of unparalleled usefulness for the study of the Qur'ān. Meanwhile other translations of the Qur'ān have appeared in greater frequency. Whereas the translation of the Qur'ān was a matter of great controversy in Muslim circles in the early twentieth century, it was eventually embraced as Muslim scholars such as Muhammad Marmaduke Pickthall (1930), Yusuf Ali (1938), and Muhammad Asad (1980) translated the Qur'ān into English. Today several translations of the Qur'ān, of varying quality and diverse ideological perspectives, are published each year. While most translators of the Qur'ān were not accomplished scholars of Qur'ānic Studies, and some translations are mere paraphrases of earlier translations, others have academic value, including the 2013 work of A. J. Droge, which includes notes with relevant cross-references, biblical parallels, and insights into the meaning of qur'ānic vocabulary. Numerous translations report the views of traditional Muslim commentators in their annotations but avoid entirely questions of source criticism.

In recent decades, scholarly interest in the Qur'ān, and not only in translating the Qur'ān, has grown rapidly. This is due, in part, to a revived interest in biblical texts—especially Syriac Christian texts—that are related to the Qur'ān. However, it is also due to a rise in interest in the Qur'ān in general, inspired in part by a general appreciation of its importance in the life of Muslims and Islamic societies and in part by the greater participation of Muslims in the Western academy. Indeed, all areas of Qur'ānic Studies today, one can say without exaggeration, are flourishing. If scholars of the Qur'ān often find themselves in sharp disagreement, that disagreement itself is a sign of the vibrancy of the field.

Perhaps the area of scholarship in the field which has received the most attention recently is that which explores the relationship of Jewish, and especially Christian, texts and traditions and the Qur'ān. Christoph Luxenberg's 2000 work *Die syro-aramäische Lesart des Koran*, later translated into English as *The Syro-Aramaic Reading of the Koran* (2007), led many scholars to reexamine the traditional doctrine (defended by Nöldeke) that the Qur'ān is written in classical Arabic, and to consider the possibility that new meanings of the text could be derived by understanding certain qur'ānic terms according to a possible Syriac meaning. While Luxenberg was criticized for focusing too narrowly on individual terms, other scholars began to look more broadly at the intersection of elements of the Qur'ān—such as the account of the prostration of the angels before Adam, or of the Companions of the Cave—and Syriac tradition. Emran El-Badawi, Sidney Griffith, Gabriel Reynolds, and Joseph Witztum have all worked on this question, while Holger Zellentin has studied the possibility that not only the narrative, but also the legal material in the Qur'ān might have a particular connection to Christian, or Jewish-Christian, communities who wrote in Syriac. Kevin Van Bladel and Tommaso Tesei have drawn attention to the Syriac Alexander legend and its connection to the *Dhū'l-Qarnayn* account of Sūrat al-Kahf.

In general, such scholars have been moving away from a model in which this or that feature of the text is identified as biblical and in which discrepancies are viewed as errors on the part of the Qur'ān, to a model in which qur'ānic departures from biblical material are understood to occur for particular reasons. In some ways we might say that such scholars have discovered the Qur'ān's independent, creative, and sometimes polemical voice. The Qur'ān does not simply borrow: it adapts, develops, modifies, and criticizes earlier traditions. For example, the way in which the Qur'ān insists that the Israelites did not crucify Jesus (Q Nisā' 4:157) is today rarely approached as a vestige of the heresy of the Docetists, but rather as a reflection of the qur'ānic teaching on the inability of a prophet's enemies to defeat him.

The Corpus Coranicum project, which began in 2007 under the leadership of Angelika Neuwirth, has avoided the language of influence by reference to "intertexts" that are related in some fashion to the Qur'ān but perhaps only indirectly. A number of scholars, including Neuwirth, have come to speak about the Qur'ān within the larger context of Late Antiquity. They mean thereby to highlight the Qur'ān's relationship to Jewish, Christian, and other Near Eastern traditions without implying a hierarchy, or the superiority of one tradition over the others. Effectively, this late antique emphasis means enlarging one's view of the Qur'ān's historical context from only Mecca and Medina (and then only from 610–632) to the Near East generally over a broader sweep of time.

Another major area of research is that of qur'ānic manuscripts. Until recently, scholars had only paid attention to complete manuscripts, and had therefore concluded, tentatively and clearly incorrectly, that it would not be possible to say much about the textual transmission of the Qur'ān on the basis of manuscripts before ca. 900 CE. Bergsträsser and Pretzl, together with the Australian Arthur Jeffery, worked in the early/mid-twentieth century on the collection and study of early Qur'ān manuscripts along with the study of medieval Islamic literature on qur'ānic readings, with the aim of producing a critical edition of the Qur'ān. In part, their work was inspired by the appearance and diffusion of the 1924 Cairo edition of the Qur'ān, produced on the basis of medieval Islamic literature alone. While they never completed their project, the study of manuscripts has accelerated in recent decades. With the discovery of fragments of early Qur'ān manuscripts in Yemen and with the assiduous study of fragments extant in collections in European libraries and libraries throughout the Islamic world by François Déroche, Gerd Puin, Elisabeth Puin, Alba Fedeli, Behnam Sadeghi, Asma Hilali, and others, significant advances have been made. The aforementioned Corpus Coranicum project has organized a database of qur'ānic manuscripts with the goal of allowing scholars to see ancient variants to standard readings of the text. Together this work has shown that the study of manuscripts in conversation with Islamic *qirā'āt* literature can advance our knowledge of the early history of the qur'ānic text, if not lead to a critical edition which reflects the text's original shape.

Attention to calligraphy, decoration, format, and other physical features in addition to the text has made it possible to provide a chronology of qur'ānic manuscripts that will make it possible to determine the type and provenance of other early fragments. This scholarship has moved the frontier of our knowledge of the qur'ānic text back over a century earlier: whereas scholars a century ago were reluctant to say anything about the history of qur'ānic manuscripts before about 300 A.H., modern investigation has revealed elements of the textual history of the Qur'ān going back to the Umayyad period. It has in some cases confirmed what is known from the traditional science of *qirā'āt*, and in other cases not.

Another area of fruitful research has been on the stylistic and aesthetic features of the qur'ānic text. Carl Ernst, Navid Kermani, Michael Sells, Devin Stewart, and Shawkat Toorawa have in different ways highlighted the Qur'ān's acoustic features, the importance of its rhyme, and its literary qualities.

Yet another major area of research is the structure of *sūrahs*. Hamiduddin Farahi (d. 1930), Amin Ahsan Islahi (d. 1997), and others have attempted to argue for the unity of the *sūrah*, including long, Medinan *sūrahs*, against the critiques of earlier European scholars—notably Bell—who claimed that the Qur'ān, or at least particular *sūrahs*, were mixed compositions of originally discrete passages put together without careful attention to logical progression. They have sought to do this by identifying the central theme of each *sūrah* for all of the *sūrahs* of the Qur'ān. Mustansir Mir has made much of the scholarship of Islahi available to scholars in the Western academy. Other scholars such as Neal Robinson, Mathias Zahniser, Marianna Klar, Nevin El Tahery, and others have examined in particular long *sūrahs*, such as Sūrat al-Baqarah and Sūrat al-Nisā', in order to argue for their unity.

A particular trend in this scholarship has invoked the term "Semitic rhetoric" (developed by Roland Meynet in Biblical Studies) and tried to show that a number of *sūrahs* exhibit ring structure: that sections of the text mirror each other around a central pivot. The founding figure of Semitic rhetoric studies as applied to the Qur'ān is the Belgian Michel Cuypers. In his 2007 book *Le festin: une lecture de la sourate al-Mâ'ida*, translated into English as *The Banquet: A Reading of the Fifth Sura of the Qur'an* (2009), Cuypers argues for the coherence of Sūrat al-Mā'idah and maintains that a richer understanding of the Qur'ān's message generally is achieved by detecting ring structures therein. Not all scholars have accepted the method of Semitic rhetoric; some have insisted that this method is so flexible that the insights into the text which it seems to achieve might in fact be the construction of the researcher and say little about the original composition of the Qur'ān.

Meanwhile other scholars have focused on certain features of the qur'ānic text that are found across a variety of *sūrahs*. Both Daniel Madigan (who reapplies some of the semantic analysis of Toshihiko Izutsu) and Anne-Sylvie Boisliveau have emphasized the uniqueness of the Qur'ān's self-referentiality, or meta-textuality. The Qur'ān frequently refers to itself in a way that is unusual for most late antique texts (although it has some precedence in Syriac Christian homilies). These references are often taken by traditional Muslim scholars as allusions to a complete version of the Qur'ān that existed already in heaven before it was brought down to earth. Madigan, however, has argued that the Qur'ān's references to a "book" or a "recitation" (*qur'ān*) reflect more closely a notion of oral revelation (that is, the Arabic word *kitāb* in the Qur'ān need not always refer to a written book). Boisliveau has emphasized that the Qur'ān's self-referentiality is a manifestation of its apologetic and argumentative nature: it is concerned to defend its claims of revelation to a skeptical audience (which included Jews and Christians who were familiar with the category of prophecy). The concern with argument is also prominent in the work of Mehdi Azaiez on the Qur'ān's counter-discourse. Azaiez has examined the voice that the Qur'ān gives to its opponents in the Qur'ān and raised the question of whether it is actually quoting its opponents or attributing to them those opinions which it wishes to refute. Again through Azaiez's scholarship, one has the sense of discovery of the Qur'ān's unique voice. The Qur'ān, such studies show, is intimately connected to the biblical tradition but independent in its religious perspective and rhetorical constructions.

Some historians have called many of the agreed-upon features of the Qur'ān and early Islamic history into question by focusing on non-Islamic sources, instead of the familiar Islamic literature. This trend was begun by *Hagarism*, a work published in 1977 by Patricia Crone and Michael Cook that, despite criticism, has inspired later scholars such as Fred Donner, Stephen Shoemaker, Guillaume Dye, Yehuda Nevo, and the scholars of the Inarah group in Germany. One of the key facts made much of in this trend is that accounts of the Islamic invasions do not call the invaders of the seventh century conquests Muslims but rather *mhaggrāyē* (Hagarenes, or perhaps *muhājirūn*) or *ṭayyāyē*. Others have looked at the Dome of the Rock, an idiosyncratic building that seems to have been associated with Abraham before being associated with Muḥammad's ascension into heaven, and which includes quotations from the Qur'ān that seem to deviate from the standard reading, as a vestige of primitive or proto-Islam. Both Shoemaker and Dye have argued that the Kathisma Church in Jerusalem (after which the Dome of the Rock was apparently modeled) may help explain why Sūrat Maryam associates the birth of Jesus with the miracle of the palm tree (a miracle associated instead with the flight to Egypt in early Christian legend). Some scholars, most recently Robert Hoyland, suggest that we should speak of the Arab, not Islamic, conquests. Collectively this research suggests that we should not think of the Qur'ān emerging from a fully formed religious community but rather a community still in development. Fred Donner has suggested as much in his 2012 work, *Muhammad and the Believers*.

Finally, we might note that scholarship on the Qur'ān produced in Islamic languages, including investigations of qur'ānic rhetoric and themes, whether theological, social, or political, is too often unknown to researchers working in Western languages. As a learned society, and particularly through its international conferences, IQSA will seek to build bridges between different scholarly communities.

In recent years a number of observers have noted that Qur'ānic Studies is a field with deep ideological divides. Some have suggested that the field as a whole is barely coherent or even chaotic. In our opinion, however, the ideological divides in Qur'ānic Studies, which reflect the general increase in interest in the Qur'ān, make for constructive academic discussions. At the same time, it will no doubt be useful for scholars of the Qur'ān to have a learned society that will host those discussions and allow for the serious and rigorous debates which ultimately redound to their benefit. Accordingly, the foundation of IQSA is an auspicious development for a field which in many ways is already thriving.

JIQSA MISSION AND CALL FOR PAPERS

The *Journal of the International Qur'anic Studies Association* (*JIQSA*) is a peer-reviewed annual journal devoted to the scholarly study of the Qur'ān. Our goals are:

- To publish scholarship of high technical quality on the Qur'ān, addressing such concerns as its historical context; its relationship to other scriptural, parascriptural, and commentary traditions; and its literary, material, and cultural reception;
- To cultivate Qur'ānic Studies as a growing field with a distinctive identity and focus, and with relevant linkages to the study of the Bible as well as Islamic tradition, including *tafsīr*;
- To facilitate crucial conversations about the state-of-the-art in Qur'ānic Studies and its future;
- To connect diverse scholarly communities from around the world on issues of common concern in the study of the Qur'ān.

We invite submission of original, quality research articles for consideration for publication in *JIQSA*. Methodologies of particular interest to the journal include historical-critical, contextual-comparative, and literary approaches to the Qur'ān. We especially welcome articles that explore the Qur'ān's origins in the religious, cultural, social, and political contexts of Late Antiquity; its connections to various literary precursors, especially the scriptural and parascriptural traditions of older religious communities; the historical reception of the Qur'ān in the West; the hermeneutics and methodology of qur'ānic exegesis and translation (both traditional and modern); the transmission and evolution of the *textus receptus*; Qur'ān manuscripts and material culture; and the application of various literary and philological modes of investigation into qur'ānic style, compositional structure, and rhetoric.

The field of Qur'ānic Studies is rich, diverse, and dynamic, and currently comprises a wide array of approaches and concerns. Articles to be considered for publication may reflect a variety of disciplinary perspectives, but should be:

- Located in and engaged with the relevant scholarly literature, building on existing knowledge;
- Conscious of authorial perspective and positionality, and explicit about aims, theoretical posture, and methodology;

- Reflective about their potential impact on larger issues and debates in the academic field of Qur'ānic Studies and in broader scholarly and public discourses around the Qur'ān and Islam.

To submit an article for consideration for publication in *JIQSA*, please e-mail complete manuscript (in the range of 8,000–12,000 words) and abstract (approx. 150 words) to jiqsa@iqsaweb.org. Authors are encouraged to conform their submission to our current style guidelines, available at https://iqsaweb.files.wordpress.com/2014/10/jiqsa-guidelines-and-style-sheet.pdf.

JIQSA 1 (2016): 187–192

القرآن: ما بعد أبي زيد وما قبل المصحف

علي مبروك†

موجز

هذا البحث القصير يستكمل عمل نصر حامد أبو زيد ويناقش موضوع التطابق بين قرآن"المصحف" وقرآن "اللوح المحفوظ." ويجد الدكتور علي مبروك في التراث الإسلامي نفسه ما ينفي ذلك التطابق المفترض، بل وأن "الشرط الإنساني" لعب دوراً هامّاً في إعطاء قرآن المصحف الشكل الذي استقرّ عليه بعد وفاة النبيّ محمّد. ويستشهد تحليله بأقوال الصحابة في أمر الاختلاف بين مصاحفهم على مستوى السور والآيات والكلمات. ويشير البحث أنّ عدم وجود التطابق الراهن قد يعني أنّ محمّداً النبيّ أراد أن يترك القرآن خطاباً مفتوحاً.

THE QUR'ĀN: BETWEEN ABŪ ZAYD AND THE *MUṢḤAF*

ALI MABROUK†

Abstract

This paper is inspired by the work of Nasr Hamid Abu Zayd (d. 2010) and inquires whether the extant text of the Qur'ān (*muṣḥaf*) is identical to the Qur'ān of the divine "preserved tablet" (*al-lawḥ al-maḥfūẓ*). Dr. Ali Mabrouk finds within Islamic tradition itself evidence against such a correspondence and, furthermore, that the "human factor" played an important role in giving shape to the current qur'ānic text after the death of the Prophet Muḥammad. The paper cites traditions ascribed to the Companions of Muḥammad, demonstrating differences in the number and order of *sūrah*s, as well as the number of verses and words. In conclusion, the paper asks if the cited differences and the lack of correspondence means that Muḥammad considered the Qur'ān an open and continuing discourse.

doi: http://dx.doi.org/10.5913/jiqsa.1.2017.a010

علي مبروك (١٩٦١ - ٢٠١٦)

توفي الدكتور والمفكر الكبير علي مبروك، أستاذ الفلسفة الإسلامية والكلام بجامعة القاهرة، يوم ٢٠ مارس / آذار، ٢٠١٦ م. كان الدكتور علي معروفاً بإنتاجه الفكري الواسع والذي تضمن كتاب "نصوص حول القرآن: في السعي وراء القرآن الحي" (٢٠١٤). حظيت جامعات ومؤسسات دولية عديدة بحراكه الفكري الثري، إذ كان يستكمل عمل أستاذه المرحوم والمفكر الكبير أيضاً الدكتور نصر حامد أبو زيد. وكانت آخر هدية استقبلتها الجمعية الدولية للدراسات القرآنية من الدكتور علي مبروك هي هذا المقال الوجيز.

***

إذا كانت مقاربة أبي زيد للقرآن قد ابتدأت من التعاطي معه كنص، ثم تطورت إلى حيث راح يقاربه كخطاب، فإن أهم ما يمكن ملاحظته على هذه المقاربة أنها – في مستوييها – تنطلق من القرآن كواقعة مكتملة في المصحف. وإذ تكاد المقاربة النصيّة للقرآن تنبني على كونه "مدونٌ بين دفتي المصحف،" فإنه يبدو أن الوقت لم يتوفر لأبي زيد[1] لقراءة المآلات التي تنشأ عن مقاربته للقرآن كخطاب؛ وبالخصوص على صعيد لغته وتاريخه. وإذن فالأمر في حاجة لمتابعة التداعيات المصاحبة لسيرورة الانتقال من قرآن (النبي) إلى مصحف (عثمان).

وهنا يلزم التنويه بما يكاد أن يكون من الثوابت الراسخة في وعي المسلمين على العموم أن الشكل الذي استقر عليه القرآن (تركيباً وترتيباً ولغةً) في المصحف هو ذات الشكل الذي تركه عليه النبي الكريم؛ وبما يعنيه ذلك من الاعتقاد الجازم في تطابق القرآن مع المصحف. ولسوء الحظ، فإن ثمة ما يخلخل هذا التصور المستقر، ويفتح الباب أمام افتراض عدم التطابق بينهما؛ حيث إن خمس عشرة سنةً تفصل بين القرآن الذي تركه النبي عند وفاته وبين المصحف الإمام الذي أقره الخليفة الثالث عثمان (بعد عامين تقريباً من ابتداء ولايته) كانت زاخرة – سواء على مستوى التركيب أو اللغة – بما يحيل إلى اختلاف المسلمين في القرآن "حتى كاد يكون بينهم فتنة."[2] وبالطبع فإن بلوغ الاختلاف إلى حد الفتنة إنما يعكس مدى اتساعه وشموله على هذا النحو المُهدد.

---

1. في دراسته المُعنونة: مقاربة جديدة للقرآن: من النص إلى الخطاب، يقول أبو زيد: "سأحاول في ما يلي إبراز بعض الخصائص الخطابية في القرآن؛ لأن دراسة مستفيضة تحتاج إلى مجلد أضخم، أتمنى أن تكون الأمثلة التالية بمثابة مخطط لهذا المشروع." انظر: نصر حامد أبو زيد، التجديد والتحريم والتأويل (بيروت: المركز الثقافي العربي، 2010)، ص 216.

2. ابن ابي داود السجستاني، كتاب المصاحف، تحقيق: محب الدين عبد السبحان واعظ (ط 2؛ بيروت: دار البشائر الإسلامية، 2002)، ص 202. حيث يرُوى عن عثمان أنه "خطب الناس ثم قال: إنما قبُض نبيكم منذ خمس عشرة سنة، وقد اختلفتم في القرآن." انظر: المصدر السابق، ص 209.

وبالرغم من الخطر الداهم للفتنة على وحدة الجماعة، فإنه يبدو أن اختلاف المسلمين حول القرآن تبدى، من جهة، في تعدد القراءات (على أن يكون مفهوماً أن الأمر بخصوص هذا الاختلاف لا يتصل بالتباين حول مخارج الألفاظ وكيفية نطقها، بل يتجاوزه إلى إبدال الألفاظ والحروف بأخرى غيرها)، وفي الشكل أو التركيب (البنائي) والترتيب الذي استقر عليه القرآن في المصحف. وبالطبع فإن ذلك يعني أن الفترة السابقة على تثبيت القرآن في المصحف قد اتسعت لضروبٍ من التدخل الإنساني في القرآن؛ على النحو الذي يحيل إلى استحالة أن يكون المصحف مطابقاً للقرآن الذي تركه النبي قبل وفاته. فالاختلاف الذي حفظته المصادر حول اللغة والتركيب البنائي يعني أن وجهاً واحداً من هذه الاختلافات هو الذي جرى تثبيته في المصحف، وأنه لا يوجد ما يقطع بأن هذا الوجه، دون غيره، كان هو ذلك الذي تركه النبي عند وفاته. وغنيٌّ عن البيان أن ذلك يعني أن الشكل الذي جرى به تثبيت القرآن في المصحف (لغةً وتركيباً) قد شهد نوعاً من التدخل من الإنساني؛ على النحو الذي يؤول إلى استحالة النظر إلى هذا الشكل على أنه انعكاسٌ مطابق للقرآن القائم في الأزل، بما هو صفة الله القديمة.

إنَّ "القرآن الكريم الذي يتداوله المسلمون اليوم بين دفتي المصحف لم يكن على هذا الترتيب في حياة الرسول صلى الله عليه وسلم. فقد قُبِضَ عليه السلام ولم يكن القرآن جُمِعَ في شيء."[3] فقد "كان القرآن كُتب كله في عهد رسول الله صلى الله عليه وسلم، لكن غير مجموع في موضعٍ واحد، ولا مُرَتب السور."[4] وكان مما ترتب على ذلك أن أصبح لكل واحدٍ من الصحابة الكبار مجموعه الذي يخصه من القرآن؛ والذي اصطُلِحَ على تسميته بالمصحف.[5] وهكذا تعددت المصاحف المنسوبة لأصحابها؛ والتي كانت نسبتها لأصحابها مرتبطةً بمخالفتها للمصحف الإمام الذي جرى الإجماع عليه؛ فإنما "قلنا مصحف فلان لِما خالف مصحفنا (يعني الإمام) من الخط أو الزيادة أو النقصان."[6] بل إنه وحتى بعد وضع المصحف الإمام، فإن ثمة من أصحاب هذه المصاحف من تمسك بمصحفه، رغم مخالفته لمصحف عثمان؛ ومن هنا ما قيل من أن "ابن مسعود لما حضر مصحف عثمان إلى الكوفة لم يوافق على

3. ابن الزبير الغرناطي، البرهان في ترتيب سور القرآن، دراسة وتحقيق: محمد شعباني (المغرب: وزارة الأوقاف والشؤون الإسلامية، 1990)، ص 21 من المقدمة.

4. جلال الدين السيوطي، الإتقان في علوم القرآن، تحقيق: شعيب الأرنؤوط (دمشق: مؤسسة الرسالة ناشرون، 1429/2008)، ص 129.

5. أورد السيوطي عن كتاب المصاحف لابن إشتة أن "أول من جمع القرآن في مصحف (هو) سالم مولى أبي حُذيفة، أقسم لا يرتدي برداء حتى يجمعه، فجمعه، ثم ائتمِروا: ما يسمونه؟ فقال بعضهم: سموه السفر، قال: ذلك اسمٌ تسميه اليهود، فكرهوه، فقال: رأيت مثله بالحبشة يُسمى المصحف، فاجتمع رأيهم على أن يسموه المصحف." انظر: السيوطي، الإتقان في علوم القرآن (سبق ذكره)، ص 130.

6. السجستاني، كتاب المصاحف (سبق ذكره)، ص 283–284.

الرجوع عن قراءته، ولا على إعدام مصحفه، فكان تأليف (ترتيب) مصحفه مغايراً لتأليف مصحف عثمان"[7]؛ وبما لابد أن يدل عليه ذلك من أن الشكل أو الترتيب الراهن الذي استقر عليه القرآن لم يكن هو الشكل الذي تركه عليه النبي، وذلك على فرض أن الترتيب الذي تركه عليه قد كان أصلاً هو ترتيبه في اللوح المحفوظ. وبالرغم من ذلك فإن ثمة من يقطع – وأعني به البغوي في <شرح السنَّة> – بأن القرآن "مكتوبٌ في اللوح المحفوظ على هذا الترتيب."[8]

وفي تفسير عدم جمع النبي للقرآن في المصحف، فإن ثمة من مضى إلى أنه "إنما لم يَجمع (النبي) صلى الله عليه وسلم القرآن في المصحف لما كان يترقبه من ورود ناسخ لبعض أحكامه أو تلاوته."[9] وبالطبع فإنه كان يمكن قبول مثل هذا التفسير لو أن النبي كان قد قُبض قبل أن يكتمل نزول الوحي؛ وهو ما تعارضه الرواية عن ابن عباس من أنه "كان بين نزول آخر آية (من القرآن) وبين موت النبي صلى الله عليه وسلم أحد وثمانون يوماً."[10] وحتى على فرض أن المدة الفاصلة بين نزول آخر آية من القرآن وبين موت النبي كانت – حسب رواية أخرى – بضع أيام فقط، فإن ترك النبي للقرآن على غير الشكل والترتيب الذي استقر عليه بعد رحيله إنما يعني أنه قد أراد للقرآن أن يظل خطاباً مفتوحاً.[11] ولقد ظل القرآن هكذا لمدة خمس عشرة سنة حتى اتخذ الشكل والترتيب الراهن الذي استقر عليه مع الخليفة الثالث عثمان؛ وهو الترتيب الذي جرى التأكيد على أنه من فعل البشر. حيث إنه "لما كُتِب مصحف عثمان رتبوه (يعني الناس) على ما هو عليه الآن."[12] ومما استدل به على أن ترتيب السور كان باجتهاد الصحابة "اختلاف مصاحف السلف في ترتيب السور؛ فمنهم من رتبها على النزول، وهو مصحف عليّ، كان أوله *اقرأ* ثم البواقي على ترتيب نزول المكي ثم المدني، ثم كان أول مصحف ابن مسعود *البقرة* ثم *النساء* ثم *آل عمران* على اختلاف شديد، وكذا مصحف أُبيّ بن كعب وغيره."[13] وهنا يلزم التنويه بأنه إذا كان القائلون بأن ترتيب سور القرآن هو باجتهاد من الصحابة يستندون إلى وقائع عينية

---

7. ابن حجر العسقلاني، فتح الباري بشرح صحيح البخاري، تحقيق: عبد القادر شيبة الحمد (المملكة السعودية: مطبعة العبيكان، 2001)، ج 8 ص 668.

8. المصدر السابق، ص 137.

9. المصدر السابق، ص 921. وانظر: الزركشي، البرهان في علوم القرآن، تحقيق: محمد أبو الفضل إبراهيم (القاهرة: دار التراث، 1957)، ج 1 ص 235.

10. المصدر السابق، ص 67.

11. لعل من المفيد الإشارة إلى أن كلمة سورة مُشتقة من "سور المدينة، لإحاطتها بآياتها واجتماعها، كاجتماع البيوت بالسور، ومنه السوار لإحاطته بالساعد." وبالطبع فإن وظائف السور تتجاوز مجرد الإحاطة بالشيء إلى إغلاقه وتحصينه أمام أي تدخل بالرفع منه بالذات. انظر: المصدر السابق، ص 118.

12. العسقلاني، فتح الباري (سبق ذكره)، ج 8 ص 668.

13. السيوطي، أسرار ترتيب القرآن، تحقيق: عبد القادر أحمد عطا (القاهرة: دار الاعتصام، 1976)، ص 68 .

تتعلق بوجود مصاحف مختلفة الترتيب (لعليٍّ وابن مسعود وأُبيّ)[14]، فإن أصحاب الرأي القائل بأن هذا الترتيب قد كان بتوقيف من النبي لا يجدون ما يستندون إليه في هذا التقرير إلا بعض الروايات التي تجري نسبتها إلى النبي؛ وعلى النحو الذي توضع معه "الرواية" في مواجهة "الواقعة".

ولعل هذا الانفتاح الذي ترك النبي عليه القرآن هو ما يقف وراء ضروب الاختلاف حول عدد سور القرآن وآياته وكلماته وحروفه.[15] فأما سوره "فقال أبو الحسين بن المنادي: جميع سور القرآن في تأليف زيد بن ثابت على عهد الصدِّيق وذي النورين مائة وأربع عشرة سورة، فيهن الفاتحة والتوبة والمعوذتان، وذلك هو الذي في أيدي أهل قبلتنا. وجملة سوره على ما ذُكِر عن أُبيّ بن كعب رضيّ الله عنه مائة وست عشرة سورة. وكان ابن مسعود رضيّ الله عنه يُسقِط المعوذتين، فنقصت جملته سورتين عن جملة زيد. وكان أُبيّ بن كعب يلحقهما ويُزيد إليهما سورتين هما الحَفد والخَلع."[16] وبخصوص الآيات، فإن "عدد آي القرآن مُختَلَفٌ فيه على حسب اختلاف العادّين. والعدد منسوبٌ إلى خمسة بلدان هي مكة والمدينة والكوفة والبصرة والشام."[17] وإذ يُقال إنَّ "سبب اختلاف السلف في عدد الآي: أن النبي صلى الله عليه وسلم كان يقف على رؤوس الآي للتوقيف، فإذا عُلِم محلها وصل للتمام، فيحسب

---

14. وحين يتعلق الأمر بأُبي ابن كعب بالذات فإنه يلزم اعتباره من الحجج أصحاب السيادة العليا في كل ما يتعلق بالقرآن؛ وبمعنى أنه يستحيل اعتباره من الذين فات عليهم العلم بترتيب سور القرآن الموقوف عليه من النبي. فقد "جاء في الحديث الصحيح أن النبي صلى الله عليه وسلم قال لأبيّ ابن كعب: إن الله أمرني أن أقرأ عليك القرآن، قال: آلله سماني؟ قال: نعم، وقد ذُكرت عند رب العالمين، قال: وذرفت عيناه. اشتهر بين الناس بأن أُبيّ أقرؤكم." وبالطبع فإنه يستحيل فيمن طلب الله من النبي أن يقرأ عليه القرآن أن يغيب عنه الترتيب الذي جعله الله أو النبي للقرآن. وقد قيل في سبب قراءة النبي للقرآن على أُبيّ أن "المُراد العرض على أُبيّ ليتعلم منه القراءة ويتثبّت فيها، وليكون عرض القرآن سنة، وللتنبيه على فضيلة أُبيّ ابن كعب وتقدمه في حفظ القرآن." انظر: ابن حجر العسقلاني، فتح الباري (سبق ذكره)، ج 7 ص 96.

15. ولا يقف الأمر عند مجرد ذلك، بل يتجاوز إلى ترتيب العقوبات المقررة على حسب احتياج الواقع؛ وذلك ما جرى تقريباً بخصوص العقوبات المقررة للزنا. فإذ استقرت المدونة التقليدية على أن الإمساك والحبس في البيوت كان أولاً ثم تلاه الإيذاء باللسان، فالجلد أخيراً، فإن "فرقة قالت: بل كان الإيذاء هو الأول، ثم نُسخ بالإمساك (في البيوت)، ولكن التلاوة قدَّمت وأخَّرت (كما) ذكر ابن فورك." وهكذا فإن التقديم والتأخير في ترتيب التلاوة قد انعكس على ترتيب العقوبة؛ وبما يعنيه ذلك من أن ترتيب التلاوة يتجاوب مع منطق الاحتياج الإنساني. انظر: سعد المرصفي، شبهات حول أحاديث الرجم وردها (الكويت: مكتبة المنار الإسلامية، 1994)، ص 17.

16. ابن الجوزي، فنون الأفنان في عيون علوم القرآن، تحقيق: حسن ضياء الدين عمر (بيروت: دار البشائر الإسلامية، 1987)، ص 234–235. وقد أورد السيوطي ما يفيد أن عليّ بن أبي طالب قد علَّم سورتي الحَفد والخَلع الزائدتين عند أُبيّ بن كعب، وأن عمر بن الخطاب قد قَنت بهما. انظر: السيوطي، الإتقان (سبق ذكره)، ص 143–144.

17. ابن الجوزي، فنون الأفنان (سبق ذكره)، ص 632–732.

السامع حينئذ أنها ليست فاصلة."[18] وهكذا فإن الشرط الإنساني يدخل في تعداد الآيات؛ وبما يعنيه ذلك من أن التعداد المتحقق في المصاحف المتباينة، لآي القرآن، يخلخل فكرة أن يكون عدد الآيات في المصحف القائم بأيدي المسلمين الآن هو نفس عددها في اللوح المحفوظ، بحسب ما يروج أصحاب القول بأن ما في المصحف هو انعكاسٌ مطابق لما في اللوح المحفوظ من دون أن يكون للشرط الإنساني الخاص بالمتلقين أدنى تأثير في ذلك.

وإذا جاز قبول الاختلاف بخصوص عدد السور والآيات لارتباطه بالشرط الإنساني المتمثل في طريقة أداء النبي للقرآن من جهة، وفي كيفية تلقي السامعين له من جهة أخرى، فإن الاختلاف لا يجوز أبداً بخصوص عدد كلمات القرآن. إذ تبقى الكلمات بمثابة الوحدات الأولية الصغرى التي يمكن أن تدخل في تراكيب (آيات وسور) يجوز الاختلاف بشأن أعدادها، بينما ينبغي أن تظل أعدادها – هي نفسها – ثابتة وغير قابلة للتغيُّر. فالتراكيب قد تتباين عدداً بحسب طرائق التعامل معها، بينما تظل الوحدات الأولية التي تتشكَّل منها هذه التراكيب ثابتة. ولسوء الحظ فإن الاختلاف حول عدد كلمات القرآن ليس من النوع الذي يمكن تجاهله؛ لضآلة الفارق بين التعدادات المذكورة للكلمات. إذ يروي "المنهال بن عمرو عن ابن مسعود أنه قال: كلام القرآن سبعٌ وسبعون ألف كلمة وتسعمائة كلمة وأربع وثلاثون كلمة. وروي عن مجاهد وابن جبير: سبع وسبعون ألف كلمة وأربعمائة وسبع وثلاثون كلمة. وروي عن عطاء بن يسار: تسع وسبعون ألف كلمة ومائتان وسبع وسبعون كلمة. وعن أبي المعافي يزيد بن عبد الواحد الضرير أنه قال: ست وسبعون ألف كلمة."[19] وهكذا يصل الفارق بين بعض العادّين إلى أكثر من ثلاثة آلاف كلمة تقريباً؛ وهو ما يجاوز حجم سورة متوسطة الطول من القرآن. وبالطبع فإنه لو كان النبي، قبل رحيله، قد وضع للقرآن شكله النهائي الذي كان يريد له أن يستقر عليه لما كان لمثل هذه الاختلافات أن تنشأ أبداً. لكنه يبقى أن هذه الاختلافات تظل كاشفةً عن دورٍ للمتلقين في تركيب القرآن على النحو الذي استقر عليه في المصحف؛ وبكيفية يتأكد فيها عدم التطابق بين قرآن "المصحف" وقرآن "اللوح المحفوظ." ولعل غياب مثل هذا التطابق يبدو حجر الزاوية في السعي إلى استعادة "الطبيعة التداولية للقرآن بوصفه خطابات متعددة السياقات من جهة، ومتعددة المستقبلين التاريخيين من جهة أخرى."[20]

18. السيوطي، الإتقان (سبق ذكره)، ص 146.
19. ابن الجوزي، فنون الأفنان (سبق ذكره)، ص 245.
20. أبو زيد، التجديد (سبق ذكره)، ص 200.